OLE Wizardry: Programming OLE Applications and Custom Controls Using Wizards

OLE Wizardry: Programming OLE Applications and Custom Controls Using Wizards

William H. Murray III
Chris H. Pappas

Osborne **McGraw-Hill**

Berkeley New York St. Louis San Francisco
Auckland Bogotá Hamburg London Madrid
Mexico City Milan Montreal New Delhi Panama City
Paris São Paulo Singapore Sydney Tokyo Toronto

Osborne **McGraw-Hill**
2600 Tenth Street
Berkeley, California 94710
U.S.A.

For information on translations or book distributors outside of the U.S.A., please write to Osborne **McGraw-Hill** at the above address.

OLE Wizardry: Programming OLE Applications and Custom Controls Using Wizards

1234567890 DOC 998765

ISBN 0-07-882102-9

Publisher
Lawrence Levitsky

Acquisitions Editor
Jeffrey Pepper

Project Editors
Wendy Rinaldi
Emily Rader

Copy Editor
Jan Jue

Proofreader
Vicki Van Ausdall

Computer Designer
Roberta Steele

Illustrator
Rhys Elliot

Series Design
Jani Beckwith

Quality Control Specialist
Joe Scuderi

Cover Design
Ted Mader Associates

To our friends
CHP: Mike and Ellen Wood
WHM: Irvin (Bud) and Anne Simser

About the Authors ...

William H. Murray, III and Chris H. Pappas are professors of computer science at the S.U.N.Y. System in Binghamton, New York. They are the authors of more than two dozen highly acclaimed computer books, including the three volume *Osborne Windows Programming Series, Windows 3.1 Programming, Application Programming for Windows NT, The Visual C++ Handbook*, and *The Borland C++ Handbook*, now in its fourth edition.

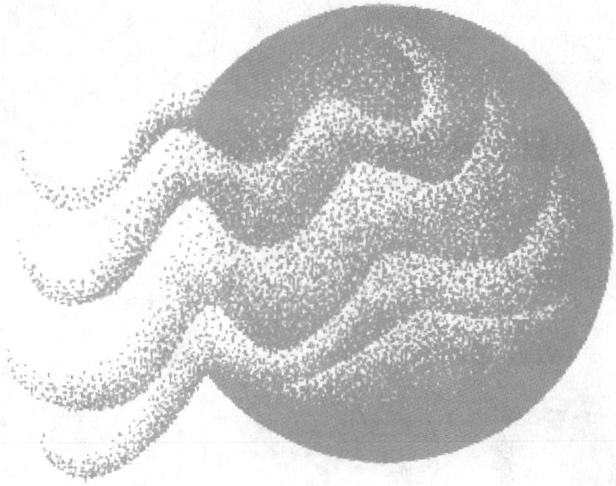

Contents At A Glance

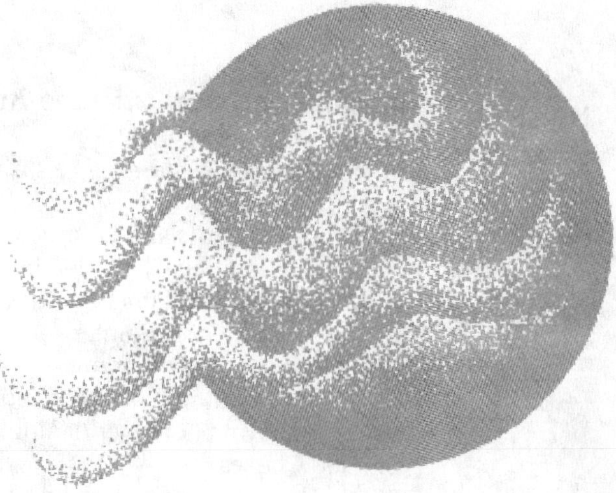

Contents

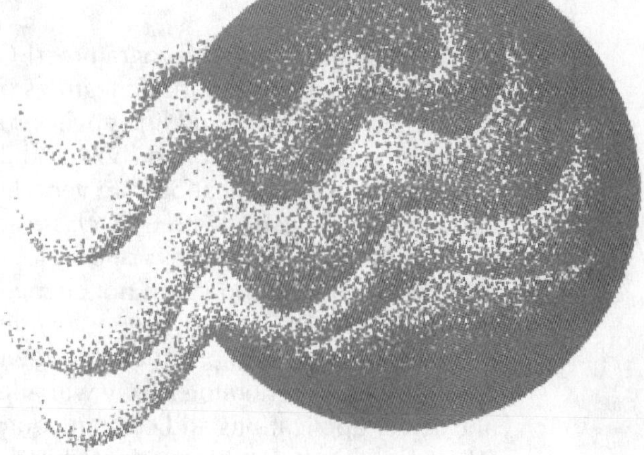

Introduction

In the summer of 1992, we attended a Microsoft Developers Conference on Windows NT in San Francisco. At this conference, Microsoft began hinting at the importance of programming with the Microsoft Foundation Class library (MFC). At that time, only a handful of programmers were taking advantage of the object-oriented features that this library provides. More recently, Microsoft has again hinted that programmers might do well by mastering the concepts of OLE and their Component Object Model, which includes the specification for OLE Custom Controls. The use of the MFC library and OLE design guidelines will be the driving force in Windows development well into the next century.

As a programmer, you may have been reluctant to master any of this material. After all, a procedure-oriented approach to Windows application development has worked just fine in the past. Hopefully, by purchasing this book you have seen the writing on the wall and are determined to stay on the cutting edge of this latest software technology. This book holds a carefully planned strategy in helping you master these new concepts in the fastest and easiest way possible.

First, as you may have discovered, object-oriented programming techniques are not mere extensions of procedure-oriented concepts. There are dues to be paid! However, once over this initial learning curve, an entire new world of programming awaits you. In terms of Windows programming, a whole collection of objects is available through the MFC library. So the first thing you need to be is an object-oriented Windows programmer! Chapters 1 and 2 will teach you the definitions, concepts and basic features of object-oriented application design in a non-threatening command line environment. Chapters 3 and 4 will entice you into a Windows environment and show you the true power of the MFC library.

Second, OLE applications are very difficult and time-consuming to write. Using traditional approaches with C++ classes or C structures means even simple applications can require days of development time. The good news is that once OLE code is developed it will not change significantly from one application to another. Thus, OLE code is a good candidate for a template. Microsoft has made template code generation an easy task with the use of Wizards. Wizards are automatic code generators. They will allow you to develop such things as client and server applications and custom controls in hours instead of days or weeks. Wizards only create object-oriented code, and in so doing, make full use of the MFC library. Chapter 5 will guide you through OLE concepts and definitions and illustrate OLE features with several examples. Chapters 6 and 7 will teach you how to use the various Wizards to create basic server and client applications. You'll also learn how to enhance this template code to create your own unique application(s).

Third, with the first release of Visual Basic, Windows developers began to move away from the use of stock Windows controls such as pushbuttons, scroll bars, radio buttons, etc., to custom controls. Custom controls give an application a unique look and flair. While custom controls were relatively simple to design in Visual Basic, that was not the case with early releases of Visual C++. The latest version of Visual C++, with the help of Wizards, allows you to develop the new standard in custom controls, OLE controls. Chapter 8 will help you understand what OLE custom controls are, how they differ from VDX controls, and their importance. In Chapters 9 and 10 you will learn how to use a control Wizard to develop simple and complex OLE custom controls. You will learn how custom controls fulfill the OLE Component Object Model for reusable components

This book makes certain assumptions about you as a developer/programmer and about the software and hardware platforms that you will be developing your applications on. As a C or C++ programmer, you should be familiar with procedure-oriented Windows programming such as that found in *Windows 3.1 Programming* by Murray and Pappas and published by Osborne/McGraw-Hill. Your computer should be running Win95 or Windows NT as its operating system. You must also have the latest version of Microsoft's Visual C++ compiler and Microsoft's OLE Custom Control Developer's Kit (CDK—currently supplied with the compiler) installed on your system. Note: When installing the Visual C++ compiler, we selected all available development options. For hardware, we strongly recommend a 50 Mhz - 100 Mhz, 80486 or Pentium computer with double or triple speed CD-ROM, 16 MB RAM, and a 500 MB hard drive. At this speed, full compiles will typically be under 1 minute.

Congratulations! By declaring your interest in this important area of Windows application development, you are setting yourself apart from many developers/programmers and are staying on the cutting edge of an exciting software technology.

— The Authors

This book is based on information on Windows 95 made public by Microsoft as of 2/6/95. Since this information was made public before the release of the product, we encourage you to visit your local bookstore after the product is released for updated books on Windows 95.

If you have a modem or access to the Internet, you can always get up-to-the-minute information on Windows 95 direct from Microsoft on WinNews:

On CompuServe:	GO WINNEWS
On the Internet:	ftp://ftp.microsoft.com/PerOpSys/Win_News/Chicago
	http://www.microsoft.com
On AOL:	keyword WINNEWS
On Prodigy:	jumpword WINNEWS
On GEnie:	WINNEWS file area on Windows RTC

You can also subscribe to Microsoft's WinNews electronic newsletter by sending Internet e-mail to enews@microsoft.nwnet.com and putting the words SUBSCRIBE WINNEWS in the text of the e-mail.

CHAPTER 1

An Introduction to Object-Oriented Concepts

To help you quickly master the concepts of OLE Application and Custom Control Development, this book has been divided into three major sections. This building-block approach allows you to master the fundamental concepts behind the more automatic features of Microsoft's integrated development environment should you need to customize an application.

Chapters I through 4 introduce the fundamental concepts associated with all object-oriented languages and then moves on to a simple example application. This application uses Microsoft's Foundation Class Library.

Chapters 5 through 7 expand upon this information by discussing the concepts involved in OLE application development and include examples of how to use Microsoft's Wizards. *Wizards* allow you to automatically generate many of the components necessary to create an OLE application.

Chapters 8 through 10 explain what custom controls are and how to generate application-specific interfaces. This section of the book also demonstrates the steps necessary to incorporate third-party commercial custom controls into an application.

In this chapter you will learn the various object-oriented programming (OOPs) concepts. You'll discover the differences between the traditional procedure-oriented programming approach to a problem and the object-oriented approach. Also discussed are definitions and terms associated with C++ and object-oriented programming. These terms include, among others, objects, encapsulation, hierarchy, inheritance, and polymorphism.

Later in the chapter simple examples will show that the C++ **class** type is an outgrowth of the C **struct** type. In the following chapter you will learn the details of how the C++ **class** type forms the foundation for object-oriented programming.

It All Runs on the Same Chip

Advertisers know that a product will sell better if the word *new* appears somewhere on the product's label. But object-oriented programming is not really a new programming concept.

For example, the machine code that instructs an 80486 chip is not structured code, procedure-oriented code, or object-oriented code—it is just a sequence of numeric instructions that tell the microprocessor what to do next. The most that can be said about the machine code is that it is executed in a classical top-down programming approach.

Put another way, regardless of a program's original "orientation," the code is eventually converted to a sequence of machine code instructions. If the conversion is performed optimally, the final code will be the same regardless of the original high-level language. To get a feel for this concept, use Microsoft's CodeView debugger, load a C or C++ program, and examine the optimized machine code counterpart.

Early programmers, growing up with the BASIC language, often wrote large programs without the use of structured programming concepts. Pages and pages of programming code were tied together with one- or two-letter variables that had a global scope. **Goto** statements abounded. The code was a nightmare to read, understand, and debug. Adding new features to such a program was like unlocking Pandora's box. The code, to say the least, was very difficult to maintain.

In the 1960s, structured programming concepts were introduced. These suggested using meaningful variable names, global and local variable scope, and a procedure-oriented top-down programming approach. The concepts made code easier to read, understand, and debug. Program maintenance was improved, because the program could now be studied and altered one procedure at a time. Programming languages such as Ada, C, and Pascal encourage a structured approach to programming problems.

Although C++ is the foundational language for object-oriented programming, it is still possible to write unstructured code or procedure-oriented code. The choice is yours. Bjarne Stroustrup, who developed C++ at Bell Labs, may well be the father of object-oriented programming as we know it in C++.

There might not be anything new in "programming concepts," but this chapter will introduce you to the most elegant *packaging* method for a programming concept that you have ever seen. At last, with languages such as C++, we truly have the tools to enter the age of object-oriented programming. The good news is that all this raw programming horsepower still runs on the same microprocessor you already drive.

Normal Structured Programming

If you have been programming in a language such as Pascal, you have probably been using a structured procedure approach to solve programming problems. You have also seen that a procedure-oriented C or C++ program is structured in such a way that there is typically a main function and possibly one or more functions (subroutines, if you will), which are called from the main function.

In this top-down approach the main function is typically short, shifting the work to the remaining functions in the program. Here program execution flows from the top of the main function and terminates at the bottom of the same function. In this approach, code and data are separate. Procedures define what is to happen to data, but the two never become one. You'll see that this will change in object-oriented programming. Again, a procedural approach is common among all structured languages including C, C++, Pascal, and PL/I.

The procedural approach suffers from several disadvantages, the chief of which is heavy program maintenance requirements. When additions or deletions must be made to the program code, such as in a database program, often the entire program must be reworked to include the new routines. This approach takes enormous amounts of time in both development and debugging. A better approach toward program maintenance is needed.

Switching to Object-Oriented Programming

Object-oriented programs (OOPs), on the other hand, function differently from the traditional procedural approach. They require a new programming strategy that is often difficult for traditional procedure-oriented programmers to grasp. During the next four chapters you will be introduced to the concepts that make up object-oriented programming in C++.

If you have already written or examined program code for Microsoft Windows or the OS/2 Presentation Manager, then you've tried one of the techniques used in object-oriented programming. In object-oriented programming, a program consists of a group of often-related objects.

With C++, objects are formed with the new **class** data type. A class provides a set of *values* (data) and the *operations* (methods or member functions) that act on those values. The resulting objects are then manipulated with messages. It is the message component of object-oriented languages that is also common to Windows and Presentation Manager programs.

In object-oriented programming, objects hold not only the *data* (member data) but the *method* (member functions) for working on that data. The two items have been combined into one working concept. Simply put, objects contain data and the method for working on that data.

There are three advantages offered to the programmer by object-oriented programming. The first advantage is less program maintenance. Programs are easier to read and understand. Program complexity is controlled by allowing only the necessary details to be viewed by the programmer.

The second advantage is program *alteration* (adding or deleting features). Additions and deletions can often be made to programs, such as in a database program, by simply adding or deleting additional objects. New objects can inherit everything from a parent object and need only add or delete items that differ.

Finally, a third advantage is that objects can be used numerous times. Well-designed objects can be saved in a tool kit of useful routines that can easily be inserted in new code, with few or no changes to that code.

Actually, many C programs could be converted to C++ syntax, and vice versa, with simple program alterations. For example, **printf** would be switched to **cout** for I/O streams. This is an example of an easy switch because the conversion was from and to a procedural programming structure.

Object-oriented programming is exclusively in the C++ realm, as C does not provide the vital link—the abstract data type **class**. It is therefore more difficult to convert a procedure-oriented program solution into its object-oriented form. This can be a distinct disadvantage. Programs will have to be reworked with traditional functions being replaced with objects. In some cases, it will be easier to toss out the old program and create an object-oriented program from the ground up.

Object-Oriented Programming with C++

Object-oriented programming concepts cross language boundaries. Microsoft's Quick Pascal, for example, was one of the first languages to allow the use of objects. What does C++ have that makes it a suitable language for developing object-oriented programs? The answer, as mentioned earlier, is the **class** data type.

It is C++'s class, built upon C's **struct** type, that gives the language the ability to build objects. C++ brings several additional features to object-oriented programming over other languages that simply make use of objects. C++'s advantages include strong typing, operator overloading, and less emphasis on the preprocessor.

It is true that object-oriented programming can be done with other products and in other languages, but with C++ the benefits are outstanding! This is a language that was designed, not retrofitted, for object-oriented programming.

In the following sections of this chapter you will learn more object-oriented terminology. These terms and definitions will help you form a solid understanding of this programming technique. Hang on, these new terms will be your biggest hurdle as you enter the world of object-oriented programming.

Object-Oriented Definitions and Terminology

Much of the terminology of object-oriented programming is common to object-oriented languages such as Pascal, C++, and so on. We'll discuss terms that are more specific to C++ in Chapter 2.

Object-oriented programming is a programming technique that allows the programmer to view concepts as a variety of objects. By using objects, the programmer can represent the tasks that are to be performed, their interaction, and any conditions that must be observed. A data structure often forms the basis of an object, thus in C or C++ the **struct** type can form an elementary object.

Communicating with objects can be done with messages, as mentioned earlier. Using messages is similar to calling a function in a procedure-oriented program. When an object receives a message, methods contained within the object respond.

Methods are similar to the functions of procedure-oriented programming. However, methods are part of an object.

The C++ *class* is an extension of the C and C++ **struct** type and forms the required abstract data type for object-oriented programming. The class can contain closely related items that share attributes. In a more formal definition, an *object* is simply an instance of a class. In Figure 1-1, the **Tire** class is illustrated.

Assume that the **Tire** class is described in the program's code. This class might include a description of traits that are common to all tires, such as diameter, air pressure, weight, composition, cost, and so on, along with common functions, such as **ShowTire( ).** At run time three additional objects of the Tire class can be created. They could include, for this example, the *RainTire,* the *SnowTire,* and the *AllSeasonTire.* The additional objects might include details of features and data common to each model. For example, a *SnowTire* is an object that describes a particular type of tire. It is an instance of the **Tire** class.

If a message is sent to the **Tire** class (similar to a call to a function) with instructions to display all winter tread patterns, that message could only be used by the *SnowTire* object of the class.

Ultimately, there should emerge class *libraries* containing many object types. Instances of those object types could be used by the programmer to piece together program code. In Chapters 3 and 4 you will see exciting examples of this when we look at Windows class libraries later in the book.

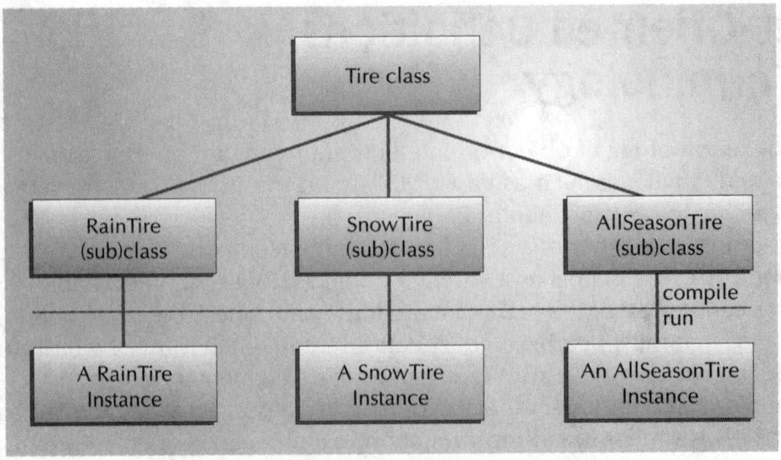

FIGURE 1-1. *A diagram of the Tire class*

Before we study these terms in closer detail, there are additional concepts that relate to C++ and object-oriented programming.

Class Hierarchy

The C++ **class** actually serves as a template or pattern for creating objects. The objects formed from the class description, are *instances* of the class. It is possible to develop a class *hierarchy* where there is a parent class and several child classes. In C++ the basis for doing this revolves around *derived* classes. Parent classes represent more generalized tasks, while derived child classes are given specific tasks to perform.

For example, the **Tire** class discussed earlier might contain data and methods common among all tires: appropriate measurements, materials, and common functions such as rolling resistance, tread wear, and heat-generation algorithms, not to mention a function to view the object (**ShowTire( )**). Child classes, derived from the parent, such as **RainTire**, **SnowTire**, and **AllSeasonTire**, could contain items specific to the derived class or subclass.

Encapsulation

Encapsulation refers to how each object combines its member data and member functions (methods) into a single structure. Figure 1-2 illustrates how data fields and methods can be combined to build an object.

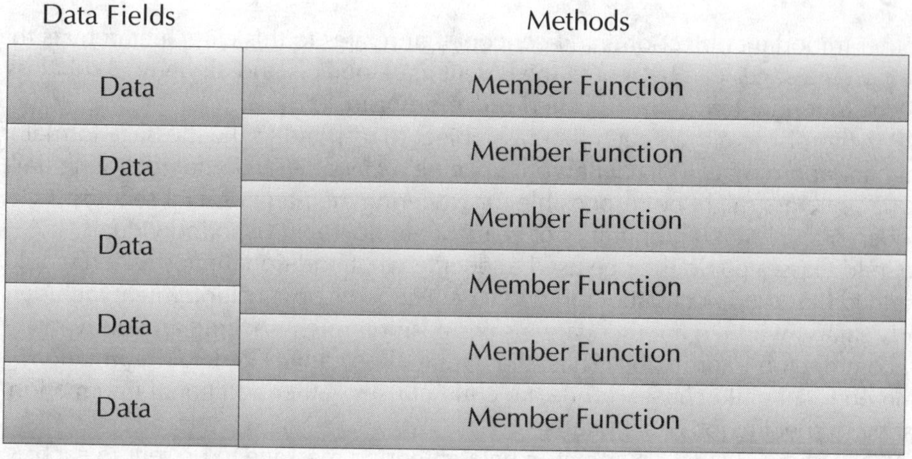

FIGURE 1-2. *Data fields and methods combined to build an object*

Typically, an object's description is part of a C++ class and describes the object's internal structure, how the object relates with other objects, and some form of protection that isolates the functional details of the object from outside of the class. The C++ class structure does all this.

In a C++ class, functional details of the object are controlled by using *public*, *private*, and/or *protected* descriptors. In object-oriented programming the public section is typically used for the interface information (methods) that makes the class reusable across applications. If data or methods are contained in the public section, they are available outside of the class. The private section of a class limits the availability of data or methods to the class itself. A protected section containing data or methods is limited to the class and any derived subclasses.

Inheritance

Inheritance in object-oriented programming allows an object to inherit properties from a class of objects. The parent class serves as a pattern for the derived class and can be altered in several ways. In the next chapter you will learn that member functions can be overloaded, new member functions can be added, and member access privileges can be changed.

If an object inherits its attributes from a single parent, it is called *single* inheritance. If an object inherits its attributes from multiple parents, it is called *multiple* inheritance. Inheritance is an important concept—it allows reuse of a class definition without requiring major code changes. Inheritance encourages the reuse of code, since child classes are extensions of parent classes.

Polymorphism

Another important object-oriented concept that relates to this class hierarchy is that common messages can be sent to the parent class objects and all derived subclass objects. In formal terms, this is called *polymorphism*.

Polymorphism allows each subclass object to respond to the message format in a manner appropriate to its definition. Imagine a class hierarchy for gathering data. The parent class might be responsible for gathering the name, social security number, occupation, and number of years of employment of an individual.

Child classes could then be used to decide what additional information would be added based on occupation. In one case a supervisory position might include yearly salary, while in another case a sales position might include an hourly rate and commission information. Thus, the parent class gathers general information common to all child classes, while the child classes gather additional information relating to specific job descriptions.

Polymorphism allows a common data-gathering message to be sent to each class. Both the parent and child classes respond in an appropriate manner to the message. Polymorphism encourages extendibility of existing code.

Virtual Functions

Polymorphism gives objects the ability to respond to messages from routines when the object's type is not known. In C++, this ability is a result of late binding. Late binding is accomplished with virtual functions. With *late binding,* the addresses are determined dynamically at run time, rather than statically at compile time.

With traditional compiled languages, binding is *static* (fixed) at compile time. Here function names are replaced with memory addresses. This static method is often called *early binding.*

Virtual functions are defined in the parent class when subsequent derived classes will overload the function by redefining the function's implementation. When virtual functions are used, messages are passed as a pointer that points to the object instead of being passed directly to the object.

Virtual functions use a table for address information. The table is initialized at run time using a constructor. A *constructor* is invoked whenever an object of its class is created. The job of the constructor here is to link the virtual function with the table of address information. During the compile operation, the address of the virtual function is not known. Rather, it is given the position in the table of addresses that will contain (determined at run time) the address for the function.

Your First C++ Class

We have alluded to the fact that the C++ **class** type is an extension of C's **struct** type. In the following section, you will learn how the **struct** type can be used in C++ to form a primitive class, complete with data and members.

Next you'll examine the formal syntax for defining a class and see several simple examples of its implementation. The differences between a primitive **struct** class type and an actual C++ class will be discussed. Several simple examples will be used to illustrate class concepts. The next chapter is devoted to a detailed analysis of the C++ class as it is applied to object-oriented programming.

Creating Classes Out of Structures

In many respects, the structure in C++ is an elementary form of class. The keyword **struct** is used to define a structure. Examine the following code:

```
//
//   SQROOT.CPP
//   C++ program using the keyword "struct" to illustrate a
//   primitive form of class. Here several member functions
```

```
//  are defined within the structure.
//  William H. Murray and Chris H. Pappas
//

#include <iostream.h>
#include <math.h>

struct math_operations {
  double data_value;

  void set_value(double ang) {data_value=ang;}
  double get_square(void) {double answer;
                           answer=data_value*data_value;
                           return (answer);}
  double get_square_root(void) {double answer;
                                answer=sqrt(data_value);
                                return (answer);}
} math;

main()
{
  // set numeric value to 31.20
  math.set_value(31.20);

  cout << "The square of the number is: "
       << math.get_square() << endl;
  cout << "The square root of the number is: "
       << math.get_square_root() << endl;
  return (0);
}
```

The first thing to notice in this code is that the structure definition contains member data and functions. While you might be used to seeing data declarations as part of a structure, this is probably the first time you have seen member functions defined within the structure definition. These member functions can act upon the data contained in the structure (or class) itself.

Recall that a class can contain member data and functions. By default, in a **struct** declaration in C++, member data and functions are public. A public section means that the data and the functions are available outside of the structure. Here is the output sent to the screen when the program is executed:

```
The square of the number is: 973.44
The square root of the number is: 5.5857
```

In this example, the structure definition contains a single data value.

```
double data_value;
```

Next, three member functions are defined. Actually, the code for each function is contained within the structure.

```
void set_value(double ang) {data_value=ang;}
double get_square(void) {double answer;
                          answer=data_value*data_value;
                          return (answer);}
double get_square_root(void) {double answer;
                               answer=sqrt(data_value);
                               return (answer);}
```

The first member function is responsible for initializing the variable *data_value*. The remaining two member functions return the square and square root of *data_value*. Notice that the member functions are not passed a value; *data_value* is available to them as members of the structure. Both member functions return a **double**.

The program's **main( )** function sets the value of *data_value* to 31.20 with a call to the member function, **set_value**.

```
math.set_value(31.20);
```

Notice the name *math* has been associated with the structure **math_operations**. The remaining two member functions return values to the *cout* stream.

```
cout << "The square of the number is: "
     << math.get_square() << endl;
cout << "The square root of the number is: "
     << math.get_square_root() << endl;
```

This example contains a structure with member data and functions. The functions are contained within the structure definition. It won't get any simpler than this example.

In the next program, the **struct** keyword will still be used to develop a primitive class, but this time the member functions will be written outside of the structure. This is the way you will most commonly see structures and classes defined.

The next example contains a structure definition with one data member, *data_value*, and seven member functions. The member functions return information for various trigonometric values.

```
//
//  TSTRUC.CPP
```

```
//  C++ program using the keyword "struct" to illustrate a
//  primitive form of class. This program uses a structure
//  to obtain trigonometric values for an angle.
//  William H. Murray and Chris H. Pappas
//

#include <iostream.h>
#include <math.h>

const double DEG_TO_RAD=0.0174532925;

struct degree {
  double data_value;

  void set_value(double);
  double get_sine(void);
  double get_cosine(void);
  double get_tangent(void);
  double get_secant(void);
  double get_cosecant(void);
  double get_cotangent(void);
} deg;

void degree::set_value(double ang)
{
  data_value=ang;
}

double degree::get_sine(void)
{
  double answer;

  answer=sin(DEG_TO_RAD*data_value);
  return (answer);
}

double degree::get_cosine(void)
{
  double answer;

  answer=cos(DEG_TO_RAD*data_value);
  return (answer);
```

```
}

double degree::get_tangent(void)
{
  double answer;

  answer=tan(DEG_TO_RAD*data_value);
  return (answer);
}

double degree::get_secant(void)
{
  double answer;

  answer=1.0/sin(DEG_TO_RAD*data_value);
  return (answer);
}

double degree::get_cosecant(void)
{
  double answer;

  answer=1.0/cos(DEG_TO_RAD*data_value);
  return (answer);
}

double degree::get_cotangent(void)
{
  double answer;

  answer=1.0/tan(DEG_TO_RAD*data_value);
  return (answer);
}

main()
{
  // set angle to 30.0 degrees
  deg.set_value(30.0);

  cout << "The sine of the angle is: "
       << deg.get_sine() << endl;
  cout << "The cosine of the angle is: "
```

```
        << deg.get_cosine() << endl;
  cout << "The tangent of the angle is: "
        << deg.get_tangent() << endl;
  cout << "The secant of the angle is: "
        << deg.get_secant() << endl;
  cout << "The cosecant of the angle is: "
        << deg.get_cosecant() << endl;
  cout << "The cotangent of the angle is: "
        << deg.get_cotangent() << endl;
  return (0);
}
```

Notice that the structure definition contains the prototypes for the member functions. The variable *deg* is associated with the **degree** structure type.

```
struct degree {
  double data_value;

  void set_value(double);
  double get_sine(void);
  double get_cosine(void);
  double get_tangent(void);
  double get_secant(void);
  double get_cosecant(void);
  double get_cotangent(void);
} deg;
```

Immediately after the structure is defined, the various member functions are developed and listed. The member functions are associated with the structure or class by using the *scoping operator* (::). Other than using the scoping operator, the member functions resemble normal functions.

Examine the first part of the **main( )** function.

```
  // set angle to 30.0 degrees
  deg.set_value (30.0);
```

Here the value 30.0 is being passed as an argument to the **set_value** function. Observe the syntax for this operation. The **set_value** function, itself, is very simple.

```
void degree::set_value(double ang)
{
  data_value=ang;
}
```

The function accepts the argument and assigns the value to the class variable *data_value*. This is one way of initializing class variables. From this point forward, in the class *data_value* is accessible by each of the six member functions. The job of the member functions is to calculate the sine, cosine, tangent, secant, cosecant, and cotangent of the given angle. The respective values are printed to the screen from the **main( )** function with statements similar to the following:

```
cout << "The sine of the angle is: "
     << deg.get_sine() << endl;
```

The member functions are accessed with the dot notation commonly used for structures. Pointer variables can also be assigned to a structure or class, in which case, the arrow operator is used. You will see examples of this in Chapter 2.

C++ Class Syntax

The definition of a C++ class begins with the keyword **class**. The class name (tag type) immediately follows the keyword. The framework of the class is very similar to the **struct** type definition that you have already seen.

```
class type {
  type var1;
  type var2;
  type var3;
       .
       .
       .
public:
  member function 1;
  member function 2;
  member function 3;
  member function 4;
       .
       .
       .
} name associated with class type;
```

Member variables immediately follow the class declaration. These variables are private, by default, to the class and can only be accessed by the member functions that follow. Member functions typically follow a public declaration. This allows access to the member functions from calling routines external to the class. All class member functions have access to public, private, and protected parts of a class.

The following shows a class that will be used in the next programming example.

```
class degree {
  double data_value;

public:
  void set_value(double);
  double get_sine(void);
  double get_cosine(void);
  double get_tangent(void);
  double get_secant(void);
  double get_cosecant(void);
  double get_cotangent(void);
} deg;
```

This class has a *type* (tag name) **degree**. A private variable, *data_value*, will share degree values among the various member functions. Seven functions make up the function members of the class. They are **set_value**, **get_sine**, **get_cosine**, **get_tangent**, **get_secant**, **get_cosecant**, **get_cotangent**. The name that is associated with this class type is *deg*. Unlike this example, the association of a variable name with the class name is most frequently made in the **main( )** function.

Does this class definition look familiar? It is basically the structure definition, from the previous example, converted to a true class.

A Simple Class

In a C++ class, the visibility of class members is by default private. That is, member variables are accessible only to member functions of the class. If the member functions are to have visibility beyond the class, that visibility must be explicitly specified.

The conversion of the last program's structure to a true C++ class is both simple and straightforward. First, the **struct** keyword is replaced by the **class** keyword. Second, the member functions that are to have public visibility are separated from the private variable of the class with the use of a public declaration. Examine the complete program.

```
//
//  TCLASS.CPP
//  C++ program illustrates a simple but true class and
//  introduces the concept of private and public.
//  This program uses a class to obtain the trigonometric
//  value for a given angle.
```

```
//  William H. Murray and Chris H. Pappas
//

#include <iostream.h>
#include <math.h>

const double DEG_TO_RAD=0.0174532925;

class degree {
  double data_value;

public:
  void set_value(double);
  double get_sine(void);
  double get_cosine(void);
  double get_tangent(void);
  double get_secant(void);
  double get_cosecant(void);
  double get_cotangent(void);
} deg;

void degree::set_value(double ang)
{
  data_value=ang;
}

double degree::get_sine(void)
{
  double answer;

  answer=sin(DEG_TO_RAD*data_value);
  return (answer);
}

double degree::get_cosine(void)
{
  double answer;

  answer=cos(DEG_TO_RAD*data_value);
  return (answer);
}
```

```
double degree::get_tangent(void)
{
  double answer;

  answer=tan(DEG_TO_RAD*data_value);
  return (answer);
}

double degree::get_secant(void)
{
  double answer;

  answer=1.0/sin(DEG_TO_RAD*data_value);
  return (answer);
}

double degree::get_cosecant(void)
{
  double answer;

  answer=1.0/cos(DEG_TO_RAD*data_value);
  return (answer);
}

double degree::get_cotangent(void)
{
  double answer;

  answer=1.0/tan(DEG_TO_RAD*data_value);
  return (answer);
}

main()
{
  // set angle to 30.0 degrees
  deg.set_value(30.0);

  cout << "The sine of the angle is: "
       << deg.get_sine() << endl;
  cout << "The cosine of the angle is: "
       << deg.get_cosine() << endl;
  cout << "The tangent of the angle is: "
```

```
        << deg.get_tangent() << endl;
    cout << "The secant of the angle is: "
        << deg.get_secant() << endl;
    cout << "The cosecant of the angle is: "
        << deg.get_cosecant() << endl;
    cout << "The cotangent of the angle is: "
        << deg.get_cotangent() << endl;
    return (0);
}
```

In this example, the body of the program remains the same. The structure definition has been converted to a true, but elementary, class definition with private and public parts.

Note that the variable *data_value* is private to the class (by default) and as a result is only accessible to the member functions of the class. The member functions, themselves, have been declared public in visibility and are accessible from outside of the class. Each class member, however, whether public or private, has access to all other class members public or private.

Here is the output from the program:

```
The sine of the angle is: 0.5
The cosine of the angle is: 0.866025
The tangent of the angle is: 0.57735
The secant of the angle is: 2
The cosecant of the angle is: 1.1547
The cotangent of the angle is: 1.73205
```

Again, class member functions are usually defined immediately after the class has been defined and before the **main( )** function of the program. Nonmember class functions are still defined after the function **main( )** and are prototyped in the normal fashion.

In the following chapter, we'll look at the details of C++ classes more closely.

CHAPTER 2

Developing Object-Oriented Applications

There are two major components involved in designing an object-oriented solution to any programming problem. The first component is the *design philosophy*. The design philosophy is the logical dissection of the problem into smaller, more manageable steps, followed by the ordering of those steps into a working solution.

The second component is the *language construct* that supports an object-oriented solution. For example, in a procedural design approach, the function or procedure is the fundamental language construct used to encode the solution. However, an object-oriented design approach relies heavily on a new construct, the *object*.

Learning the syntax of OOP (object-oriented programming) is the easier of the two, since it is just a matter of mastering and applying a set of rules. Understanding how to solve a problem using OOP design philosophy is a bit more difficult. The problem-solving ability will come by understanding OOP syntax, combined with studying this syntax as applied in the many example programs throughout this book.

In this chapter you will learn the syntax for those features provided by C++ that will enable you to create, encode, and manipulate objects. Your understanding of how to solve a problem by using OOP technology will take a major leap forward as soon as you learn how objects are created and used.

The C++ Classes

In the previous chapter you learned that a primitive C++ class could be created with the use of the **struct** keyword. Next, several elementary C++ classes were created using the **class** keyword. Both types of examples illustrated the simple fact that classes can contain both member data and member functions that act on that data.

In this chapter you will learn more about C++ classes. This information includes the nesting of classes and structures, the use of constructors and destructors, overloading member functions, friend functions, operator overloading, derived classes, virtual functions, and other miscellaneous topics. These class structures create objects that form the foundation of object-oriented programs.

As you have studied C and C++ programming, consider the increase in programming power you have gained with each new data type: *vectors,* or one-dimensional arrays, allow a group of like data types to be held together. Next, *structures* allow related items of different data types to be combined in a group. Finally, the C++ *class* concept takes us one step further with abstract data types. A class allows the user to implement a member data type and to associate member functions with the data. A programmer using classes has the storage concept associated with a structure along with the member functions to operate on the member variables.

Remember that a C++ class, or object, retains the benefits of a structure along with the ability to limit access to specific data to functions that are also members of the class. As a result, classes are one of the single greatest contributions made by C++ to programming. The added features of the class include the ability to initialize and protect sensitive functions and data.

Advanced Class Features

In the last chapter you learned the syntax for creating an elementary C++ class. Classes have extended capabilities that go far beyond this simple syntax. This section is devoted to exploring these capabilities with an eye toward object-oriented programming.

Nesting

C++ allows you to nest structure definitions. This is also true for C++ classes. When using nested classes, take care not to make the resulting declaration more complicated than necessary. The following example illustrates nesting.

The program demonstrates how two structures can be nested within a class definition. Using nesting in this fashion is both common and practical. The **class** keyword can also be used in this manner.

```
//
//  WAGES.CPP
//  C++ program illustrates the use of nesting concepts
//  in classes. This program calculates the wages for
//  the named employee.
//  William H. Murray and Chris H. Pappas
//

#include <iostream.h>

char newline;

class employee {
  struct emp_name {
    char firstname[20];
    char middlename[20];
    char lastname[20];
  } name;
  struct emp_hours {
    double hours;
    double base_sal;
    double overtime_sal;
  } hours;

public:
```

```
  void emp_input(void);
  void emp_output(void);
};

void employee::emp_input(void)
{
  cout << "Enter first name of employee: ";
  cin >> name.firstname;
  cin.get(newline);     // flush carriage return
  cout << "Enter middle name of employee: ";
  cin >> name.middlename;
  cin.get(newline);
  cout << "Enter last name of employee:  ";
  cin >> name.lastname;
  cin.get(newline);

  cout << "Enter total hours worked:   ";
  cin >> hours.hours;
  cout << "Enter hourly wage (base rate):  ";
  cin >> hours.base_sal;
  cout << "Enter overtime wage (overtime rate): ";
  cin >> hours.overtime_sal;
  cout << "\n\n";
}

void employee::emp_output(void)
{
  cout << name.firstname << " " << name.middlename
       << " " << name.lastname << endl;
  if (hours.hours <= 40)
    cout << "Base Pay:  $"
         << hours.hours * hours.base_sal << endl;
    else {
      cout << "Base Pay:  $"
           << 40 * hours.base_sal << endl;
      cout << "Overtime Pay: $"
           << (hours.hours-40) * hours.overtime_sal
           << endl;
    }
}

main()
```

```
{
  employee acme_corp;     // associate acme_corp with class

  acme_corp.emp_input();
  acme_corp.emp_output();
  return (0);
}
```

In this example, two structures (primitive C++ classes) are nested within the **employee** class definition. As you can see, the use of nesting can be quite straightforward.

```
class employee {
  struct emp_name {
    char firstname[20];
    char middlename[20];
    char lastname[20];
  } name;
  struct emp_hours {
    double hours;
    double base_salary;
    double overtime_sal;
  } hours;
```

The **employee** class includes two nested structs (classes), **emp_name** and **emp_hours**. The nested classes, while part of the private section of **employee** class, are actually available outside of the class. In other words, the visibility of the nested classes is the same as if they were defined outside of the **employee** class. The individual member variables, for this example, are accessed through the member functions (public, by default), **emp_input** and **emp_output**.

Both member functions **emp_input** and **emp_output** are of type **void**, and do not accept arguments. The **emp_input** function prompts the user for employee data that will be passed to the nested structures (classes). The data collected includes the employee's full name, the total hours worked, the regular pay rate, and the overtime pay rate. Output is generated when the **emp_output** function is called. The employee's name, base pay, and overtime pay will be printed to the screen.

```
Enter first name of employee: Bob
Enter middle name of employee: Fitzgerald
Enter last name of employee: Azimith
Enter total hours worked: 55
Enter hourly wage (base rate): 8.00
Enter overtime wage (overtime rate): 10.00
```

```
Bob Fitzgerald Azimith
Base Pay:  $320.00
Overtime Pay: $150.00
```

The length of the **main( )** function in this program is fairly short. This is because most of the work is being done by the member functions of the class.

```
employee acme_corp;     // associate acme_corp with class

  acme_corp.emp_input();
  acme_corp.emp_output();
```

First, the variable, *acme_corp*, representing the Acme Computer Corporation, is associated with the **employee** class. To request a member function, the dot operator is used. Next, **acme_corp.emp_input()** is called to collect the employee information and then **acme_corp.emp_output()** is used to calculate and print the payroll results.

Constructors and Destructors

A *constructor* is a class member function. Constructors are useful for initializing class variables or allocating memory storage. The constructor always has the same name as the class it is defined within.

Constructors have additional versatility; they can accept arguments and be overloaded. A constructor is executed automatically when an object of the **class** type is created. *Free store* objects are objects created with the **new** operator and serve to allocate memory for the objects created. Constructors are generated by Microsoft's Visual C/C++ compiler if they are not explicitly defined.

A *destructor* is a class member function typically used to return memory allocated from free store memory. The destructor, like the constructor, has the same name as the class it is defined in, preceded by the tilde character (~). Destructors are the complement to their constructor counterparts.

A destructor is automatically called when the **delete** operator is applied to a class pointer, or when a program passes beyond the scope of a class object. Destructors, unlike their constructor counterparts, cannot accept an argument and may not be overloaded. Destructors are also generated by Microsoft's C/C++ compiler if they are not explicitly defined.

Creating a Simple Constructor and Destructor

In the first example, involving the use of constructors and destructors, a constructor and destructor will be used to signal the start and end of a coin conversion example. This program illustrates that constructors and destructors are called automatically.

```
//
//  COINS.CPP
//  C++ program illustrates the use of constructors and
//  destructors in a simple program.
//  This program converts cents into appropriate coins:
//  (quarters, dimes, nickels, and pennies).
//  William H. Murray and Chris H. Pappas
//

#include <iostream.h>

const int QUARTER=25;
const int DIME=10;
const int NICKEL=5;

class coins {
  int number;

public:
  coins() {cout << "Begin Conversion!\n";}       // constructor
  ~coins() {cout << "\nFinished Conversion!";}  // destructor
  void get_cents(int);
  int quarter_conversion(void);
  int dime_conversion(int);
  int nickel_conversion(int);
};

void coins::get_cents(int cents)
{
  number=cents;
  cout << number << " cents, converts to:"
       << endl;
}

int coins::quarter_conversion(void)
{
  cout << number/QUARTER << " quarter(s), ";
  return(number%QUARTER);
}
```

```
int coins::dime_conversion(int d)
{
  cout << d/DIME << " dime(s), ";
  return(d%DIME);
}

int coins::nickel_conversion(int n)
{
  cout << n/NICKEL << " nickel(s), and ";
  return(n%NICKEL);
}

main()
{
  int c,d,n,p;

  cout << "Enter the cash, in cents, to convert: ";
  cin >> c;

  // associate cash_in_cents with coins class.
  coins cash_in_cents;

  cash_in_cents.get_cents(c);
  d=cash_in_cents.quarter_conversion();
  n=cash_in_cents.dime_conversion(d);
  p=cash_in_cents.nickel_conversion(n);
  cout << p << " penny(ies).";
  return (0);
}
```

This program uses four member functions. The first function passes the number of pennies to the private class variable, *number*. The remaining three functions are used to convert cash, given in cents, to the equivalent cash in quarters, dimes, nickels, and pennies. Notice, in particular, the placement of the constructor and destructor in the class definition.

The constructor and destructor function descriptions contain nothing more than a message that will be printed to the screen. The constructors are not specifically called by the program. Their appearance on the screen is our key that the constructor and destructor were automatically called when the object was created and destroyed.

```
public:
  coins() {cout << "Begin Conversion!\n";}          // constructor
  ~coins() {cout << "\nFinished Conversion!";}  // destructor
```

Here is an example of the output from this program.

```
Enter the cash, in cents, to convert: 230
Begin Conversion!
230 cents, converts to:
9 quarter(s), 0 dime(s), 1 nickel(s), and 0 penny(ies).
Finished Conversion!
```

In this example, the function definition is actually included within the constructor and destructor. When the function definition is included with member functions, it is said to be implicitly defined. Member functions can be defined in the typical manner or declared explicitly as inline functions.

Using Constructors to Initialize Member Variables

Another practical use for constructors is for initialization of private class variables. In the previous examples, class variables were set by utilizing separate member functions. In the next example, the original class of the previous program is modified slightly to eliminate the need for user input. In this case, the variable, *number*, will be initialized to 522 pennies.

```
class coins {
  int number;

public:
  coins() {number=522;}                              // constructor
```

The route to private class variables is always through class member functions. Remember that the constructor is considered a member function.

Creating a Pointer Class

The next example illustrates another use for constructors and destructors while also teaching you how to incorporate the features of the Microsoft Mouse in your programs. Study the complete program listing that follows, and pay particular attention to the definition of the **pointer** class. Note in particular that the constructor and destructor are defined, like member functions, outside the class definition.

```
//
//  MOUSE.CPP
//  C++ program creates a pointer class which will allow
//  the use of the Microsoft Mouse for DOS mode programs.
//  A constructor initializes the mouse, while a
//  destructor hides the mouse pointer.
//  William H. Murray and Chris H. Pappas
//

#include <iostream.h>
#include <dos.h>          // for mouse
#include <process.h>      // for exit

class pointer {
  int l_button;
  int r_button;

public:
  pointer();
  ~pointer();
  void p_latent(void);
  void p_visible(void);
  int p_lbinfo(void);
  int p_rbinfo(void);
  int p_xinfo(void);
  int p_yinfo(void);
} ms_mouse;               // instance of the class

pointer::pointer(void)
{
  union REGS regs;

  regs.x.ax=0;
  int86(0x33,&regs,&regs);
}

pointer::~pointer(void)
{
  union REGS regs;

  regs.x.ax=2;
  int86(0x33,&regs,&regs);
}
```

```
void pointer::p_latent(void)
{
  union REGS regs;

  regs.x.ax=2;
  int86(0x33,&regs,&regs);
}

void pointer::p_visible(void)
{
  union REGS regs;

  regs.x.ax=1;
  int86(0x33,&regs,&regs);
}

int pointer::p_lbinfo(void)
{
  union REGS regs;

  l_button=0;
  regs.x.ax=3;
  int86(0x33,&regs,&regs);
  if(regs.x.bx & 1)
    l_button=1;
  return(l_button);
}

int pointer::p_rbinfo(void)
{
  union REGS regs;

  r_button=0;
  regs.x.ax=3;
  int86(0x33,&regs,&regs);
  if(regs.x.bx & 2)
    r_button=1;
  return(r_button);
}

int pointer::p_xinfo(void)
```

```
{
  union REGS regs;

  regs.x.ax=3;
  int86(0x33,&regs,&regs);
  return(regs.x.cx);
}

int pointer::p_yinfo(void)
{
  union REGS regs;

  regs.x.ax=3;
  int86(0x33,&regs,&regs);
  return(regs.x.dx);
}

main()
{
  ms_mouse.p_visible();    // start with mouse visible

  for(;;) {
    if(ms_mouse.p_lbinfo()==1)
      ms_mouse.p_visible();
      cout << ms_mouse.p_xinfo() << "\t"
           << ms_mouse.p_yinfo() << endl;
    if(ms_mouse.p_rbinfo()==1)
      ms_mouse.p_latent();
      cout << ms_mouse.p_xinfo() << "\t"
           << ms_mouse.p_yinfo() << endl;
    if(ms_mouse.p_lbinfo()==1 && ms_mouse.p_rbinfo()==1)
      exit(0);
  }
  return (0);
}
```

The **pointer** class uses a constructor, *pointer()*, and a destructor, *~pointer()*. To use the Microsoft Mouse, under DOS, an interrupt 33h is used in conjunction with the **int86** function.

By sending various values to specific registers, the mouse can be made to do many tasks. Under DOS, the mouse can be initialized by passing a 0 in the **ax** register, as shown in the constructor's definition.

```
pointer::pointer(void)
{
  union REGS regs;

  regs.x.ax=0;
  int86(0x33,&regs,&regs);
}
```

Here a **union** is used to allow communication with the system's registers.

A unique application available with destructors can be seen, during execution, when the mouse pointer is automatically erased when the destructor is called. The destructor passes a 2 to the **ax** register and then calls the mouse interrupt.

```
pointer::~pointer(void)
{
  union REGS regs;

  regs.x.ax=2;
  int86(0x33,&regs,&regs);
}
```

The remaining class member functions return information on mouse buttons and *x,y* screen coordinate positions for the mouse. The structure of these remaining member functions is fairly consistent and makes good use of **unions**.

If you execute this program, the *x* and *y* screen coordinates will be continuously printed to the screen. If you push the right mouse button, the mouse pointer will disappear from the screen. You will still be able to track the mouse's position, you just won't be able to see the mouse pointer on the screen. The mouse's pointer can be made visible again by pushing the left mouse button.

Pushing both buttons at the same time will terminate the execution of the program and also erase the mouse pointer. Can you think of any applications that you might want to write that might make good use of the mouse?

Using Constructors and Destructors for Creating and Deleting Free Store Memory

Perhaps the most significant reason for using a constructor is in utilizing free store memory. In the next example, a constructor is used to allocate memory for the *string1* pointer with the **new** operator. A destructor is also used to release the allocated memory back to the system when the object is destroyed. This is accomplished with the use of the **delete** operator.

```
class string_operation {
  char *string1;
  int  string_len;

public:
  string_operation(char *) {string1=new char[string_len];}
  ~string_operation() {delete string1;}
  void input_data(char *);
  void output_data(char *);
};
```

The memory allocated by **new** to the pointer, *string1*, can only be deallocated with a subsequent call to **delete**. For this reason, you will usually see memory allocated to pointers in constructors and deallocated in destructors. This also ensures that if the variable assigned to the class passes out of its scope, the allocated memory will be returned to the system. These operations make memory allocation dynamic and are most useful in programs that use linked lists.

Overloading Class Member Functions

Class member functions, like ordinary C++ functions, can be overloaded. *Overloading* (functions) means that more than one function can have the same function name in the current scope. It becomes the compiler's responsibility to select the correct function based upon the number and type of arguments used during the function call.

The first example in this section illustrates the overloading of a class function named **number()**. This overloaded function will return the absolute value of an integer or double with the use of the math functions **abs()**, which accepts and returns integer values, and **fabs()**, which accepts and returns double values. With an overloaded function, the argument types determine which member function will actually be used.

```
//
//   ABSOL.CPP
//   C++ program illustrates member function overloading.
//   Program determines the absolute value of an integer
//   and a double.
//   William H. Murray and Chris H. Pappas
//

#include <iostream.h>
```

```
#include <math.h>
#include <stdlib.h>

class absolute_value {
public:
  int number(int);
  double number(double);
};

int absolute_value::number(int test_data)
{
  int answer;

  answer=abs(test_data);
  return (answer);
}

double absolute_value::number(double test_data)
{
  double answer;

  answer=fabs(test_data);
  return (answer);
}

main()
{
  absolute_value neg_number;

  cout << "The absolute value is "
       << neg_number.number(-165) << endl;
  cout << "The absolute value is "
       << neg_number.number(-165.2314) << endl;
  return (0);
}
```

Notice that the dot operator is used in conjunction with the member function name to pass a negative integer and negative double values. The program selects the proper member function based upon the type (integer or double) of argument passed along with the function name. The positive value, returned by each function, is printed to the screen.

```
the absolute value is 165
the absolute value is 165.2314
```

In another example, angle information is passed to member functions in one of two formats—a double or a string. With member function overloading, it is possible to process both types.

```
//
//  OVERLD.CPP
//  C++ program illustrates overloading two class member
//  functions. The program allows an angle to be entered
//  in decimal or deg/min/sec formats. One member function
//  accepts data as a double, the other, as a string. The
//  program returns the sine, cosine, and tangent.
//  William H. Murray and Chris H. Pappas
//

#include <iostream.h>
#include <math.h>
#include <string.h>

const double DEG_TO_RAD=0.0174532925;

class trigonometric {
  double angle;
  double answer_sine;
  double answer_cosine;
  double answer_tangent;

public:
  void trig_calc(double);
  void trig_calc(char *);
};

void trigonometric::trig_calc(double degrees)
{
  angle=degrees;
  answer_sine=sin(angle * DEG_TO_RAD);
  answer_cosine=cos(angle * DEG_TO_RAD);
  answer_tangent=tan(angle * DEG_TO_RAD);
  cout << "\nFor an angle of " << angle
       << " degrees." << endl;
  cout << "The sine is " << answer_sine << endl;
```

```
  cout << "The cosine is " << answer_cosine << endl;
  cout << "The tangent is " << answer_tangent << endl;
}

void trigonometric::trig_calc(char *dat)
{
  char *deg,*min,*sec;

  deg=strtok(dat,"°");
  min=strtok(0,"' ");
  sec=strtok(0,"\"");
  angle=atof(deg)+((atof(min))/60.0)+((atof(sec))/360.0);
  answer_sine=sin(angle * DEG_TO_RAD);
  answer_cosine=cos(angle * DEG_TO_RAD);
  answer_tangent=tan(angle * DEG_TO_RAD);
  cout << "\nFor an angle of " << angle
       << " degrees." << endl;
  cout << "The sine is " << answer_sine << endl;
  cout << "The cosine is " << answer_cosine << endl;
  cout << "The tangent is " << answer_tangent << endl;
}

main()
{
  trigonometric data;

  data.trig_calc(75.0);
  data.trig_calc("35° 75' 20\"");   //make ° with alt-248
  data.trig_calc(145.72);
  data.trig_calc("65° 45' 30\"");
  return (0);
}
```

This program uses a very powerful built-in function, **strtok()**, prototyped in STRING.H. The syntax for using **strtok()** is straightforward.

```
char *strtok(string1,string2);  //locates token in string1
char *string1;                  //string which has token(s)
const char *string2;            //string with delimiter chars
```

The **strtok()** function will scan the first string, *string1*, looking for a series of character tokens. For this example, the tokens representing degrees, minutes, and seconds are used. The actual length of the tokens can vary.

The second string, *string2*, contains a set of delimiters. Spaces, commas, or other special characters can be used for delimiters. The tokens in *string1* are separated by the delimiters in *string2*.

Because of this, all of the tokens in *string1* can be retrieved with a series of calls to the **strtok()** function. **Strtok()** alters *string1* by inserting a null character after each token is retrieved. The function returns a pointer to the first token the first time it is called. Subsequent calls return a pointer to the next token, and so on. When there are no more tokens in the string, a null pointer is returned.

This example permits angle readings formatted as decimal values or formatted as degrees, minutes, and seconds of arc. For the latter format **strtok()** uses the degree symbol (°) to find the first token. For minutes, a minute symbol (′) will pull out the token containing the number of minutes. Finally, a \" symbol is used to retrieve seconds. The last delimiter uses two symbols because the double quote by itself is used for terminating strings.

This program produces the following formatted output:

```
For an angle of 75 degrees.
The sine is 0.965926
The cosine is 0.258819
The tangent is 3.732051

For an angle of 36.305565 degrees.
The sine is 0.592091
The cosine is 0.805871
The tangent is 0.734722

For an angle of 145.72 degrees.
The sine is 0.653238
The cosine is -0.826295
The tangent is -0.681642

For an angle of 65.833333 degrees.
The sine is 0.912358
The cosine is 0.409392
The tangent is 2.228658
```

Class member function overloading gives programs and programmers flexibility when dealing with different data formats. If you are not into math or engineering programs, can you think of any applications that interest you where this feature might be helpful? Consider this possibility: if you are the cook in your household, you could develop an application that modifies recipes. You could write a program that would accept data as a decimal value or in mixed units. For example, the program might allow you to enter *3.75 cups, 1 pint 1.75 cups,* or *1 pint 1 cup 12 tbs.*

Using Friend Functions to Access Private Class Variables

One important feature of classes is their ability to hide data. Recall that member data is *private* by default in classes—that is, sharable only with member functions of the class. It will appear almost ironic, then, that there exists a category of functions specifically designed to override this feature. Functions of this type are called *friend* functions.

Friend functions allow the sharing of private class information with nonmember functions. Friend functions, not defined in the class itself, can share the same class resources as member functions. Friend functions offer the advantage that they are external to the class definition.

```
//
//  SECS.CPP
//  C++ program illustrates the use of friend functions.
//  Program will collect a string of date and time
//  information from system. Time information will
//  be processed and converted into seconds.
//  William H. Murray and Chris H. Pappas
//

#include <iostream.h>
#include <time.h>     // for tm & time_t structure
#include <string.h>   // for strtok function prototype
#include <stdlib.h>   // for atol function prototype

class time_class {
  long secs;
  friend char * present_time(time_class);  //friend
public:
  time_class(char *);
};

time_class::time_class(char *tm)
{
  char *hours,*minutes,*seconds;

  // data returned in the following string format:
  // (day month date hours:minutes:seconds year)
  // Thus, need to skip over three tokens, i.e.,
  // skip day, month, and date
```

```
  hours=strtok(tm," ");
  hours=strtok(0," ");
  hours=strtok(0," ");

  // collect time information from string
  hours=strtok(0,":");
  minutes=strtok(0,":");
  seconds=strtok(0," ");

  // convert data to long type and accumulate seconds.
  secs=atol(hours)*3600;
  secs+=atol(minutes)*60;
  secs+=atol(seconds);
}

char * present_time(time_class);  // prototype

main()
{
  // get the string of time & date information
  struct tm *ptr;
  time_t ltime;
  ltime=time(NULL);
  ptr=localtime(&ltime);

  time_class tz(asctime(ptr));

  cout << "The date/time string information: "
       << asctime(ptr) << endl;
  cout << "The time converted to seconds: "
       << present_time(tz) << endl;
  return (0);
}

char * present_time(time_class tz)
{
  char *ctbuf;
  ctbuf=new char[40];
  long int seconds_total;

  seconds_total=tz.secs;
  ltoa(seconds_total,ctbuf,10);
```

```
    return (ctbuf);
}
```

Notice in the class definition the use of the keyword **friend** along with the description of the **present_time** function. When you examine the program listing, you will notice that this function, external to the class, appears after the **main()** function description. In other words, it is written as a traditional C++ function, external to member functions of the defined class.

This program has a number of additional interesting features. In the function **main()**, the system's time is obtained with the use of **time_t** and its associated structure *tm*. In this program, *ltime* is the name of the variable associated with *time_t*. Local time is initialized and retrieved into the pointer, *ptr*, with the next two lines of code. By using *asctime(ptr)*, the pointer will point to an ASCII string of date and time information.

```
struct tm *ptr;
time_t ltime;
ltime=time(NULL);
ptr=localtime(&ltime);

time_class tz(asctime(ptr));
```

The date and time string is formatted in this manner:

day month date hours:minutes:seconds year \n \0

For example:

```
        Tue Jan 11  12:10:05 1995
```

The string information that is retrieved is sent to the class by associating *tz* with the class **time_class**.

```
time_class tz(asctime(ptr));
```

A constructor, *time_class(char *)*, is used to define the code required to convert the string information into integer data. This is accomplished by using the **strtok()** function.

The date/time information is returned in a rather strange format. To process this information, **strtok()** must use a space as the delimiter in order to skip over the day, month, and date information in the string.

In this program the variable *hours* initially serves as a junk collector for unwanted tokens. The next delimiter is a colon, ":", which is used in collecting both hour and minute tokens from the string. Finally, the number of seconds can be retrieved by reading the string until another space is encountered.

The string information is then converted to a **long** type and converted to the appropriate number of seconds. The variable *secs is* private to the class, but accessible to the friend function.

The friend function takes the number of accumulated seconds, *tz.seconds,* and converts it back to a character string. The memory for storing the string is allocated with the **new** operator. This newly created string results from using the friend function.

The program prints two pieces of information.

```
The date/time string information: Fri Feb 23 16:01:55 1995

The time converted to seconds: 57715
```

First, **cout** sends the string produced by **asctime()** to the screen. This information is obtainable from the **time_t()** function and is available to the **main()** function. Second, the system time is printed by passing *present_time* to the **cout** stream.

While friend functions offer some interesting programming possibilities when programming with C++ classes, they should be used with caution.

Using the this Pointer

The keyword **this** is used to identify a self-referential pointer that is implicitly declared in C++, as:

```
class_name *this;    //class_name is class type.
```

The **this** pointer is used to point to the object for which the member function is invoked.

Here is an example, used in a class definition:

```
class class_name {
  char chr;

public:
  void begin_conv(char k) {chr=k;}
  char conv_chr(void) {return (this -> chr);}
};
```

In this case, the pointer **this** is used to access the private class variable member, *chr.*

There are additional uses for the **this** pointer. The **this** pointer can be used to include a link on a doubly linked list, or when writing constructors and destructors involving memory allocations. Examine the following example:

```
class class_name {
  int x,y;
  char chr;

public:
  class_name(int size) {this=new(size);}
  ~class_name(void) {delete(this);}
};
```

Using Operator Overloading

Earlier in this chapter you learned that it was possible to overload member functions in a class. In this section, you will learn that it is also possible to overload C++ operators. In C++ new definitions can be applied to such familiar operators as +, -, *, and / in a given class.

The idea of operator overloading is familiar in numerous programming languages, even if it is not specifically implemented. For example, all compiled languages make it possible to add two integers, two floats, or two doubles (or their equivalent types) with the + operator. This is the essence of operator overloading—using the same operator on different data types.

In C++ it is possible to extend this simple concept even further. In most compiled languages it is not possible, for example, to take complex numbers, matrices, or character strings and add them by using the + operator.

These operations are valid in all programming languages:

5 + 2
1.1 + 9.6

These operations are typically not valid operations:

(1 - k8) + (7 + k23)
(11° 30′ 15") + (44° 21′ 32")
"combine " + "strings"

If the last three operations were possible with the + operator, the workload of the programmer would be greatly reduced when designing new applications. The good news is that in C++ the + operator can be overloaded and the previous three operations can be made valid!

Many additional operators can also be overloaded. Operator overloading is used extensively in C++. You will find examples throughout the various Microsoft C++ libraries.

Overloading Operators and Function Calls

In C++, the following operators can be overloaded:

```
+  -  *  /  =  <  >  +=  -=
*=  /=  <<  >>  >>=  <<=  ==  !=  <=
>=  ++  --  %  &  ^  !  |  ~
&=  ^=  |=  &&  ||  %=  []  ()  new
delete
```

The main restrictions are that the syntax and precedence of the operator must remain unchanged from its originally defined meaning. Another important point is that operator overloading is only valid within the scope of the class in which overloading occurs.

The Syntax of Overloading

To overload an operator, the **operator** keyword is followed by the operator itself:

```
type operator opr(param list)
```

For example:

```
angle_value operator +(angle_argument);
```

Here, *angle_value* is the name of the class type, followed by the **operator** keyword, the operator itself (+), and a parameter to be passed to the overloaded operator.

Within the scope of a properly defined class, several angles specified in degrees/minutes/seconds could be directly added together:

```
angle_value angle1("37° 15' 65\"");
angle_value angle2("10° 44' 44\"");
angle_value angle3("75° 17' 59\"");
angle_value angle4("130° 32' 54\"");
angle_value sum_of_angles;
```

```
sum_of_angles=angle1+angle2+angle3+angle4;
```

As you know from earlier examples, the symbol for seconds is the double quote mark ("). This symbol is also used to signal the beginning and end of a character string. The quote symbol can be printed to the screen if it is preceded by a backslash (\). This format will be used for the input, such as that shown in the previous listing.

There is another problem that must be taken into account in programs such as this; the *carry* information from seconds-to-minutes and from minutes-to-hours must be handled properly. A carry occurs in both cases when the total number of seconds or minutes exceeds 59. This has nothing directly to do with operator overloading, but the program must take this into account to produce a correct total.

```
//
//  OPOVER.CPP
//  C++ program illustrates operator overloading.
//  Program will overload the "+" operator so that
//  several angles,in the format degrees minutes seconds,
//  can be added directly.
//  William H. Murray and Chris H. Pappas
//

#include <strstrea.h>
#include <stdlib.h>
#include <string.h>

class angle_value {
  int degrees,minutes,seconds;

  public:
  angle_value(void) {degrees=0,
                     minutes=0,
                     seconds=0;}  // constructor
  angle_value(char *);
  angle_value operator +(angle_value);
  char * info_display(void);
};

angle_value::angle_value(char *angle_sum)
{
  degrees=atoi(strtok(angle_sum,"° "));
  minutes=atoi(strtok(0,"' "));
```

```
   seconds=atoi(strtok(0,"\""));
}

angle_value angle_value::operator+(angle_value angle_sum)
{
   angle_value ang;
   ang.seconds=(seconds+angle_sum.seconds)%60;
   ang.minutes=((seconds+angle_sum.seconds)/60+
               minutes+angle_sum.minutes)%60;
   ang.degrees=((seconds+angle_sum.seconds)/60+
               minutes+angle_sum.minutes)/60;
   ang.degrees+=degrees+angle_sum.degrees;
   return ang;
}

char * angle_value::info_display()
{
   char *ang[20];
   // strstream.h required for in core formatting
   ostrstream(*ang,sizeof(ang)) << degrees << "° "
                                << minutes << "' "
                                << seconds << "\""
                                << ends;
   return *ang;
}

main()
{
   angle_value angle1("37° 15' 65\"");    //make ° with alt-248
   angle_value angle2("10° 44' 44\"");
   angle_value angle3("75° 17' 59\"");
   angle_value angle4("130° 32' 54\"");
   angle_value sum_of_angles;

   sum_of_angles=angle1+angle2+angle3+angle4;
   cout << "the sum of the angles is "
        << sum_of_angles.info_display() << endl;
   return (0);
}
```

The details of how the mixed units are added together are included in the small piece of code, which declares that the + operator is to be overloaded.

```
angle_value angle_value::operator+(angle_value angle_sum)
{
  angle_value ang;
  ang.seconds=(seconds+angle_sum.seconds)%60;
  ang.minutes=((seconds+angle_sum.seconds)/60+
              minutes+angle_sum.minutes)%60;
  ang.degrees=((seconds+angle_sum.seconds)/60+
              minutes+angle_sum.minutes)/60;
  ang.degrees+=degrees+angle_sum.degrees;
  return ang;
}
```

Here, divide and modulo operations are performed on the sums to ensure correct carry information.

Further details of the program's operation will be omitted, since you have seen most of the functions and modules in earlier examples. However, it is important to remember when overloading operators that proper operator syntax and precedence must be maintained.

The output from the **this** program shows the sum of the four angles to be

```
the sum of the angles is 253° 51' 33"
```

Is this answer correct?

Derived Classes

A *derived* class can be considered an extension or inheritance of an existing class. The original class is known as a base or parent class, and the derived class as a subclass or child class. As such, a derived class provides a simple means for expanding or customizing the capabilities of a parent class, without the need for re-creating the parent class itself. With a parent class in place, a common interface is possible to one or more of the derived classes.

Any C++ class can serve as a parent class, and any derived class will reflect its description. The derived class can add additional features to those of the parent class. For example, the derived class can modify access privileges, add new members, or overload existing ones.

When a derived class overloads a virtual function declared in the parent class, it is said to be a *virtual* member function. You will see that virtual member functions are very important to the concept of object-oriented programming.

The Syntax of a Derived Class

A derived class is described using the following syntax:

```
class   derived-class-type:(public/private/protected) . . .
        parent-class-type { . . . .};
```

For example, in creating a derived class, you might write:

```
class retirement:public consumer { . . . .};
```

In this case, the derived class tag is *retirement*. The parent class has public visibility and its tag is *consumer*.

A third visibility specifier is often used with derived classes—**protected**. A **protected** specifier is the same as a **private** specifier with the added feature that derived classes and friends of derived classes are given access to the class. **Private** members are not visible to derived classes.

Creating Derived Classes

The next program will be used to depict the concept of a derived class. The parent class collects and reports information on a consumer's name, address, city, state, and ZIP code.

Two similar child classes are derived. One child class maintains information on a consumer's accumulated airline mileage, while the second derived child class reports information on a consumer's accumulated rental car mileage. Both derived child classes inherit information from the parent class. Study the listing and see what you can discern about these derived classes.

```
//
//  DERCLS.CPP
//  C++ program illustrates derived classes.
//  The parent class contains name, street, city,
//  state, and ZIP information. Derived classes add
//  either airline or rental car mileage information
//  to parent class information.
//  William H. Murray and Chris H. Pappas
//

#include <iostream.h>
#include <string.h>
```

```
char newline;

class consumer {
  char name[60],
       street[60],
       city[20],
       state[15],
       zip[10];
public:
  void data_output(void);
  void data_input(void);
};

void consumer::data_output(void)
{
  cout << "Name: " << name << endl;
  cout << "Street: " << street << endl;
  cout << "City: " << city << endl;
  cout << "State: " << state << endl;
  cout << "Zip: " << zip << endl;
}

void consumer::data_input(void)
{
  cout << "Enter The Consumer's Full Name: ";
  cin.get(name,59,'\n');
  cin.get(newline);       //flush carriage return
  cout << "Enter The Street Address: ";
  cin.get(street,59,'\n');
  cin.get(newline);
  cout << "Enter The City: ";
  cin.get(city,19,'\n');
  cin.get(newline);
  cout << "Enter The State: ";
  cin.get(state,14,'\n');
  cin.get(newline);
  cout << "Enter The Five-Digit ZIP Code: ";
  cin.get(zip,9,'\n');
  cin.get(newline);
}

class airline:public consumer {
```

```
  char airline_type[20];
  float acc_air_miles;
public:
  void airline_consumer(void);
  void disp_air_mileage(void);
};

void airline::airline_consumer(void)
{
  data_input();
  cout << "Enter Airline Type: ";
  cin.get(airline_type,19,'\n');
  cin.get(newline);
  cout << "Enter Accumulated Air Mileage: ";
  cin >> acc_air_miles;
  cin.get(newline);       //flush carriage return
}

void airline::disp_air_mileage(void)
{
  data_output();

  cout << "Airline Type: " << airline_type
       << endl;
  cout << "Accumulated Air Mileage: "
       << acc_air_miles << endl;
}

class rental_car:public consumer {
  char rental_car_type[20];
  float acc_road_miles;
public:
  void rental_car_consumer(void);
  void disp_road_mileage(void);
};

void rental_car::rental_car_consumer(void)
{
  data_input();
  cout << "Enter Rental_car Type: ";
  cin.get(rental_car_type,19,'\n');
  cin.get(newline);       //flush carriage return
```

```
    cout << "Enter Accumulated Road Mileage: ";
    cin >> acc_road_miles;
    cin.get(newline);
  }

  void rental_car::disp_road_mileage(void)
  {
    data_output();

    cout << "Rental Car Type: "
         << rental_car_type << endl;
    cout << "Accumulated Mileage: "
         << acc_road_miles << endl;
  }

main()
{
  //associate variable names with classes
  airline jetaway;
  rental_car varooom;

  //get airline information
  cout << "\n--Airline Consumer--\n";
  jetaway.airline_consumer();


  //get rental_car information
  cout << "\n--Rental Car Consumer--\n";
  varooom.rental_car_consumer();

  //now display all consumer information
  cout << "\n--Airline Consumer--\n";
  jetaway.disp_air_mileage();
  cout << "\n--Rental Car Consumer--\n";
  varooom.disp_road_mileage();

  return (0);
}
```

In the example, the parent class is type **consumer**. The private part of this class accepts consumer information for name, address, city, state, and ZIP code. The public part describes two functions, **data_output()** and **data_input()**. We have used functions similar to these to gather class information in earlier programs. The first derived child class is **airline**.

```
class airline:public consumer {
  char airline_type[20];
  float acc_air_miles;
public:
  void airline_consumer(void);
  void disp_air_mileage(void);
};
```

This derived child class contains two functions, **airline_consumer()** and **disp_air_mileage()**. The first function, **airline_consumer()**, uses the parent class to obtain the name, address, city, state, and ZIP code, and attaches the airline type and accumulated mileage.

```
void airline::airline_consumer(void)
{
  data_input();
  cout << "Enter Airline Type: ";
  cin.get(airline_type,19,'\n');
  cin.get(newline);
  cout << "Enter Accumulated Air Mileage: ";
  cin >> acc_air_miles;
  cin.get(newline);        //flush carriage return
}
```

Do you understand how the derived class is being used? A call to the function, **data_input()**, is a call to a member function that is part of the parent class. The remainder of the derived class is involved with obtaining the additional airline type and accumulated mileage.

The information on accumulated air mileage can be displayed for a consumer in a similar manner. The parent class function, **data_output()**, prints the information gathered by the parent class (name, address, and so on), while **disp_air_mileage()** attaches the derived child class's information (airline type and mileage) to the output. The process is repeated for the rental car consumer.

Thus, one parent class serves as the data-gathering base for two derived child classes, each obtaining their own specific information.

I/O in C++

Now that you understand the concepts and syntax for object-oriented classes, constructors, destructors, member functions, and operators, you are ready for a deeper understanding of C++ I/O.

Just like C, C++ does not have any built-in I/O routines. Instead, all C++ compilers come bundled with object-oriented iostream classes. These standard I/O class objects have a cross-compiler syntax consistency because they were developed by the authors of the C++ language.

If you are trying to write a C++ application that is portable to other C++ compilers, then you will want to use these iostream classes. The Microsoft C/C++ compiler provides the following five ways to perform C/C++ I/O:

- *Unbuffered C library I/O* The C compiler provides unbuffered I/O through functions such as **read()** and **write()**. These functions are very popular with C programmers due to their efficiency and the ease with which they can be customized.
- *ANSI C buffered I/O* C also supports buffered functions such as **fread()** and **fwrite()**. These STDIO.H library functions perform their own buffering before calling the direct I/O base routines.
- *C console and port I/O* C provides additional I/O routines that have no C++ equivalent, such as **getch()**, **_ungetch()**, and **_kbhit()**. All non-Windows applications can use these functions that give the programmer direct access to the hardware.
- *Microsoft iostream class library* The iostream class library provides C++ programs with object-oriented I/O. You can use them in place of functions such as **scanf()**, **printf()**, **fscanf()**, and **fprintf()**. However, while these iostream classes are not required by C++ programs, many of the character mode objects such as **cin**, **cout**, **cerr**, and **clog** are incompatible with the Windows graphical user interface.
- *Microsoft Foundation Class Library* The Microsoft CFile class found in the foundation class library provides C++ and especially Windows applications with objects for disk I/O. Using this library of routines will guarantee that your application will be easy to maintain and portable.

iostream Class List

With the exception of the stream buffer classes, all of the I/O objects defined in the **iostream** class library share the same abstract stream base class called **ios**. These derived classes fall into four categories:

Input Stream Classes	
istream	Used for general-purpose input or as a parent class for other derived input streams
ifstream	Class used for file input
istream_ withassign	Class used for **cin** input
istrstream	Class used for string input
Output Stream Classes	
ostream	Used for general-purpose output or as a parent class for other derived output streams
ofstream	Class used for file output
ofstream_ withassign	Class used for **cout**, **cerr**, and **clog**
ostrstream	Class used for string output
Input/Output Stream Classes	
iostream	Used for general-purpose input and output, or as a parent class for other derived I/O streams
fstream	File I/O stream class
strstream	String I/O stream class
stdiostream	Standard I/O stream class
Stream Buffer Classes	
streambuf	Used as a parent class for derived objects
filebuf	Disk file stream buffer class
strstreambuf	Stream buffer class for strings
stdiobuf	Stream buffer class for standard file I/O

All **ios**-derived **iostream** classes use a **streambuf** class object for the actual I/O processing. The **iostream** class library uses the following three derived buffer classes with streams:

filebuf	Provides buffered disk file I/O
strstreambuf	Provides an in-memory array of bytes to hold the stream data
stdiobuf	Provides buffered disk I/O with all buffering done by the standard I/O system

Remember, all derived classes usually expand upon their inherited parent class definitions. This explains why you will often be using an operator or member function for a derived class that doesn't appear to be in the derived class's definition. This means that if you are going to fully understand how any derived class operates, you will have to research back to the root or parent class definition.

All of the example programs that follow use a derived class based on some parent class. Some of the example program code will use derived class member functions, while other statements use inherited characteristics. Understanding this approach will help you appreciate derived classes. While the whole concept of inheritance may seem frustrating to you at first, just remember that with one simple derived class definition, you can instantly inherit a parent class's latent functionality.

Input Stream Classes

The **ifstream** class used in the next example program is derived from **fstreambase** and **istream**. It provides input operations on a *filebuf*. The program concentrates on text stream input.

```
//
//  ISFTRM.CPP
//  C++ program demonstrating how to use ifstream class,
//  derived from the istream class.
//  William H. Murray and Chris H. Pappas
//
//  Valid member functions for ifstream include:
//        ifstream::open       ifstream::rdbuf
//
//  Valid member functions for istream include:
//        istream::gcount      istream::get
//        istream::getline     istream::ignore
//        istream::istream     istream::peek
//        istream::putback     istream::read
//        istream::seekg       istream::tellg
```

```
#include <fstream.h>
#define iCOLUMNS 80

void main(void)
{
  char cOneLine[iCOLUMNS];

  ifstream ifMyInputStream("ISFTRM.CPP",ios::in);
  while(ifMyInputStream) {
    ifMyInputStream.getline(cOneLine,iCOLUMNS);
    cout << '\n' << cOneLine;
  }
 ifMyInputStream.close();
}
```

The first statement in the program uses the *ifstream* constructor to create an *ifstream* object and connect it to an open file descriptor, *ifMyInputStream*. The syntax uses the name of a file, including a path if necessary *"IFSTRM.CPP"*, along with an open mode (**ios::in** ¦ **ios::nocreate** ¦ **ios::binary**). The default is text input. The optional **ios::nocreate** parameter tests for the file's existence. The *ifMyInputStream* file descriptor's integer value can be used in logical tests such as **if** and **while** statements, and is automatically set to 0 on **EOF**.

The **getline()** member function inherited from the **iostream** class allows a program to read whole lines of text up to a terminating null character. Function **getline()** has three formal parameters, a **char** *, the number of characters to input—including the null character, and an optional delimiter (default = **'\n'**).

Since char array names are technically pointers to characters, *cOneLine* meets the first parameter requirement. The number of characters to be input matches the array's definition, or *iCOLUMNS*. No optional delimiter was defined. However, if you knew your input lines were delimited by a special character, for example, '*', you could have written the **getline()** statement like this:

```
ifMyInputStream.getline(cOneLine,iCOLUMNS,'*');
```

The example program continues by printing the string and then manually closes the file: *ifMyInputStream.close()*.

Output Stream Classes

All **ofstream** classes are derived from **fstreambase** and **ostream**, and allow a program to perform formatted and unformatted output to a *streambuf*.

The program use of the *ofstream* constructor is very similar to its *ifstream* counterpart just described. It expects the name of the output file, *MYOSTRM.OUT,* and open mode, **ios::out**.

```
//
// OSTRM.CPP
// C++ program demonstrating how to use the ofstream class
// derived from the ostream class.
// William H. Murray and Chris H. Pappas

// Valid ofstream member functions include:
//        ofstream::open      ofstream::rdbuf

// Valid ostream member functions include:
//        ostream::flush      ostream::ostream
//        ostream::put        ostream::seekp
//        ostream::tellp      ostream::write

#include <fstream.h>
#include <string.h>
#define iSTRING_MAX 40

void main(void)
{
  int i=0;
  long ltellp;
  char pszString[iSTRING_MAX] = "Sample test string\n";

  // file opened in the default text mode
  ofstream ofMyOutputStream("MYOSTRM.OUT",ios::out);


  // write out string character by character
  // notice that '\n' is translated into 2 characters

  while(pszString[i] != '\0') {
    ofMyOutputStream.put(pszString[i]);
    ltellp = ofMyOutputStream.tellp();
    cout << "\ntellp value: " << ltellp;
    i++;
  }
```

```
// write out entire string with write member function

ltellp = ofMyOutputStream.tellp();
cout << "\ntellp's value before writing 2nd string: "
     << ltellp;
ofMyOutputStream.write(pszString,strlen(pszString));
ltellp = ofMyOutputStream.tellp();
cout << "\ntellp's updated value: " << ltellp;

ofMyOutputStream.close();

}
```

The first **while** loop prints out the *pszString* character-by-character with the **put()** member function. After each character is output, the variable *ltellp* is assigned the current *put* pointer's position as returned by the call to the **tellp()** member function. It is important that you stop at this point to take a look at the following output generated by the program.

The string variable, *pszString,* is initialized with 19 characters plus a '\0', null terminator, bringing the count to a total of 20. However, though the program output generates a **tellp()** count of 1..20, the 20th character isn't the '\0' null terminator. This is because, in text mode, the *pszString*'s '\n' is translated into a two-byte output—one for the carriage return (19th character), the second for the line feed (20th character). The null terminator is not output.

The last portion of the program calculates the output pointer's position before and after using the **write()** member function to print *pszString* as a whole string. Notice that the **tellp()** values printed show that the function **write()** also translates the single null terminator into a two-character output. If the character translation had not occurred, **tellp's** last value would be 39 (assuming **put()** left the first count at 20, not 19). The abbreviated output from the program looks like this:

```
tellp value: 1
tellp value: 2
tellp value: 3
      .
      .
      .
tellp value: 17
tellp value: 18
tellp value: 20
tellp's value before writing 2nd string: 20
tellp's updated value: 40
```

Fortunately, **istream**-derived class member functions such as **get()** and **read()** automatically convert the two bytes output back to a single '\n'. The program highlights the need for caution when dealing with file I/O. Had the file created by this program been used later on as an input file, opened in binary mode, disaster awaited.

Buffered Stream Classes

Any derived classes based on the **ios** class inherit a pointer to a **streambuf**. The **filebuf** class is derived from **streambuf** and modifies the parent class to handle files.

The program begins by defining two **filebuf** handles, *fbMyInputBuf* and *fbMyOutputBuf*, using the **open()** member function to create each text file. Assuming there were no file-creation errors, each handle is then associated with an appropriate *istream* (input) and *ostream* (output) object. With both files opened, the **while** loop performs a simple echo print from the input stream *is.get()* to the output stream *os.put()*, counting the number of linefeeds, '\n'. The overloaded **close()** member function manually closes each file.

```
//
//  FILBUF.CPP
//  C++ program demonstrating how to use filebuf class.
//  William H. Murray and Chris H. Pappas
//
//  Valid member functions include:
//        filebuf::attach        filebuf::close
//        filebuf::fd            filebuf::~filebuf
//        filebuf::filebuf       filebuf::is_open
//        filebuf::open          filebuf::overflow
//        filebuf::seekoff       filebuf::setbuf
//        filebuf::sync          filebuf::underflow
//

#include <fstream.h>
#include <fcntl.h>
#include <process.h> // exit prototype

void main(void)
{
  char ch;
  int iLineCount=0;
  filebuf fbMyInputBuf, fbMyOutputBuf;
```

```
fbMyInputBuf.open("FILBUF.CPP",O_RDONLY ¦ O_TEXT);
if(fbMyInputBuf.is_open() == 0) {
  cerr << "Can't open input file";
  exit (1);
}

istream is(&fbMyInputBuf);

fbMyOutputBuf.open("output.dat",O_WRONLY ¦ O_TEXT);
if(fbMyOutputBuf.is_open() == 0) {
  cerr << "Can't open output file";
  exit (2);
}

ostream os(&fbMyOutputBuf);

while(is) {
  is.get(ch);
  os.put(ch);
  iLineCount += ch == '\n';
}

fbMyInputBuf.close();
fbMyOutputBuf.close();

cout << "You had " << iLineCount << " lines in your file";
}
```

String Stream Class

The **streambuf** class is the foundation for C++ stream I/O. This general class defines all of the basic operations that can be performed with character-oriented buffers. The **streambuf** class is also used to derive file buffers (**filebuf** class) and the **istream** and **ostream** classes that contain pointers to **streambuf** objects.

You can use the **streambuf** class to extend the capabilities of the **iostream** class. It is the **ios** class that provides the derived classes with the programming interface and formatting features. However, it is the **streambuf** public members and virtual functions that do all the work. All derived **ios** classes make calls to these routines.

All buffered **streambuf** objects manage a fixed memory buffer called *a reserve area*. This reserve area can be divided into a *get* area for input and a *put* area for output. If your application requires, the *get* and *put* areas may overlap. Your program can use protected member functions to access and manipulate the two separate *get* and *put* pointers for character I/O. Each application determines the behavior of the buffers and pointers based on the program's implementation of the derived class.

There are two constructors for **streambuf** objects. Their syntax looks like:

streambuf::streambuf();

streambuf::streambuf(char* pr, int nLength);

The first constructor is used indirectly by all **streambuf**-derived classes. It sets all the internal pointers of the **streambuf** object to NULL. The second constructor creates a **streambuf** object that is attached to an existing character array. The following program demonstrates how to declare a string *strstreambuf* object derived from the **streambuf** base class. Once the *stbMyStreamBuf* object is created, the program outputs a single character using the **sputc()** member function and then reads the character back in with the **sgetc()** member function.

```
//
//  STRBUF.CPP
//  C++ program demonstrating how to use the streambuf class.
//  William H. Murray and Chris H. Pappas
//

#include <strstrea.h>
#define iMYBUFFSIZE 1024

void main(void)
{
  char c;

  strstreambuf stbMyStreamBuf(iMYBUFFSIZE);
  stbMyStreamBuf.sputc('A');  // output single character
  c = stbMyStreamBuf.sgetc();
  cout << c;
}
```

Just remember that there are two separate pointers for **streambuf**-based objects, a *put* to, and a *get* from. Each is manipulated independently of the other. The reason that the **sgetc()** member function retrieved the 'A' is because the class initializes the pointer to the beginning of the buffer. Even though **sputc()** has moved the *put* pointer one byte into the buffer, the *get* pointer still sits at the beginning of the memory location. Once the **sgetc()** statement is executed, the *get* pointer is updated one byte into the buffer.

Working in an Object-Oriented Environment

There are several object-oriented languages available to programmers in addition to C++. However, each language produces object-oriented code that shares these common features:

- Object-based modularization
- Abstract data types
- Memory management (automatic)
- Classes
- Inheritance
- Polymorphism
- Inheritance (multiple)

From your current study of C++ classes, you have learned that Microsoft Visual C/C++ provides these features to the object-oriented programmer. In fact, you might conclude that to do true object-oriented programming, you must work in a language such as C++ that is itself object-oriented. There are valid arguments against this notion, as you shall see later in this book. For example, programs written for Microsoft's Windows contain many of the seven previously mentioned features, even though they can be written in C.

An Object-Oriented Stack in C++

So far, you have learned that the C++ class—an abstract data type—provides the encapsulation of data structures and the operations on those structures (member functions). As such, the C++ class serves as the mechanism for forming objects. In the following listing, the implementation of an object-oriented stack is a simple example of object creation with a C++ class.

Stack operations, in this example, are carried out in the traditional FILO (first in last out) manner. The **stack** class provides six member functions, including **clear()**, **top()**, **empty()**, **full()**, **push()**, and **pop()**. Examine the following listing and observe how these member functions are implemented.

```
//
//  STACK.CPP
//  C++ program illustrates object-oriented programming
//  with a classical stack operation using a string of
//  characters.
//  William H. Murray and Chris H. Pappas
//

#include <iostream.h>
#include <string.h>

#define maxlen 80

class stack {
  char str1[maxlen];
  int  first;

public:
  void clear(void);
  char top(void);
  int  empty(void);
  int  full(void);
  void push(char chr);
  char pop(void);
};

void stack::clear(void)
{
  first=0;
}

char stack::top(void)
{
  return (str1[first]);
}

int stack::empty(void)
{
  return (first==0);
}

int stack::full(void)
{
```

```
  return (first==maxlen-1);
}

void stack::push(char chr)
{
  str1[++first]=chr;
}

char stack::pop(void)
{
  return (str1[first--]);
}

main()
{
  stack mystack;
  char str[11]="0123456789";

  // clear the stack
  mystack.clear();

  // load the string, char-by-char, on the stack
  cout << "\nLoad character data on stack" << endl;
  for(int i=0;i<strlen(str);i++) {
    if (!mystack.full())
      mystack.push(str[i]);
      cout << str[i] << endl;
  }

  // unload the stack, char-by-char
  cout << "\nUnload character data from stack" << endl;
  while (!mystack.empty())
    cout << mystack.pop() << endl;

  return (0);
}
```

In this program, characters from a string are pushed, one character at a time, onto the stack. Next, the stack is unloaded one character at a time. Loading and unloading is done from the stack top, so the first character information loaded on the stack is pushed down the deepest in the stack.

Observe in the following listing that the character for the number zero (0) was pushed onto the stack first. It should be no surprise that it is the last character popped off the stack.

```
Load character data on stack
0
1
2
3
4
5
6
7
8
9

Unload character data from stack
9
8
7
6
5
4
3
2
1
0
```

While this simple example lacks many of the more advanced object-oriented concepts such as memory management, inheritance, and polymorphism, it is, nevertheless, a simple object-oriented program.

An Object-Oriented Linked List in C++

Most programmers agree that when using a traditional procedural approach to design a linked list, you create a data structure that is difficult to alter and maintain. In this section, a linked-list program using objects will be developed that will allow you to create a list of employee information. It will be possible to also add and delete employees from the list.

To limit the size of the linked-list program, no user interface will be used for gathering employee data. Data for the linked list has been "hard-wired" in the **main()** function. Examples of how to make this program interactive and able to accept information from the keyboard have been shown in earlier chapters. In addition to linked-list concepts, you will find that it includes all seven of the object-oriented concepts listed earlier in the "Working in an Object-Oriented Environment" section.

Creating a Parent Class

This program will use several child classes derived from a common parent class. The parent class for this linked-list example is named **NNR**. **NNR** represents the Nineveh National Research Company, developers of fine computer-related books and software. The linked-list program is a database that will keep pertinent information and payroll data on company employees. The purpose of the parent class, **NNR**, is to gather information common to all subsequent derived child classes. For this example, that common information includes an employee's last name, first name, occupation title, social security number, and year hired at the company. The parent class, **NNR**, has two levels of isolation: public and private. The *protected* section of this class shows the structure for gathering data common to each derived child class. The *public* section (member functions) shows how that information will be intercepted from the function **main()**.

```
// PARENT CLASS
class NNR {

friend class payroll_list;

protected:
  char lstname[20];
  char fstname[15];
  char job_title[30];
  char social_sec[12];
  int year_hired;
  NNR *pointer;
  NNR *next_link;

public:
  NNR(char *lname,char *fname,char *ss,
      char *job,int y_hired)
  {
    strcpy(lstname,lname);
```

```
    strcpy(fstname,fname);
    strcpy(social_sec,ss);
    strcpy(job_title,job);
    year_hired=y_hired;
    next_link=0;
  }
      .
      .
      .
      .
```

The parent class and all derived child classes will utilize a friend class named **payroll_list**. When you study the full program listing, later in this chapter, notice that all derived child classes share this common variable, too.

Remember how the terms *private* and *public* relate to encapsulation concepts used by object-oriented programmers!

A Derived Child Class

This program uses four derived child classes. Each of these is derived from the parent class, **NNR**, shown in the last section. In this segment we'll look at one child class, which represents the points common to all four derived classes. The **salespersons** class will serve as this example. A portion of this derived class is shown next. The derived child class satisfies the object-oriented concept of inheritance.

```
//SUB OR CHILD DERIVED CLASS
class salespersons:public NNR {

friend class payroll_list;

private:
  float disk_sales;
  int comm_rate;

public:
  salespersons(char *lname,char *fname,char *ss,
               char *job,int y_hired,
               float d_sales,int c_rate):
               NNR(lname,fname,ss,
               job,y_hired)
  {
```

```
    disk_sales=d_sales;
    comm_rate=c_rate;
  }
      .
      .
      .
      .
```

In this case, the **salespersons** child class gathers information and adds it to the information already gathered by the parent class. This, in turn, forms a data structure comprised of last name, first name, social security number, year hired, the total sales, and the appropriate commission rate.

Now take a look at the remainder of the child class description.

```
      .
      .
      .
      .

  void fill_sales(float d_sales)
  {
    disk_sales=d_sales;
  }

  void fill_comm_rate(int c_rate)
  {
    comm_rate=c_rate;
  }

  void add_info()
  {
    pointer=new salespersons(lstname,
                             fstname,
                             social_sec,
                             job_title,
                             year_hired,
                             disk_sales,
                             comm_rate);
  }

  void send_info()
  {
    NNR::send_info();
```

```
    cout << "\n Sales (disks): " << disk_sales;
    cout << "\n Commission Rate: " << comm_rate;
  }

};
```

Add_info() sets aside memory for each additional linked-list node by using the **new** free store operator. The node is being assigned a pointer to a variable, *pointer*, that in turn points to an *NNR* node. The use of the free store operator provides the automatic memory management required by object-oriented programs.

When you examine the full program listing, you will also see that the **delete** free store operator is used in the **payroll_list** class when items are deleted from the linked list. This automatically frees system memory.

Output information on a particular employee is constructed in a unique manner. In the case of the **salespersons** class, notice that **send_info()** makes a request to the **NNR**'s **send_info()** *function*. **NNR**'s function prints the information common to each derived class, and then the **salespersons**' **send_info()** function prints the information unique to the particular child class. For this example, this information includes the sales and the commission rate.

It would also have been possible to print the information about the salesperson completely from within the child class, but this has allowed another advantage of object-oriented programming to be illustrated—the use of virtual functions.

Using a Friend Class

The friend class, **payroll_list**, contains the means for printing the linked list and for inserting and deleting employees from the list. Here is a small portion of this class:

```
//FRIEND CLASS
class payroll_list {

private:
  NNR *location;

public:
  payroll_list()
  {
    location=0;
  }

  void print_payroll_list();
```

```
  void insert_employee(NNR *node);

  void remove_employee_id(char *social_sec);

};
     .
     .
     .
     .
```

Notice that messages that are sent to the member functions **print_payroll_list()**, **insert_employee()**, and **remove_employee_id()** form the functional part of the linked-list program.

Consider the function **print_payroll_list()**, which begins by assigning the pointer to the list to the pointer variable *present*. While the pointer, *present*, is not 0 it will continue to point to employees in the linked list, direct them to **send_info**, and update the pointer until all employees have been printed. See how this is achieved in the next section of code:

```
     .
     .
     .
     .
void payroll_list::print_payroll_list()
{
  NNR *present=location;

  while(present!=0) {
    present->send_info();
    present=present->next_link;
  }
}
     .
     .
     .
```

You might recall, from an earlier discussion, that the variable *pointer* contains the memory address of nodes inserted via **add_info()**. This value is used by **insert_employee()** to form the link with the linked list. The insertion technique inserts alphabetically by an employee's last name. Thus, the linked list is always ordered alphabetically by last name.

A correct insertion is accomplished by comparing the last name of a new employee with those already in the list. When a name (*node->lstname*) already in the list is found that is greater than the *current_node->lstname*, the first **while** loop ends. This is a standard linked-list insert procedure which leaves the pointer variable, *previous_node*, pointing to the node behind where the new node is to be inserted and leaves *current_node* pointing to the node which will follow the insertion point for the new node.

When the insertion point is determined, a new link or node is created by calling *node->add_info().* The *current_node* is linked to the new node's *next_link*. The last decision which must be made is whether the new *node* is to be placed as the front node in the list or between existing nodes. This is established by examining the contents of the pointer variable *previous_node*.

If the pointer variable is 0, then it cannot be pointing to a valid previous node, so *location* is updated to the address of the new *node*. If *previous_node* contains a nonzero value, it is assumed to be pointing to a valid previous node. In this case, *previous_node->next_link* is assigned the address of the new node's address or *node->pointer*.

```
        .
        .
        .
        .
void payroll_list::insert_employee(NNR *node)
{
  NNR *current_node=location;
  NNR *previous_node=0;

  while (current_node != 0 &&
         strcmp(current_node->lstname,node->lstname) < 0) {
    previous_node=current_node;
    current_node=current_node->next_link;
  }
  node->add_info();
  node->pointer->next_link=current_node;
  if (previous_node==0)
    location=node->pointer;
  else
    previous_node->next_link=node->pointer;
}
        .
        .
        .
        .
```

Items can only be removed from the linked list by knowing the employee's social security number. This technique adds a level of protection against accidentally deleting an employee.

As you examine **remove_employee_id()**, shown in the next listing, note that the structure used for examining the nodes in the linked list is almost identical to that of **insert_employee()**. However, the first **while** loop leaves the *current_node* pointing to the node to be deleted, not the node after the one to be deleted.

```
  .
  .
  .
  .
void payroll_list::remove_employee_id(char *social_sec)
{
  NNR *current_node=location;
  NNR *previous_node=0;

  while(current_node != 0 &&
        strcmp(current_node->social_sec,
        social_sec) != 0) {
    previous_node=current_node;
    current_node=current_node->next_link;
  }

  if(current_node != 0 && previous_node == 0) {
    location=current_node->next_link;
    delete current_node;
  }
  else if(current_node != 0 && previous_node != 0) {
    previous_node->next_link=current_node->next_link;
    delete current_node;
  }
}
```

The first compound **if** statement takes care of deleting a node in the front of the list. This is accomplished by examining the contents of *previous_node* to see if it contains a 0. If this is true, then the front of the list, *location,* needs to be updated to the node following the one to be deleted. This is achieved with:

```
current_node->next_link
```

The second **if** statement takes care of deleting a node between two existing nodes. This requires the *previous_node->next_link* to be assigned the address of the node after the one being deleted, as seen in the following statement:

```
previous_node->next_link=current_node->next_link.
```

Now that the important pieces of the program have been examined, they will be put together to form a complete program.

Examining the Complete Program

The following listing is the complete operational C++ object-oriented linked-list program. The only thing that it lacks is an interactive user interface. When the program is executed, it will add nine employees, each with different *job_titles*, to the linked list and then print the list. Next, the program will delete two employees from the list. This is accomplished by supplying their social security numbers. The altered list is then printed. The **main()** function contains information on which employees are added and deleted.

```
//
//   NNR.CPP
//   C++ program illustrates object-oriented programming
//   with a linked list.  This program keeps track of
//   employee data at Nineveh National Research (NNR).
//   William H. Murray and Chris H. Pappas
//

#include <iostream.h>
#include <string.h>

// PARENT CLASS
class NNR {

friend class payroll_list;

protected:
  char lstname[20];
  char fstname[15];
  char job_title[30];
  char social_sec[12];
  int year_hired;
  NNR *pointer;
```

```
   NNR *next_link;
public:
   NNR(char *lname,char *fname,char *ss,
      char *job,int y_hired)
   {
     strcpy(lstname,lname);
     strcpy(fstname,fname);
     strcpy(social_sec,ss);
     strcpy(job_title,job);
     year_hired=y_hired;
     next_link=0;
   }

   NNR(void)
   {
     lstname[0]=NULL;
     fstname[0]=NULL;
     social_sec[0]=NULL;
     job_title[0]=NULL;
     year_hired=0;
     next_link=0;
   }

   void fill_lstname(char *l_name)
   {
     strcpy(lstname,l_name);
   }

   void fill_fstname(char *f_name)
   {
     strcpy(fstname,f_name);
   }

   void fill_social_sec(char *soc_sec)
   {
     strcpy(social_sec,soc_sec);
   }

   void fill_job_title(char *o_name)
   {
     strcpy(job_title,o_name);
```

```
  }

  void fill_year_hired(int y_hired)
  {
    year_hired=y_hired;
  }

  virtual void add_info(void) {
  }

  virtual void send_info(void)
  {
    cout << "\n\n" << lstname << ", " << fstname
      << "\n Social Security: #" << social_sec;
    cout << "\n Job Title: " << job_title;
    cout << "\n Year Hired: " << year_hired;
  }

};


//SUB OR CHILD DERIVED CLASS
class administration:public NNR {

friend class payroll_list;

private:
  float yearly_salary;

public:
  administration(char *lname,char *fname,char *ss,
                 char *job,int y_hired,
                 float y_salary):
                 NNR(lname,fname,ss,
                 job,y_hired)
  {
    yearly_salary=y_salary;
  }

  administration(void):NNR(void)
  {
    yearly_salary=0.0;
```

```
  }

  void fill_yearly_salary(float salary)
  {
    yearly_salary=salary;
  }

  void add_info(void)
  {
    pointer=new administration(lstname,
                               fstname,
                               social_sec,
                               job_title,
                               year_hired,
                               yearly_salary);
   }

  void send_info(void)
  {
    NNR::send_info();
    cout << "\n Yearly Salary: $" << yearly_salary;
  }

};


//SUB OR CHILD DERIVED CLASS
class salespersons:public NNR {

friend class payroll_list;

private:
  float disk_sales;
  int comm_rate;

public:
  salespersons(char *lname,char *fname,char *ss,
               char *job,int y_hired,
               float d_sales,int c_rate):
               NNR(lname,fname,ss,
               job,y_hired)
  {
```

```
    disk_sales=d_sales;
    comm_rate=c_rate;
  }

  salespersons(void):NNR(void)
  {
    disk_sales=0.0;
    comm_rate=0;
  }

  void fill_sales(float d_sales)
  {
    disk_sales=d_sales;
  }

  void fill_comm_rate(int c_rate)
  {
    comm_rate=c_rate;
  }

  void add_info(void)
  {
    pointer=new salespersons(lstname,
                             fstname,
                             social_sec,
                             job_title,
                             year_hired,
                             disk_sales,
                             comm_rate);
  }

  void send_info(void)
  {
    NNR::send_info();
    cout << "\n Sales (disks): " << disk_sales;
    cout << "\n Commission Rate: " << comm_rate;
  }

};


//SUB OR CHILD DERIVED CLASS
```

```
class technicians:public NNR {

friend class payroll_list;

private:
  float hourly_salary;

public:
  technicians(char *lname,char *fname,char *ss,char *job,
              int y_hired,float h_salary):
              NNR(lname,fname,ss,job,y_hired)
  {
    hourly_salary=h_salary;
  }

  technicians(void):NNR(void)
  {
    hourly_salary=0.0;
  }

  void fill_hourly_salary(float h_salary)
  {
    hourly_salary=h_salary;
  }

  void add_info()
  {
    pointer=new technicians(lstname,
                            fstname,
                            social_sec,
                            job_title,
                            year_hired,
                            hourly_salary);
  }

  void send_info(void)
  {
    NNR::send_info();
    cout << "\n Hourly Salary: $" << hourly_salary;
  }

};
```

```
//SUB OR CHILD DERIVED CLASS
class supplies:public NNR {

friend class payroll_list;

private:
  float hourly_salary;

public:
  supplies(char *lname,char *fname,char *ss,char *job,
           int y_hired,float h_salary):
           NNR(lname,fname,ss,
           job,y_hired)
  {
    hourly_salary=h_salary;
  }

  supplies(void):NNR(void)
  {
    hourly_salary=0.0;
  }

  void fill_hourly_salary(float h_salary)
  {
    hourly_salary=h_salary;
  }

  void add_info(void)
  {
    pointer=new supplies(lstname,
                         fstname,
                         social_sec,
                         job_title,
                         year_hired,
                         hourly_salary);
  }

  void send_info(void)
  {
    NNR::send_info();
```

```
    cout << "\n Hourly Salary: $" << hourly_salary;
  }

};


//FRIEND CLASS
class payroll_list {

private:
  NNR *location;

public:
  payroll_list(void)
  {
    location=0;
  }

  void print_payroll_list(void);

  void insert_employee(NNR *node);

  void remove_employee_id(char *social_sec);

};

void payroll_list::print_payroll_list(void)
{
  NNR *present=location;

  while(present!=0) {
    present->send_info();
    present=present->next_link;
  }
}

void payroll_list::insert_employee(NNR *node)
{
  NNR *current_node=location;
  NNR *previous_node=0;

  while (current_node != 0 &&
```

```
         strcmp(current_node->lstname,node->lstname) < 0) {
    previous_node=current_node;
    current_node=current_node->next_link;
  }
  node->add_info();
  node->pointer->next_link=current_node;
  if (previous_node==0)
    location=node->pointer;
  else
    previous_node->next_link=node->pointer;
}

void payroll_list::remove_employee_id(char *social_sec)
{
  NNR *current_node=location;
  NNR *previous_node=0;

  while(current_node != 0 &&
     strcmp(current_node->social_sec,social_sec) != 0) {
    previous_node=current_node;
    current_node=current_node->next_link;
  }

  if(current_node != 0 && previous_node == 0) {
    location=current_node->next_link;
    delete current_node;
  }
  else if(current_node != 0 && previous_node != 0) {
    previous_node->next_link=current_node->next_link;
    delete current_node;
  }
}

main()
{
  payroll_list workers;

  // static data to add to linked list
  salespersons salesperson1("Samantha","Samantha","111-65-1111",
                            "Salesperson",1985,5.3,6.2);
  salespersons salesperson2("Muscle","Mark","222-22-2222",
                            "Salesperson",1985,3.0,3.2);
```

```
salespersons salesperson3("Ripoff","Randle","543-21-1010",
                          "Salesperson",1987,9.6,6.8);
technicians techperson1("Altogether","Alice","234-87-7612",
                          "Technician",1989,12.55);
technicians techperson2("Tightwad","Terry","682-67-5312",
                          "Technician",1992,10.34);
administration vice_president1("Stuckup","Stewart",
                          "782-45-1122","Vice President",
                           1980,40000.00);
administration vice_president2("Genius","Gary",
                          "987-99-9653","Vice President",
                           1984,45000.00);
supplies supplyperson1("Together","Al","443-89-3772",
                          "Supplies",1983,8.55);
supplies supplyperson2("Plenty","Sparkle","111-44-5399",
                          "Supplies",1988,7.5);

// add the nine workers to the linked list
workers.insert_employee(&techperson1);
workers.insert_employee(&vice_president1);
workers.insert_employee(&salesperson1);
workers.insert_employee(&supplyperson1);
workers.insert_employee(&supplyperson2);
workers.insert_employee(&salesperson2);
workers.insert_employee(&techperson2);
workers.insert_employee(&vice_president2);
workers.insert_employee(&salesperson3);

// print the linked list
workers.print_payroll_list();

// remove two workers from the linked list
workers.remove_employee_id("782-45-1122");
workers.remove_employee_id("543-21-1010");

cout << "\n\n***********************************";

// print the revised linked list
workers.print_payroll_list();

return (0);
}
```

Study the complete listing and see if you understand how workers are inserted and deleted from the list. If it is still a little confusing, go back and study each major section of code discussed earlier.

Linked-List Output

The linked-list program sends output to the monitor. The first section of the list contains the nine employee names that were used to create the original list. The last part of the list shows the list after two workers are deleted. Here is a sample output sent to the screen.

```
Altogether, Alice
 Social Security: #234-87-7612
 Job Title: Technician
 Year Hired: 1989
 Hourly Salary: $12.55

Together, Al
 Social Security: #443-89-3772
 Job Title: Supplies
 Year Hired: 1983
 Hourly Salary: $8.55

Muscle, Mark
 Social Security: #222-22-2222
 Job Title: Salesperson
 Year Hired: 1985
 Sales (disks): 3
 Commission Rate: 3

Slick, Samantha
 Social Security: #111-65-1111
 Job Title: Salesperson
 Year Hired: 1985
 Sales (disks): 5.3
 Commission Rate: 7

Genius, Gary
 Social Security: #987-99-9653
 Job Title: Vice President
 Year Hired: 1984
 Yearly Salary: $45000
```

```
Plenty, Sparkle
 Social Security: #111-44-5399
 Job Title: Supplies
 Year Hired: 1988
 Hourly Salary: $6.2

Ripoff, Randle
 Social Security: #543-21-1010
 Job Title: Salesperson
 Year Hired: 1987
 Sales (disks): 9.6
 Commission Rate: 6

Stuckup, Stewart
 Social Security: #782-45-1122
 Job Title: Vice President
 Year Hired: 1980
 Yearly Salary: $40000

Tightwad, Terry
 Social Security: #682-67-5312
 Job Title: Technician
 Year Hired: 1992
 Hourly Salary: $10.34

***********************************

Altogether, Alice
 Social Security: #234-87-7612
 Job Title: Technician
 Year Hired: 1989
 Hourly Salary: $12.55

Together, Al
 Social Security: #443-89-3772
 Job Title: Supplies
 Year Hired: 1983
 Hourly Salary: $8.55

Muscle, Mark
 Social Security: #222-22-2222
 Job Title: Salesperson
 Year Hired: 1985
 Sales (disks): 3
 Commission Rate: 3
```

```
Slick, Samantha
 Social Security: #111-65-1111
 Job Title: Salesperson
 Year Hired: 1985
 Sales (disks): 5.3
 Commission Rate: 7

Genius, Gary
 Social Security: #987-99-9653
 Job Title: Vice President
 Year Hired: 1984
 Yearly Salary: $45000

Plenty, Sparkle
 Social Security: #111-44-5399
 Job Title: Supplies
 Year Hired: 1988
 Hourly Salary: $6.2

Tightwad, Terry
 Social Security: #682-67-5312
 Job Title: Technician
 Year Hired: 1992
 Hourly Salary: $10.34
```

CHAPTER 3

Windows Programming: The Microsoft Foundation Class Library

The techniques presented in this chapter are different from those used by C programmers developing Windows code. Many books and magazine articles show a procedural approach when developing applications in the C language. Applications created in C++ can have a similar structure and appearance, but they can also include the advantages of object-oriented coding and Microsoft's foundation classes.

Microsoft's foundation classes give you access to reusable code—a chief advantage of C++. This chapter concentrates on the use of the Microsoft Foundation Class (MFC) library when writing C++ Windows applications. You'll find using the library classes intuitive, and your application code even easier to construct and read.

Microsoft has provided a foundation class library containing a new set of tools for the development of C++ and C++ Windows applications. The MFC library holds two groups of important classes: one group contains more than two dozen class definitions for Windows; the other group contains more than three dozen OLE classes.

The first group is designed specifically for Windows applications, while the second group can be used in both C++ and Windows development. This chapter will focus on the Windows library classes. When these classes are used in conjunction with the Windows concepts and tools, the result will be simplified code development and program maintenance.

Even the simplest Windows applications, when created with the standard API function calls, are difficult and time-consuming to develop. For example, a bare-bones Windows application template contains more than two pages of C code and Windows function calls. Most of that code is used repeatedly from application to application and is required just to establish a window on the screen. While Windows applications have been easy to use, they have certainly not been a joy to write.

This chapter will examine the advantages of using the MFC library for Windows code development. We'll discuss terms, definitions, and techniques that can then be applied to C++ application code developed in the following chapters.

The MFC library is a new and powerful toolkit for the programmer. If conventional Windows developers have a hammer and crosscut saw in their toolkit, the C++ Windows developer, using the MFC library, is equipped with a pneumatic hammer and circular power saw.

The Need for a Foundation Class Library

The MFC library provides Windows programmers with easy-to-use objects. Windows, from its very inception, has followed many principles of object-oriented programming design, within the framework of a non-object-oriented language like C. These features were discussed in the first two chapters. The marriage of C++ and Windows allows developers to take full advantage of object-oriented features. The MFC library development team designed a comprehensive implementation of the

Windows application program interface (API). This C++ library encapsulates the most important data structures and API function calls within a group of approximately 70 reusable classes.

Class libraries, such as the MFC library, offer many advantages over the traditional function libraries used by C programmers. This list includes many of the usual advantages of C++ classes, such as:

- Encapsulation of code and data within the class
- Inheritance
- Elimination of function and variable name collisions
- Classes that appear to be natural extensions of the language
- Reduced code size from well-designed class libraries

With the use of the MFC library, the code required to establish a window is one-third the length of a conventional application. This allows you, the developer, to spend less time communicating with Windows and more time developing your application's code.

Foundation Class Library Design Considerations

The MFC library design team set rigorous design principles that had to be followed in the implementation of the MFC library. Some of these principles and guidelines include:

- Utilize the power of C++ without overwhelming the programmer.
- Make the transition from standard API function calls to the use of class libraries as simple as possible.
- Allow the mixing of traditional function calls with the use of new class libraries.
- Balance power and efficiency in the design of class libraries.
- Produce a class library that can migrate easily to new platforms, such as Windows NT.

The design team felt that good code design had to start with the MFC library itself. The C++ foundation classes are designed to be small and to execute fast. Their simplicity makes them very easy to use, and their execution speed is close to the bulkier function libraries of C. When all the MFC library classes are compiled by using the small memory model, they consume less than 45K of total object code.

These classes require minimal relearning of function names for seasoned Windows programmers. This was achieved by carefully naming and designing class features. The MFC library team also designed the MFC library to allow *mixed-mode* operation. That is, classes and traditional function calls can be intermixed in the same source code.

Microsoft was also aware that class libraries should be usable. Some class libraries are designed with too high a level of abstraction. These *heavy classes*, as Microsoft calls them, tend to produce applications that are large and execute slowly. The MFC library provides a reasonable level of abstraction while keeping code sizes small. Microsoft claims only a 5 percent speed penalty when using MFC library classes over traditional C function calls.

With Windows NT, the development team designed the class library to be dynamic rather than static. The dynamic architecture will allow classes to be scaled to a growing Windows environment in the future.

Key Foundation Class Library Features

Class libraries, for Windows, are available from other C++ compiler manufacturers, but Microsoft claims several real advantages for its MFC library:

- Complete support for all Windows functions, controls, messages, GDI graphics primitives, menus, and dialog boxes.
- The same naming convention as the conventional Windows API. Thus, the action of a class is immediately recognized by its name.
- Elimination of switch/case statements that are a source of error. All messages are mapped to member functions, within a class. This direct message-to-method mapping is available for all messages.
- Better diagnostics support through the ability to send information about objects to a file. Also included is the ability to validate member variables.
- An extensive exception-handling design makes application code less subject to failure. Support for "out of memory," and so on, is provided.
- Determination of the type of a data object at run time. This allows for a dynamic manipulation of a field when classes are instantiated.

- Small code with a fast implementation. As mentioned earlier, the MFC library adds less than 45K of object code overhead and executes only 5 percent slower than conventional C Windows applications.

The experienced Windows programmer will immediately appreciate two of these features: the familiar naming convention and the message-to-method mapping. If you reexamine the source code for most Windows applications, you will see extensive use of the error-prone switch/case statements. These applications also make extensive use of API function calls. Both groups of problems have been eliminated when using the MFC library.

Professional developers will certainly appreciate Microsoft's dedication to better diagnostics and the small code overhead imposed by the MFC library. Now programmers can take advantage of the MFC library without incurring a size penalty on their application's code.

It All Begins with CObject

Libraries, such as the MFC library, often start with a few parent classes. Additional classes are then derived from the parent classes. **CObject** is one parent class used extensively in developing Windows applications. The MFC library header files located in the MFC/INCLUDE subdirectory provide a wealth of information on defined classes.

Let's take a brief look at **CObject**, which is defined in the AFX.H header file. Our code is a slightly edited version of the actual code.

```
class CObject
{
public:

// Object model (types, destruction, allocation)
    virtual CRuntimeClass* GetRuntimeClass() const;
    virtual ~CObject();  // virtual destructors are necessary

    // Diagnostic allocations
    void* AFX_CDECL operator new(size_t, void* p);
    void* AFX_CDECL operator new(size_t nSize);
    void AFX_CDECL operator delete(void* p);

protected:
    CObject();
private:
```

```
    CObject(const CObject& objectSrc);
    void operator=(const CObject& objectSrc);

// Attributes
public:
    BOOL IsSerializable() const;
    BOOL IsKindOf(const CRuntimeClass* pClass) const;

// Overridables
    virtual void Serialize(CArchive& ar);

    // Diagnostic Support
    virtual void AssertValid() const;
    virtual void Dump(CDumpContext& dc) const;

// Implementation
public:
    static AFX_DATA CRuntimeClass classCObject;
    static CRuntimeClass* PASCAL _GetBaseClass();
};
```

Upon inspection of the **CObject** listing, notice the components that make up this class definition. First, **CObject** is divided into public, protected, and private parts. **CObject** also provides normal and dynamic type checking and serialization. Recall that dynamic type checking allows the type of object to be determined at run time. The state of the object can be saved to a storage medium, such as a disk, through a concept called *persistence*. Object persistence allows object member functions to also be persistent, permitting retrieval of object data.

CGdiObject is an example of a class derived from **CObject**. Here is the **CGdiObject** definition as found in AFXWIN.H. Again, this listing has been edited for clarity.

```
class CGdiObject : public CObject
{
    DECLARE_DYNCREATE(CGdiObject)
public:

// Attributes
    HGDIOBJ m_hObject;
    HGDIOBJ GetSafeHandle() const;

    static CGdiObject* PASCAL FromHandle(HGDIOBJ hObject);
    static void PASCAL DeleteTempMap();
```

```
    BOOL Attach(HGDIOBJ hObject);
    HGDIOBJ Detach();

// Constructors
    CGdiObject(); // must Create a derived class object
    BOOL DeleteObject();

// Operations
    int GetObject(int nCount, LPVOID lpObject) const;
    UINT GetObjectType() const;
    BOOL CreateStockObject(int nIndex);
    BOOL UnrealizeObject();

// Implementation
public:
    virtual ~CGdiObject();
#ifdef _DEBUG
    virtual void Dump(CDumpContext& dc) const;
    virtual void AssertValid() const;
#endif
};
```

CGdiObject and its member functions allow drawing items such as stock and custom pens, brushes, and fonts to be created and used in a Windows application.

Microsoft has provided complete source code for the MFC library to allow the utmost in programming flexibility and customization. However, for the beginner, it is not even necessary to know how the various classes are defined to use them efficiently.

For example, in traditional C Windows applications, the **DeleteObject()** function is called with the following syntax:

```
DeleteObject(hBRUSH);  /*hBRUSH is the brush handle*/
```

In C++, with the MFC library, the same results will be achieved by accessing the member function with the following syntax:

```
newbrush.DeleteObject(); //newbrush is current brush
```

As you can see, switching between C Windows function calls and class library objects can be intuitive! Microsoft has used this approach in developing all Windows classes, making the transition from traditional function calls to MFC library objects very easy.

Important Foundation Library Classes

Table 3-1 lists all of the important Windows foundation library classes. All of these classes are derived from CObject, except where noted.

CLASS	BASE CLASS PURPOSE
CWinApp	Holds the initialization, running, and exiting code for the application
CWnd	Parent class for all windows
CFrameWnd	Preferred base class for windows based upon the Single Document Interface
CMDIFrameWnd	Preferred base class for windows based upon the Multiple Document Interface
CMDIChildWnd	Child windows based upon the Multiple Document Interface
CDialog	Modeless dialog boxes
CModalDialog	Modal dialog boxes
CButton	Button controls
CComboBox	Combo boxes
CEdit	Edit controls
CListBox	List boxes
CScrollBar	Scroll bars
CStatic	Static controls
CDC	Display contexts
CClientDC	Client area display contexts
CMetaFileDC	Metafile device contexts
CPaintDC	Display contexts used by **OnPaint** member functions such as **LineTo**, **Ellipse**, etc.
CWindowDC	Display contexts for entire windows
CGdiObject	All GDI drawing tools
CBitmap	GDI physical bitmaps

TABLE 3-1. *Foundation Class Library Windows Classes*

CLASS	BASE CLASS PURPOSE
CBrush	GDI physical brushes
CFont	GDI physical fonts
CPalette	GDI physical palettes
CPen	GDI physical pens
CRgn	GDI physical regions
CMenu	Creating menu structures
CPoint	Coordinate points (x,y) in a device context; not derived from CObject class
CRect	Rectangular regions in a device context; not derived from CObject class

TABLE 3-1. *Foundation Class Library Windows Classes* (continued)

A Simplified Application

Before writing complicated application code, let's see what is required just to establish a window on the screen. As we mentioned, that process in C requires a program length of two pages. By using the power of the MFC library, the initial program code can be reduced to one-third this size.

In this section, we'll examine the *simplest* possible Windows application, SIMPLE.CPP. The SIMPLE application will establish a window on the screen and place a title in its title bar area.

Establishing a Window with SIMPLE.CPP

Create a project named SIMPLE, and set the project options to create a Windows executable file.

To compile this application, it will be necessary for you to enter the following file (SIMPLE.CPP):

```
//
//  SIMPLE.CPP
//  The minimum code needed to establish a window with
//  the Microsoft Foundation Class Library
```

```
//  William H. Murray and Chris H. Pappas
//

#include <afxwin.h>

class CTheApp : public CWinApp
{
public:
  virtual BOOL InitInstance();
};

class CMainWnd : public CFrameWnd
{
public:
  CMainWnd()
  {
  Create(NULL,"A MFC Window",
         WS_OVERLAPPEDWINDOW,rectDefault,NULL,NULL);
  }
};

BOOL CTheApp::InitInstance()
{
  m_pMainWnd=new CMainWnd();
  m_pMainWnd->ShowWindow(m_nCmdShow);
  m_pMainWnd->UpdateWindow();

  return TRUE;
}

CTheApp TheApp;
```

In the following sections, we'll examine how each piece of code works in establishing the window on the screen.

Using AFXWIN.H

The AFXWIN.H header file is the gateway to Windows programming with the MFC library. AFXWIN.H calls all subsequent header files, including WINDOWS.H, as they are needed. Using one header file also aids in creating precompiled header files. Precompiled header files save time when repeated compilation is being done during application development.

We recommend that you print a copy of AFXWIN.H for your reference as you develop your own applications using the MFC library. This header file is approximately 40 pages long.

Deriving a Class from CWinApp

This application starts by deriving a class, **CTheApp**, from the MFC library class **CWinApp**. This object is defined by the programmer.

```
class CTheApp : public CWinApp
{
public:
  virtual BOOL InitInstance();
};
```

Our class, **CTheApp**, overrides the member function, **InitInstance()**, of **CWinApp**. You will find that overriding member functions occurs frequently. By overriding **InitInstance()**, the programmer can customize the initialization and execution of the application. In **CWinApp**, it is also possible to override **InitApplication()**, **ExitInstance()**, and **OnIdle()**, but for most applications this will be unnecessary.

Here is an edited portion of the **CWinApp** class description, as found in the AFXWIN.H header file.

```
class CWinApp : public CWinThread
{
     DECLARE_DYNAMIC(CWinApp)
public:

// Constructor
     CWinApp(LPCTSTR lpszAppName = NULL);

// Attributes
     // Startup args (do not change)
     HINSTANCE m_hInstance;
     HINSTANCE m_hPrevInstance;
     LPTSTR m_lpCmdLine;
     int m_nCmdShow;

     // Running args (can be changed in InitInstance)
     LPCTSTR m_pszAppName;  // human readable name
     LPCTSTR m_pszRegistryKey;   // used for registry entries

     // Support for Shift+F1 help mode.
```

```
    BOOL m_bHelpMode;          // are we in Shift+F1 mode?

public:  // set in constructor to override default
    LPCTSTR m_pszExeName;        // executable name (no spaces)
    LPCTSTR m_pszHelpFilePath;   // default based on module path
    LPCTSTR m_pszProfileName;    // default based on app name

// Initialization Operations - should be done in InitInstance
protected:
    void LoadStdProfileSettings(UINT nMaxMRU = _AFX_MRU_COUNT);
    void EnableShellOpen();

    void SetDialogBkColor(COLORREF clrCtlBk = RGB(192, 192, 192),
                COLORREF clrCtlText = RGB(0, 0, 0));
        // set dialog box and message box background color

    void SetRegistryKey(LPCTSTR lpszRegistryKey);
    void SetRegistryKey(UINT nIDRegistryKey);
        // enables app settings in registry instead of INI file
        //     (registry key is usually a "company name")

    void RegisterShellFileTypes();
        // call after all doc templates are registered

// Helper Operations - usually done in InitInstance
public:
    // Cursors
    HCURSOR LoadCursor(LPCTSTR lpszResourceName) const;
    HCURSOR LoadCursor(UINT nIDResource) const;
    HCURSOR LoadStandardCursor(LPCTSTR lpszCursorName) const;
    HCURSOR LoadOEMCursor(UINT nIDCursor) const;

    // Icons
    HICON LoadIcon(LPCTSTR lpszResourceName) const;
    HICON LoadIcon(UINT nIDResource) const;
    HICON LoadStandardIcon(LPCTSTR lpszIconName) const;
    HICON LoadOEMIcon(UINT nIDIcon) const;

    // Profile settings (to the app specific .INI file,
                        or registry)
    UINT GetProfileInt(LPCTSTR lpszSection, LPCTSTR lpszEntry,
```

```
                              int nDefault);
        BOOL WriteProfileInt(LPCTSTR lpszSection, LPCTSTR lpszEntry,
                              int nValue);
        CString GetProfileString(LPCTSTR lpszSection,
                                 LPCTSTR lpszEntry,
                          LPCTSTR lpszDefault = NULL);
        BOOL WriteProfileString(LPCTSTR lpszSection,
                                LPCTSTR lpszEntry,
                          LPCTSTR lpszValue);

// Running Operations - to be done on a running application
        // Dealing with document templates
        void AddDocTemplate(CDocTemplate* pTemplate);

        // Dealing with files
        virtual CDocument* OpenDocumentFile(LPCTSTR lpszFileName);
        virtual void AddToRecentFileList(LPCTSTR lpszPathName);

        // Printer DC Setup routine, 'struct tagPD'
        // is a PRINTDLG structure

        // Command line parsing
        BOOL RunEmbedded();
        BOOL RunAutomated();

// Overridables
        // hooks for your initialization code
        virtual BOOL InitApplication();
        virtual BOOL InitInstance();

        // running and idle processing
        virtual int Run();
        virtual BOOL PreTranslateMessage(MSG* pMsg);
        virtual BOOL OnIdle(LONG lCount);
                    // return TRUE if more idle processing

        // exiting
        virtual BOOL SaveAllModified(); // save before exit
        virtual int ExitInstance(); // return app exit code

        // Advanced: to override message boxes and other hooks
        virtual int DoMessageBox(LPCTSTR lpszPrompt, UINT nType,
```

```
                                   UINT nIDPrompt);
    virtual BOOL ProcessMessageFilter(int code, LPMSG lpMsg);
    virtual LRESULT ProcessWndProcException(CException* e,
                                                const MSG* pMsg);
    virtual void DoWaitCursor(int nCode);
                // 0 => restore, 1=> begin, -1=> end

   // Advanced: Help support
    virtual void WinHelp(DWORD dwData,
                        UINT nCmd = HELP_CONTEXT);

// Command Handlers
protected:
    // map to the following for file new/open
    afx_msg void OnFileNew();
    afx_msg void OnFileOpen();

    // map to the following to enable print setup
    afx_msg void OnFilePrintSetup();

    // map to the following to enable help
    afx_msg void OnContextHelp();   // shift-F1
    afx_msg void OnHelp();          // F1 (uses current context)
    afx_msg void OnHelpIndex();     // ID_HELP_INDEX, ID_DEFAULT
    afx_msg void OnHelpUsing();     // ID_HELP_USING

// Implementation
protected:
    HGLOBAL m_hDevMode;             // printer Dev Mode
    HGLOBAL m_hDevNames;            // printer Device Names
    DWORD m_dwPromptContext;        // help context override

    int m_nWaitCursorCount;         // for wait cursor
    HCURSOR m_hcurWaitCursorRestore; // old cursor to restore

    CRecentFileList* m_pRecentFileList;

    void UpdatePrinterSelection(BOOL bForceDefaults);
    void SaveStdProfileSettings(); // save options to .INI file

public: // public for implementation access
    CPtrList m_templateList;           // list of templates
```

```
    ATOM m_atomApp, m_atomSystemTopic; // for DDE open
    UINT m_nNumPreviewPages;           // num default printed pg

    size_t  m_nSafetyPoolSize;         // ideal size

    void (CALLBACK* m_lpfnOleFreeLibraries)();
    void (CALLBACK* m_lpfnOleTerm)(BOOL);
    COleMessageFilter* m_pMessageFilter;

    void SetCurrentHandles();
    int GetOpenDocumentCount();

    // helpers for standard commdlg dialogs
    BOOL DoPromptFileName(CString& fileName, UINT nIDSTitle,
            DWORD lFlags, BOOL bOpenFileDialog,
            CDocTemplate* pTemplate);
    int DoPrintDialog(CPrintDialog* pPD);

    void EnableModeless(BOOL bEnable); // disable OLE dialogs

public:
    virtual ~CWinApp();

    void HideApplication();     // hide application before close
    void CloseAllDocuments(BOOL bEndSession);
        // close documents before exiting

protected:
    //{{AFX_MSG(CWinApp)
    afx_msg void OnAppExit();
    afx_msg void OnUpdateRecentFileMenu(CCmdUI* pCmdUI);
    afx_msg BOOL OnOpenRecentFile(UINT nID);
    //}}AFX_MSG
    DECLARE_MESSAGE_MAP()
};
```

The **CWinApp** class is responsible for establishing and implementing the Windows message loop. This action, alone, eliminates many lines of repetitive code.

CFrameWnd

The application window, established by the **CMainWnd** class, is defined from the base class, **CFrameWnd**, as shown in the following segment of code.

```
class CMainWnd : public CFrameWnd
{
public:
  CMainWnd()
  {
  Create(NULL,"A MFC Window",
         WS_OVERLAPPEDWINDOW,rectDefault,NULL,NULL);
  }
};
```

The constructor for the class, **CMainWnd**, calls the **Create()** member function to establish initial window parameters. In this application, the window's style and caption are provided as parameters. You'll see in Chapter 4 that it is also possible to specify a menu name and accelerator table when this member function is used.

Here is an edited portion of **CFrameWnd**, also found in the AFXWIN.H header file:

```
class CFrameWnd : public Cwnd
{
     DECLARE_DYNCREATE(CFrameWnd)

// Constructors
public:
     static AFX_DATA const CRect rectDefault;
     CFrameWnd();

     BOOL LoadAccelTable(LPCTSTR lpszResourceName);
     BOOL Create(LPCTSTR lpszClassName,
                    LPCTSTR lpszWindowName,
                    DWORD dwStyle = WS_OVERLAPPEDWINDOW,
                    const RECT& rect = rectDefault,
                    CWnd* pParentWnd = NULL,
                    LPCTSTR lpszMenuName = NULL,
                    DWORD dwExStyle = 0,
                    CCreateContext* pContext = NULL);

     // dynamic creation - load frame and associated resources
     virtual BOOL LoadFrame(UINT nIDResource,
                    DWORD dwDefaultStyle = WS_OVERLAPPEDWINDOW |
                                                   FWS_ADDTOTITLE,
                    CWnd* pParentWnd = NULL,
                    CCreateContext* pContext = NULL);
```

```
// Attributes
	virtual CDocument* GetActiveDocument();

	// Active child view maintenance
	CView* GetActiveView() const;       // active view or NULL
	void SetActiveView(CView* pViewNew, BOOL bNotify = TRUE);
		// active view or NULL, bNotify == FALSE focus not set

	// Active frame (for frames within frames - MDI)
	virtual CFrameWnd* GetActiveFrame();

	// For customizing the default messages on the status bar
	virtual void GetMessageString(UINT nID,
	                              CString& rMessage) const;

	BOOL m_bAutoMenuEnable;
	// TRUE => menu items without handlers will be disabled

// Operations
	virtual void RecalcLayout(BOOL bNotify = TRUE);
	virtual void ActivateFrame(int nCmdShow = -1);

	// to set text of standard status bar
	void SetMessageText(LPCTSTR lpszText);
	void SetMessageText(UINT nID);

	// control bar docking
	void EnableDocking(DWORD dwDockStyle);
	void DockControlBar(CControlBar* pBar, UINT nDockBarID = 0,
		LPCRECT lpRect = NULL);
	void FloatControlBar(CControlBar* pBar, CPoint point,
		DWORD dwStyle = CBRS_ALIGN_TOP);
	CControlBar* GetControlBar(UINT nID);

	// saving and loading control bar state
	void LoadBarState(LPCTSTR lpszProfileName);
	void SaveBarState(LPCTSTR lpszProfileName) const;

// Overridables
	virtual void OnSetPreviewMode(BOOL bPreview,
	                              CPrintPreviewState* pState);
protected:
```

```
    virtual BOOL OnCreateClient(LPCREATESTRUCT lpcs,
                                CCreateContext* pContext);

// Command Handlers
public:
    afx_msg void OnContextHelp();   // for Shift+F1 help

// Implementation
public:
    virtual ~CFrameWnd();
    int m_nWindow;  // general purpose window number - as ":n"
                    // -1 => unknown, 0 => only window viewing
                    // 1 => first of many windows documents

    HMENU m_hMenuDefault;        // default menu resource
    HACCEL m_hAccelTable;        // accelerator table
    DWORD m_dwPromptContext;     // current help prompt context
    BOOL m_bHelpMode;            // if TRUE, then Shift+F1 help
    BOOL m_bStayActive;          // if TRUE, then caption forced
    CFrameWnd* m_pNextFrameWnd; // next CFrameWnd in app global
    CRect m_rectBorder;          // for OLE 2.0 border space
    COleFrameHook* m_pNotifyHook;

    DWORD m_dwDockStyle;            // docking sites
    CPtrList m_listControlBars;     // control bar array
                                    // window as their dock site
    BOOL m_bModalDisable;           // TRUE if BeginModalState
    int m_nShowDelay;               // delay show/hide

    CMiniDockFrameWnd* CreateFloatingFrame(DWORD dwStyle);
    DWORD CanDock(CRect rect, DWORD dwDockStyle,
        CDockBar** ppDockBar = NULL); // called by CDockContext
    void AddControlBar(CControlBar *pBar);
    void RemoveControlBar(CControlBar *pBar);
    void DockControlBar(CControlBar* pBar, CDockBar* pDockBar,
        LPCRECT lpRect = NULL);
    void NotifyFloatingWindows(DWORD dwFlags);
    void ShowControlBar(CControlBar* pBar, BOOL bShow,
                        BOOL bDelay);
    void DestroyDockBars();

protected:
```

```
    UINT m_nIDHelp;                 // Help ID (0 for none)
    UINT m_nIDTracking;             // tracking command ID
    UINT m_nIDLastMessage;          // last displayed message
    CView* m_pViewActive;           // current active view
    BOOL (CALLBACK* m_lpfnCloseProc)(CFrameWnd* pFrameWnd);
    UINT m_cModalStack;             // BeginModalState depth
    HWND* m_phWndDisable;           // disabled (BeginModalState)
    HMENU m_hMenuAlt;               // menu to update
    CString m_strTitle;             // default title (original)
    BOOL m_bInRecalcLayout;         // avoid recursion RecalcLayout
    CRuntimeClass* m_pFloatingFrameClass;
    static const DWORD dwDockBarMap[4][2];

public:
    virtual BOOL IsFrameWnd() const;
    BOOL IsTracking() const;
    virtual BOOL OnCmdMsg(UINT nID, int nCode, void* pExtra,
        AFX_CMDHANDLERINFO* pHandlerInfo);
    virtual CWnd* GetMessageBar();
    virtual void OnUpdateFrameTitle(BOOL bAddToTitle);
    virtual void OnUpdateFrameMenu(HMENU hMenuAlt);
    virtual HACCEL GetDefaultAccelerator();
    virtual BOOL PreTranslateMessage(MSG* pMsg);

    // idle update of frame user interface
    enum IdleFlags
        { idleMenu = 1, idleTitle = 2, idleNotify = 4,
          idleLayout = 8 };
    UINT m_nIdleFlags;    // set of bit flags for idle processing
    virtual void DelayUpdateFrameMenu(HMENU hMenuAlt);
    void DelayUpdateFrameTitle();
    void DelayRecalcLayout(BOOL bNotify = TRUE);

    // border space negotiation
    enum BorderCmd
        { borderGet = 1, borderRequest = 2, borderSet = 3 };
    virtual BOOL NegotiateBorderSpace(UINT nBorderCmd,
                                       LPRECT lpRectBorder);

    // frame window based modality
    void BeginModalState();
    void EndModalState();
```

```
    BOOL InModalState() const;
    void ShowOwnedWindows(BOOL bShow);

   // for Shift+F1 help support
    BOOL CanEnterHelpMode();
    virtual void ExitHelpMode();

protected:
    // implementation helpers
    LPCTSTR GetIconWndClass(DWORD dwDefaultStyle,
                            UINT nIDResource);
    void UpdateFrameTitleForDocument(LPCTSTR lpszDocName);
    virtual BOOL PreCreateWindow(CREATESTRUCT& cs);
    virtual BOOL OnCommand(WPARAM wParam, LPARAM lParam);
    virtual void PostNcDestroy();   // default to delete this.
    int OnCreateHelper(LPCREATESTRUCT lpcs,
                       CCreateContext* pContext);
    void BringToTop(int nCmdShow);
        // window to top for SW_ commands which affect z-order

    // implementation helpers for Shift+F1 help mode
    BOOL ProcessHelpMsg(MSG& msg, DWORD* pContext);
    HWND SetHelpCapture(POINT point, BOOL* pbDescendant);

    // CFrameWnd list management
    void AddFrameWnd();
    void RemoveFrameWnd();

    // for loading and saving control bar state
    void SetDockState(const CDockState& state);
    void GetDockState(CDockState& state) const;

    friend class CWnd;    // for access to m_bModalDisable

    //{{AFX_MSG(CFrameWnd)
    // Windows messages
    afx_msg int OnCreate(LPCREATESTRUCT lpCreateStruct);
    afx_msg void OnDestroy();
    afx_msg void OnClose();
    afx_msg void OnInitMenuPopup(CMenu*, UINT, BOOL);
    afx_msg void OnMenuSelect(UINT nItemID, UINT nFlags,
                              HMENU hSysMenu);
```

```
    afx_msg LRESULT OnSetMessageString(WPARAM wParam,
                                       LPARAM lParam);
    afx_msg void OnIdleUpdateCmdUI();
    afx_msg void OnEnterIdle(UINT nWhy, CWnd* pWho);
    afx_msg void OnSetFocus(CWnd* pOldWnd);
    afx_msg void OnHScroll(UINT nSBCode, UINT nPos,
                           CScrollBar* pScrollBar);
    afx_msg void OnVScroll(UINT nSBCode, UINT nPos,
                           CScrollBar* pScrollBar);
    afx_msg void OnSize(UINT nType, int cx, int cy);
    afx_msg BOOL OnEraseBkgnd(CDC* pDC);
    afx_msg void OnActivate(UINT nState, CWnd* pWndOther,
                            BOOL bMinimized);
    afx_msg BOOL OnNcActivate(BOOL bActive);
    afx_msg void OnSysCommand(UINT nID, LONG lParam);
    afx_msg BOOL OnQueryEndSession();
    afx_msg void OnEndSession(BOOL bEnding);
    afx_msg void OnDropFiles(HDROP hDropInfo);
    afx_msg BOOL OnSetCursor(CWnd* pWnd, UINT nHitTest,
                             UINT message);
    afx_msg LRESULT OnCommandHelp(WPARAM wParam, LPARAM lParam);
    afx_msg LRESULT OnHelpHitTest(WPARAM wParam, LPARAM lParam);
    afx_msg LRESULT OnActivateTopLevel(WPARAM wParam,
                                       LPARAM lParam);
    afx_msg void OnEnable(BOOL bEnable);
    // standard commands
    afx_msg BOOL OnToolTipText(UINT nID, NMHDR* pNMHDR,
                               LRESULT* pResult);
    afx_msg void OnUpdateKeyIndicator(CCmdUI* pCmdUI);
    afx_msg void OnHelp();
    afx_msg void OnUpdateContextHelp(CCmdUI* pCmdUI);
    //}}AFX_MSG
public:
    afx_msg void OnUpdateControlBarMenu(CCmdUI* pCmdUI);
    afx_msg BOOL OnBarCheck(UINT nID);
protected:
    DECLARE_MESSAGE_MAP()
};
```

The first parameter in **Create()** allows a class name to be specified in compliance with the traditional Windows API **RegisterClass()** function. Normally, this will be set to NULL in the applications you develop, and a class name will not be required.

Implementing the InitInstance Member Function

Recall that the derived **CTheApp** class object overrode the **InitInstance()** member function. Here is how this application implements **InitInstance()**:

```
BOOL CTheApp::InitInstance()
{
  m_pMainWnd=new CMainWnd();
  m_pMainWnd->ShowWindow(m_nCmdShow);
  m_pMainWnd->UpdateWindow();

  return TRUE;
}
```

The **new** operator invokes the constructor, **CMainWnd**, discussed in the previous section. The *m_pMainWnd* member variable (*m_* indicates a member variable) holds the location for the application's main window. **ShowWindow()**, also a member function, is required to display the window on the screen. The parameter, *m_nCmdShow*, is initialized by the application's constructor. **UpdateWindow()** displays and paints the window being sent to the screen.

The Constructor

The last piece of code invokes the application's constructor at startup.

```
CTheApp TheApp;
```

The application code, for this example, is very simple and straightforward. The application merely establishes a window, but does not permit us to draw anything in the window.

In the next chapter, we will create a more generalized template that will allow you to use basically the same code from one application to another. This code will allow us to draw in the client area of the window.

Running SIMPLE.CPP

Figure 3-1 shows a window similar to the one that will appear on your screen. While the application didn't draw anything in the client area of the window, it did give the application a new title!

This code forms the foundation for all Windows MFC library applications developed in this book. You might want to review the important details once more, before going on to the applications created in Chapter 4.

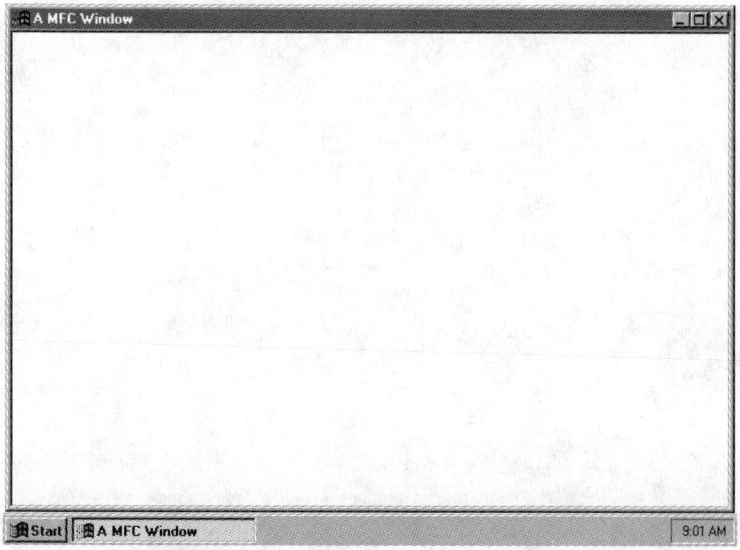

FIGURE 3-1. *Establishing a window by using the MFC library*

A Simplified Design Ensures Easy Maintenance

Reusable classes are one of C++'s main drawing cards for simplified design and application maintenance. The MFC library for Windows allows C++ to be extended in a natural way, making these classes appear to be part of the language itself. In the next chapter we'll explore many additional features of the MFC library as we develop applications that range from a simple program template to a robust bar chart program using menus and dialog boxes.

CHAPTER 4

Developing Foundation Class Library Applications

Now is the time to put your accumulated Windows theory into practice. Chapter 3 described the theory and specifications of Microsoft's Foundation Class (MFC) library. This chapter contains three complete foundation class library Windows applications that will help you understand this class library.

Each example in this chapter builds on the knowledge gained from the previous program. Various Windows and MFC library components are added to each successive example. It is imperative, therefore, to study each application in the order it appears. By the third application, you will be working with a complex

Windows application that uses several Windows resources, depends heavily on the MFC library, and produces a presentation-quality bar chart.

The program listings for each application are quite long, so enter them carefully. Remember as you type that these listings are still far shorter than their procedure-oriented function-library counterparts.

A Simple Application and Template

In Chapter 3 you learned how to establish a window on the screen with the use of the MFC library. That example serves as a gateway to all such Windows applications that use the client area for printing and drawing.

The first application in this chapter, MFCTEMP, will simply print a message in the window's client area. Before we discuss the important aspects of the application, examine a complete program listing. The following listing is a composite of the two files needed to compile this application:

- The header file, MFCTEMP.H
- The application file, MFCTEMP.CPP

Enter each file carefully and save with the filename and extension shown. When the files are entered and saved, the application can be compiled.

```
// MFCTEMP.H
class CMainWnd : public CFrameWnd
{
public:
  CMainWnd();
  afx_msg void OnPaint();
  DECLARE_MESSAGE_MAP();
};

class CMFCTEMPApp : public CWinApp
{
public:
  BOOL InitInstance();
};

//
//  MFCTEMP.CPP
```

```
//  A Simple Foundation Class Windows Application.
//  This code can serve as a template for the development
//  of other simple foundation class applications.
//  William H. Murray and Chris H. Pappas
//

#include <afxwin.h>
#include "MFCTEMP.h"

CMFCTEMPApp theApp;

CMainWnd::CMainWnd()
{
  Create(NULL,"A MFC Template For Developing Applications",
         WS_OVERLAPPEDWINDOW,rectDefault,NULL,NULL);
}

void CMainWnd::OnPaint()
{
  CPaintDC dc(this);
//---------- your routines below ----------------------//

  dc.TextOut(200,200,"Using the MFC Library",21);

//---------- your routines above ----------------------//
}

BEGIN_MESSAGE_MAP(CMainWnd,CFrameWnd)
  ON_WM_PAINT()
END_MESSAGE_MAP()

BOOL CMFCTEMPApp::InitInstance()
{
  m_pMainWnd=new CMainWnd();
  m_pMainWnd->ShowWindow(m_nCmdShow);
  m_pMainWnd->UpdateWindow();

  return TRUE;
}
```

This composite listing gives you the chance to examine all of the code necessary to produce a working application. In the next sections, we'll examine those details that are unique to this application.

Understanding the MFCTEMP Project File

The project file is responsible for directing the compiler, linker, and optional resource compiler on how to compile and link your application. In this chapter, we will use the project files generated by the integrated environment. Follow the C++ compiler's requirements for generating this file.

The Visual C++ project manager requires that you give the project a name, an application type, select a target environment, and select which files are in the project (for this example use MFCTEMP.CPP). Make certain you have the Uses MFC Library option selected. At this point you are ready to build the application.

Understanding the MFCTEMP.H Header File

We will be using two types of header files in this chapter. The first type, shown in this example, is used to contain class definitions that are unique to the application. This header file type will always be identified by the filename (MFCTEMP) and the .H extension. For example, MFCTEMP.H.

The second header file type contains menu and dialog box resource identification values. When these header files are used, they will be identified with an additional *R*, for "resource," at the end of the filename. For example, if this application had used a resource ID header file, it would have been named MFCTEMPR.H. You'll see this second type used in the final example in this chapter.

The definitions for two classes are contained here: **CMainWnd** is derived from **CWinApp**, and **CMFCTEMPApp**, from **CFrameWnd**. (Note: These were part of the body of the SIMPLE.CPP application and were explained in the last chapter. Putting them in a separate header file is just a matter of style—one encouraged by Microsoft.)

```
class CMainWnd : public CFrameWnd
{
public:
  CMainWnd();
  afx_msg void OnPaint();
  DECLARE_MESSAGE_MAP();
};

class CMFCTEMPApp : public CWinApp
{
public:
  BOOL InitInstance();
};
```

Notice, in particular, that **CMainWnd** contains a function declaration, **OnPaint()**, and the addition of a message map. For member functions, such as **OnPaint()**, the **afx_msg** keyword is used instead of **virtual**. **OnPaint()** is a member function of the **CWnd** class that the **CMainWnd** class overrides. This allows the client area of the window to be altered. The **OnPaint()** function is automatically called when a WM_PAINT message is sent to a **CMainWnd** object.

DECLARE_MESSAGE_MAP() is used in virtually all Windows applications. This line states that the class overrides the handling of certain messages (see body of application). Microsoft uses this technique, rather than virtual functions, because it is more space efficient.

The MFCTEMP.CPP Application

The majority of this application's code is the same as SIMPLE.CPP, with the addition of the **OnPaint()** message-handler function. Examine the piece of code shown next.

```
void CMainWnd::OnPaint()
{
  CPaintDC dc(this);
//---------- your routines below ----------------------//

  dc.TextOut(200,200,"Using the MFC Library",21);

//---------- your routines above ----------------------//
}
```

A device context is created for handling the WM_PAINT message. Now, any Windows GDI functions that are encapsulated in the device context can be used between the comments "your routines below" and "your routines above." This concept is similar to the template created in Chapter 3. When the **OnPaint()** function is complete, the destructor for **CPaintDC** is called automatically.

This application uses a fairly short message map, as the following code indicates.

```
BEGIN_MESSAGE_MAP(CMainWnd,CFrameWnd)
  ON_WM_PAINT()
END_MESSAGE_MAP()
```

Two classes are specified by BEGIN_MESSAGE_MAP: **CMainWnd** and **CFrameWnd**. **CMainWnd** is the target class and **CFrameWnd** is a class based on **CWnd**. The **ON_WM_PAINT()** function handles all WM_PAINT messages and directs them to the **OnPaint()** member function just discussed. In upcoming applications, you'll see many additional functions added to the message map.

The use of message maps has eliminated the need for the case/switch statements that are typical of C Windows applications.

Running MFCTEMP

If you have entered the application code and received an error-free compilation, now is the time to run the program. If you are still in the integrated development environment, you can launch the application there. If you're in Windows Program Manager, select File from the main menu and then the Run option.

The screen should be similar to the one shown in Figure 4-1.

If you want to experiment with other GDI primitives, just remove the **TextOut()** function call and insert the function of your choice into the template code. Our next example will use the template, almost without alteration, to illustrate the use of several graphics functions which will draw a line, chord, arc, and so on.

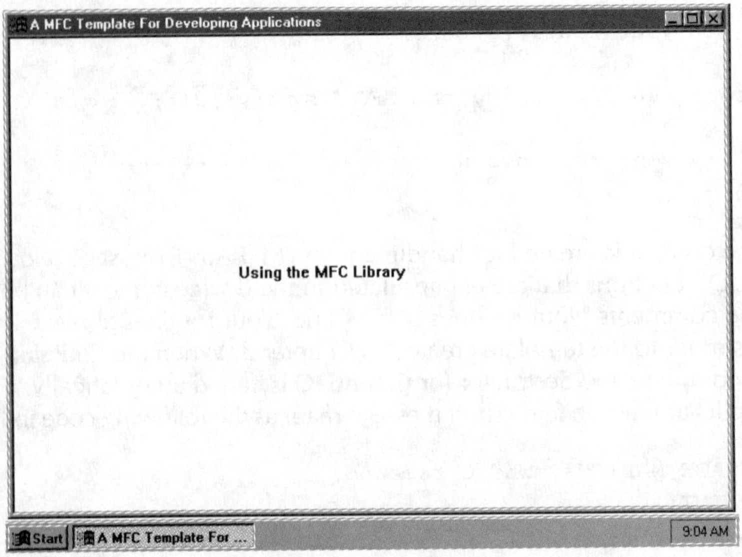

FIGURE 4-1. *The window created by the MFCTEMP application*

Drawing Graphics Primitives in a Window

The second application in this chapter, MFCGDI, will draw several graphics shapes in the window's client area. The following listing is a composite of the two files needed to compile this application:

- The header file, MFCGDI.H
- The application file, MFCGDI.CPP

Enter each file carefully. When the files are entered, the application can be compiled. Remember to generate a project file, too.

```
// MFCGDI.H
class CMainWnd : public CFrameWnd
{
public:
  CMainWnd();
  afx_msg void OnPaint();
  DECLARE_MESSAGE_MAP();
};

class CMFCGDIApp : public CWinApp
{
public:
  BOOL InitInstance();
};

//
//  MFCGDI.CPP
//  An extension of the Simple Foundation Class Windows
//  Application that allows experimenting with graphics-
//  drawing primitives.
//  William H. Murray and Chris H. Pappas
//

#include <afxwin.h>
```

```
#include "MFCGDI.h"

CMFCGDIApp theApp;

CMainWnd::CMainWnd()
{
  Create(NULL,"Using Graphics Drawing Primitives",
         WS_OVERLAPPEDWINDOW,rectDefault,NULL,NULL);
}

void CMainWnd::OnPaint()
{
  static DWORD dwColor[9]={RGB(0,0,0),           //black
                           RGB(255,0,0),         //red
                           RGB(0,255,0),         //green
                           RGB(0,0,255),         //blue
                           RGB(255,255,0),       //yellow
                           RGB(255,0,255),       //magenta
                           RGB(0,255,255),       //cyan
                           RGB(127,127,127),     //gray
                           RGB(255,255,255)};    //white

  CPen  newpen;
  CPen* oldpen;

  CPaintDC dc(this);
//---------- your routines below ----------------------//

  // draws a wide black diagonal line
  newpen.CreatePen(PS_SOLID,6,dwColor[0]);
  oldpen=dc.SelectObject(&newpen);
  dc.MoveTo(0,0);
  dc.LineTo(640,430);
  dc.TextOut(70,20,"<-diagonal line",15);
  newpen.DeleteObject();

  // draws a blue arc
  newpen.CreatePen(PS_DASH,1,dwColor[3]);
  oldpen=dc.SelectObject(&newpen);
  dc.Arc(100,100,200,200,150,175,175,150);
  dc.TextOut(125,125,"small arc->",12);

  newpen.DeleteObject();
```

```
// draws a wide green chord
 newpen.CreatePen(PS_SOLID,8,dwColor[2]);
 oldpen=dc.SelectObject(&newpen);
 dc.Chord(550,20,630,80,555,24,624,70);
 dc.TextOut(485,30,"chord->",7);

 // draws and fills a red ellipse
 newpen.CreatePen(PS_SOLID,1,dwColor[1]);
 oldpen=dc.SelectObject(&newpen);
 newbrush.CreateSolidBrush(dwColor[1]);
 oldbrush=dc.SelectObject(&newbrush);
 dc.Ellipse(180,180,285,260);
 dc.TextOut(210,215,"ellipse",7);

 // draws and fills a blue circle with ellipse function
 newpen.CreatePen(PS_SOLID,1,dwColor[3]);
 oldpen=dc.SelectObject(&newpen);
 newbrush.CreateSolidBrush(dwColor[3]);
 oldbrush=dc.SelectObject(&newbrush);
 dc.Ellipse(380,180,570,370);
 dc.TextOut(450,265,"circle",6);

 // draws a black pie wedge and fills with green
 newpen.CreatePen(PS_SOLID,1,dwColor[0]);
 oldpen=dc.SelectObject(&newpen);
 newbrush.CreateSolidBrush(dwColor[2]);
 oldbrush=dc.SelectObject(&newbrush);
 dc.Pie(300,50,400,150,300,50,300,100);
 dc.TextOut(350,80,"<-pie wedge",11);

 // draws a black rectangle and fills with gray
 newbrush.CreateSolidBrush(dwColor[7]);
 oldbrush=dc.SelectObject(&newbrush);
 dc.Rectangle(50,300,150,400);
 dc.TextOut(160,350,"<-rectangle",11);

 // draws a black rounded rectangle and fills with blue
 newbrush.CreateHatchBrush(HS_CROSS,dwColor[3]);
 oldbrush=dc.SelectObject(&newbrush);
 dc.RoundRect(60,310,110,350,20,20);
 dc.TextOut (120,310,"<------rounded rectangle",24);
```

```
// draws several green pixels
 for(xcoord=400;xcoord<450;xcoord+=3)
   dc.SetPixel(xcoord,150,0L);
 dc.TextOut(455,145,"<-pixels",8);

 // draws several wide magenta lines with polyline
 newpen.CreatePen(PS_SOLID,3,dwColor[5]);
 oldpen=dc.SelectObject(&newpen);
 polylpts[0].x=10;
 polylpts[0].y=30;
 polylpts[1].x=10;
 polylpts[1].y=100;
 polylpts[2].x=50;
 polylpts[2].y=100;
 polylpts[3].x=10;
 polylpts[3].y=30;
 dc.Polyline(polylpts,4);
 dc.TextOut(10,110,"polyline",8);

 // draws a wide cyan polygon and
 // fills with diagonal yellow
 newpen.CreatePen(PS_SOLID,4,dwColor[6]);
 oldpen=dc.SelectObject(&newpen);
 newbrush.CreateHatchBrush(HS_FDIAGONAL,dwColor[4]);
 oldbrush=dc.SelectObject(&newbrush);
 polygpts[0].x=40;
 polygpts[0].y=200;
 polygpts[1].x=100;
 polygpts[1].y=270;
 polygpts[2].x=80;
 polygpts[2].y=290;
 polygpts[3].x=20;
 polygpts[3].y=220;
 polygpts[4].x=40;
 polygpts[4].y=200;
 dc.Polygon(polygpts,5);
 dc.TextOut(70,210,"<-polygon",9);


//---------- your routines above ---------------------//
}
```

```
BEGIN_MESSAGE_MAP(CMainWnd,CFrameWnd)
  ON_WM_PAINT()
END_MESSAGE_MAP()

BOOL CMFCGDIApp::InitInstance()
{
  m_pMainWnd=new CMainWnd();
  m_pMainWnd->ShowWindow(m_nCmdShow);
  m_pMainWnd->UpdateWindow();

  return TRUE;
}
```

The MFCGDI.H Header Files

Only the application file, MFCGDI.CPP, is altered in this example. This means that except for the application's name change, the module definition and header files are identical to those of the last example. However, you will still need to make a new project file to build each new application.

The MFCGDI.CPP Application

Besides showing the use of several GDI drawing primitives, this application will also teach you how to incorporate new brushes and pens into your application. Examine the code at the start of the **OnPaint()** message-handler function. An array is established to hold the RGB values for nine brush and pen colors. You'll see how colors are picked from this array shortly.

```
static DWORD dwColor[9]={RGB(0,0,0),          //black
                         RGB(255,0,0),        //red
                         RGB(0,255,0),        //green
                         RGB(0,0,255),        //blue
                         RGB(255,255,0),      //yellow
                         RGB(255,0,255),      //magenta
                         RGB(0,255,255),      //cyan
                         RGB(127,127,127),    //gray
                         RGB(255,255,255)};   //white
```

The **CBrush** and **CPen** classes permit the brush or pen object to be passed to any **CDC** (base class for display context) member function. Brushes can be solid, hatched, or patterned, while pens can draw solid, dashed, or dotted lines. For additional combinations, refer to your Microsoft Class Libraries Reference manual. Here is the syntax we used to create a new brush and pen object.

```
CBrush newbrush;
  CBrush* oldbrush;
  CPen  newpen;
  CPen* oldpen;
```

Since each GDI primitive's code is somewhat similar, we'll just examine two typical sections. The first piece of code is used to draw a wide, black diagonal line in the window.

```
// draws a wide black diagonal line
  newpen.CreatePen(PS_SOLID,6,dwColor[0]);
  oldpen=dc.SelectObject(&newpen);
  dc.MoveTo(0,0);
  dc.LineTo(640,430);
  dc.TextOut(70,20,"<-diagonal line",15);
```

The pen object is initialized by **CreatePen()** to draw black solid lines six logical units wide. Once the pen is initialized, the **SelectObject()** member function is overloaded for the pen object class and attaches the pen object to the device context. The previously attached object is returned. The **MoveTo()** and **LineTo()** functions set the range for the diagonal line that is drawn by the selected pen. Finally, a label is attached to the figure with the use of the **TextOut()** function.

Brushes can be handled similarly. This brush is initialized to be a hatched brush filled with blue crosses (HS_CROSS). The brush object is selected in the same way the pen object was selected.

```
// draws a black rounded rectangle and fills with blue
  newbrush.CreateHatchBrush(HS_CROSS,dwColor[3]);
  oldbrush=dc.SelectObject(&newbrush);
  dc.RoundRect(60,310,110,350,20,20);
  dc.TextOut (120,310,"<------rounded rectangle",24);
```

The **RoundRect()** function draws a rounded rectangle in black at the given screen coordinates. A label is also printed for this figure.

The remaining shapes are drawn to the screen using a similar technique.

Running the MFCGDI Application

This application has a minor drawback, which you might have observed. All coordinate points for GDI functions are set to pixel values valid for VGA monitors.

What happens if you are using an EGA or Super VGA display? If you are using a monitor with a lower resolution, such as an EGA, you will get a partial image that seems magnified. If you are using a higher-resolution display, such as a Super VGA, the image will fill in only the upper-left of your screen.

To eliminate this problem, your application must determine your display's characteristics and adjust accordingly. This adds an extra layer of complexity to the application code, which we have kept as simple as possible to this point. However, the final example in this chapter will teach you how to scale your figures to fit the current display type.

If you haven't done so by this point, run the MFCGDI application. Your screen should look something like Figure 4-2 if you are using a VGA monitor.

The GDI objects are displayed in vivid colors.

A Bar Chart with Menu and Dialog Boxes

The final application in this chapter, MFCBAR, will draw a presentation-quality bar chart in the window's client area. This application also uses several Windows resources, including a menu, about dialog box, and data entry dialog box.

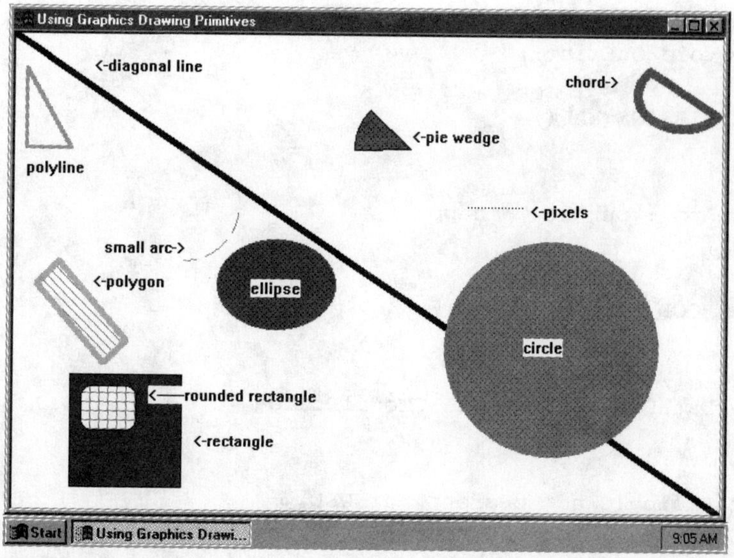

FIGURE 4-2. *Drawing several colorful GDI graphics objects with MFCGDI*

The following listing is a composite of the five files needed to compile this application:

- The header file, MFCBAR.H
- The resource header file, MFCBARR.H
- The resource script file, MFCBAR.RC
- The dialog script file, MFCBAR.DLG
- The application file, MFCTEMP.CPP

Enter each file carefully. When all five files are complete, the application can be compiled.

```
// MFCBAR.H
class CMainWnd : public CFrameWnd
{
public:
  CMainWnd();

  afx_msg void OnPaint();
  afx_msg void OnSize(UINT,int,int);
  afx_msg int  OnCreate(LPCREATESTRUCT cs);
  afx_msg void OnAbout();
  afx_msg void OnBarData();
  afx_msg void OnExit();

  DECLARE_MESSAGE_MAP()
};

class CTheApp : public CWinApp
{
public:
  virtual BOOL InitInstance();
};

class CBarDataDialog : public CModalDialog
{
public:
  CBarDataDialog(CWnd* pParentWnd=NULL)
               : CModalDialog("BarDlgBox",pParentWnd)
               {  }
  virtual void OnOK();
```

```
};

// MFCBARR.H
#define IDM_ABOUT   100
#define IDM_INPUT   200
#define IDM_EXIT    300

#define DM_TITLE    400
#define DM_XLABEL   401
#define DM_YLABEL   402
#define DM_P1       403
#define DM_P2       404
#define DM_P3       405
#define DM_P4       406
#define DM_P5       407
#define DM_P6       408
#define DM_P7       409
#define DM_P8       410
#define DM_P9       411
#define DM_P10      412


// MFCBAR.RC
#include <windows.h>
//#include <afxres.h>
#include "MFCBARR.h"

BarMenu  MENU
BEGIN
  POPUP "Bar_Chart"
  BEGIN
    MENUITEM "About Box...",  IDM_ABOUT
    MENUITEM "Bar Values...", IDM_INPUT
    MENUITEM "Exit",          IDM_EXIT
  END
END

rcinclude MFCBAR.dlg

// MFCBAR.DLG
DLGINCLUDE RCDATA DISCARDABLE
BEGIN
```

```
  "MFCBARR.H\0"
END

ABOUTDLGBOX DIALOG DISCARDABLE 14,22,200,75
STYLE WS_POPUP ¦ WS_CAPTION
CAPTION "About Box"
BEGIN
  CTEXT "A Bar Chart Application",-1,30,5,144,8
  CTEXT "A Simple Foundation Class For Windows Application",
     -1,30,17,144,8
  CTEXT "By William H. Murray and Chris H. Pappas",-1,28,28,
     144,8
  DEFPUSHBUTTON "OK",IDOK,84,55,32,14,WS_GROUP
END

BARDLGBOX DIALOG DISCARDABLE 42,-10,223,209
STYLE WS_POPUP ¦ WS_CAPTION
CAPTION "Bar Chart Data"
BEGIN
  GROUPBOX "Bar Chart Title:",100,5,11,212,89,WS_TABSTOP
  GROUPBOX "Bar Chart Heights",101,5,105,212,90,WS_TABSTOP
  LTEXT "Title: ",-1,43,35,28,8,NOT WS_GROUP
  EDITTEXT DM_TITLE,75,30,137,12
  LTEXT "x-axis label:",-1,15,55,55,8,NOT WS_GROUP
  EDITTEXT DM_XLABEL,75,50,135,12
  LTEXT "y-axis label:",-1,15,75,60,8,NOT WS_GROUP
  EDITTEXT DM_YLABEL,75,70,135,12
  LTEXT "Bar #1: ",-1,45,125,40,8,NOT WS_GROUP
  LTEXT "Bar #2: ",-1,45,140,40,8,NOT WS_GROUP
  LTEXT "Bar #3: ",-1,45,155,40,8,NOT WS_GROUP
  LTEXT "Bar #4: ",-1,45,170,40,8,NOT WS_GROUP
  LTEXT "Bar #5: ",-1,45,185,40,8,NOT WS_GROUP
  LTEXT "Bar #6: ",-1,130,125,40,8,NOT WS_GROUP
  LTEXT "Bar #7: ",-1,130,140,40,8,NOT WS_GROUP
  LTEXT "Bar #8: ",-1,130,155,40,8,NOT WS_GROUP
  LTEXT "Bar #9: ",-1,130,170,40,8,NOT WS_GROUP
  LTEXT "Bar #10:",-1,130,185,45,8,NOT WS_GROUP
  EDITTEXT DM_P1,90,120,30,12
  EDITTEXT DM_P2,90,135,30,12
  EDITTEXT DM_P3,90,150,30,12
  EDITTEXT DM_P4,90,165,30,12
  EDITTEXT DM_P5,90,180,30,12
```

```
   EDITTEXT DM_P6,180,120,30,12
   EDITTEXT DM_P7,180,135,30,12
   EDITTEXT DM_P8,180,150,30,12
   EDITTEXT DM_P9,180,165,30,12
   EDITTEXT DM_P10,180,180,30,12
   PUSHBUTTON "OK",IDOK,54,195,24,14
   PUSHBUTTON "Cancel",IDCANCEL,124,195,34,14
END

#ifdef APSTUDIO_INVOKED
///////////////////////////////////////////////////////////////
//
// TEXTINCLUDE
//

1 TEXTINCLUDE DISCARDABLE
BEGIN
    "resource.h\0"
END

2 TEXTINCLUDE DISCARDABLE
BEGIN
    "#define APSTUDIO_HIDDEN_SYMBOLS\r\n"
    "#include ""windows.h""\r\n"
    "#undef APSTUDIO_HIDDEN_SYMBOLS\r\n"
    "#include ""afxres.h""\r\n"
    "#include ""mfcbarr.h""\r\n"
    "\0"
END

3 TEXTINCLUDE DISCARDABLE
BEGIN
    "\r\n"
    "\0"
END

///////////////////////////////////////////////////////////////
#endif    // APSTUDIO_INVOKED


#ifndef APSTUDIO_INVOKED
///////////////////////////////////////////////////////////////
```

```
//
// Generated from the TEXTINCLUDE 3 resource.
//


/////////////////////////////////////////////////////////////////////////////
#endif    // not APSTUDIO_INVOKED


//
//  MFCBAR.CPP
//  A Presentation Quality Bar Chart Application
//  Using Microsoft C++ Foundation Classes
//  William H. Murray and Chris H. Pappas
//

#include <afxwin.h>
#include <string.h>
#include <math.h>
#include <stdlib.h>
#include "MFCBARR.h"   // resource ids
#include "MFCBAR.h"

#define maxnumbar 10

char szTString[80]="(bar chart title area)";
char szXString[80]="x-axis label";
char szYString[80]="y-axis label";
int iBarSize[maxnumbar]={10,30,50,20};
int m_cxClient,m_cyClient;

CTheApp theApp;

CMainWnd::CMainWnd()
{
  Create((AfxRegisterWndClass(CS_HREDRAW¦CS_VREDRAW,
         LoadCursor(NULL,IDC_CROSS),
         (HBRUSH) GetStockObject(WHITE_BRUSH),NULL)),
         "A MFC Bar Chart Application",
         WS_OVERLAPPEDWINDOW,rectDefault,NULL,"BarMenu");
}
```

```
void CMainWnd::OnSize(UINT,int x,int y)
{
  m_cxClient=x;
  m_cyClient=y;
}

void CMainWnd::OnPaint()
{
  CPaintDC dc(this);
  static DWORD dwColor[10]={RGB(0,0,0),         //black
                            RGB(255,0,0),       //red
                            RGB(0,255,0),       //green
                            RGB(0,0,255),       //blue
                            RGB(255,255,0),     //yellow
                            RGB(255,0,255),     //magenta
                            RGB(0,255,255),     //cyan
                            RGB(0,80,80),       //blend 1
                            RGB(80,80,80),      //blend 2
                            RGB(255,255,255)}; //white
  CFont newfont;
  CFont* oldfont;
  CBrush newbrush;
  CBrush* oldbrush;
  int i,iNBars,iBarWidth,iBarMax;
  int ilenMaxLabel;
  int x1,x2,y1,y2;
  int iBarSizeScaled[maxnumbar];
  char sbuffer[10],*strptr;

//---------- your routines below ----------------------//

  iNBars=0;
  for (i=0;i<maxnumbar;i++)
  {
    if(iBarSize[i]!=0) iNBars++;
  }

  iBarWidth=400/iNBars;

  // Find bar with maximum height and scale
  iBarMax=iBarSize[0];
  for(i=0;i<iNBars;i++)
```

```
    if (iBarMax<iBarSize[i]) iBarMax=iBarSize[i];

  // Convert maximum y value to a string
  strptr=_itoa(iBarMax,sbuffer,10);
  ilenMaxLabel=strlen(sbuffer);

  // Scale bars in array.  Highest bar = 270
  for (i=0;i<iNBars;i++)
    iBarSizeScaled[i]=iBarSize[i]*(270/iBarMax);

  // Create custom view port and map mode
  dc.SetMapMode(MM_ISOTROPIC);
  dc.SetWindowExt(640,400);
  dc.SetViewportExt(m_cxClient,m_cyClient);
  dc.SetViewportOrg(0,0);

 // Print text to window if large enough
  if (m_cxClient > 200) {
    newfont.CreateFont(12,12,0,0,FW_BOLD,
                       FALSE,FALSE,FALSE,OEM_CHARSET,
                       OUT_DEFAULT_PRECIS,
                       CLIP_DEFAULT_PRECIS,
                       DEFAULT_QUALITY,
                       VARIABLE_PITCH¦FF_ROMAN,
                       "Roman");
    oldfont=dc.SelectObject(&newfont);
    dc.TextOut((300-(strlen(szTString)*10/2)),
               15,szTString,strlen(szTString));
    dc.TextOut((300-(strlen(szXString)*10/2)),
               365,szXString,strlen(szXString));
    dc.TextOut((90-ilenMaxLabel*12),
               70,strptr,ilenMaxLabel);
    newfont.DeleteObject();
    newfont.CreateFont(12,12,900,900,FW_BOLD,
                       FALSE,FALSE,FALSE,
                       OEM_CHARSET,
                       OUT_DEFAULT_PRECIS,
                       CLIP_DEFAULT_PRECIS,
                       DEFAULT_QUALITY,
                       VARIABLE_PITCH¦FF_ROMAN,
                       "Roman");
    oldfont=dc.SelectObject(&newfont);
```

```
        dc.TextOut(50,200+(strlen(szXString)*10/2),
                   szYString,strlen(szYString));

        // delete font objects
        newfont.DeleteObject();

      }

    // Draw coordinate axis
     dc.MoveTo(99,49);
     dc.LineTo(99,350);
     dc.LineTo(500,350);
     dc.MoveTo(99,350);

     // Initial values
     x1=100;
     y1=350;
     x2=x1+iBarWidth;

     // Draw Each Bar
     for(i=0;i<iNBars;i++)
     {
       newbrush.CreateSolidBrush(dwColor[i]);
       oldbrush=dc.SelectObject(&newbrush);
       y2=350-iBarSizeScaled[i];
       dc.Rectangle(x1,y1,x2,y2);
       x1=x2;
       x2+=iBarWidth;
     }

     // delete brush objects
     dc.SelectObject(oldbrush);
     newbrush.DeleteObject();

//---------- your routines above ---------------------//
}

int CMainWnd::OnCreate(LPCREATESTRUCT)
{
  UpdateWindow();
  return (0);
}
```

```
void CMainWnd::OnAbout()
{
  CModalDialog about("AboutDlgBox",this);
  about.DoModal();
}

void CBarDataDialog::OnOK()
{
  GetDlgItemText(DM_TITLE,szTString,80);
  GetDlgItemText(DM_XLABEL,szXString,80);
  GetDlgItemText(DM_YLABEL,szYString,80);
  iBarSize[0]=GetDlgItemInt(DM_P1,NULL,0);
  iBarSize[1]=GetDlgItemInt(DM_P2,NULL,0);
  iBarSize[2]=GetDlgItemInt(DM_P3,NULL,0);
  iBarSize[3]=GetDlgItemInt(DM_P4,NULL,0);
  iBarSize[4]=GetDlgItemInt(DM_P5,NULL,0);
  iBarSize[5]=GetDlgItemInt(DM_P6,NULL,0);
  iBarSize[6]=GetDlgItemInt(DM_P7,NULL,0);
  iBarSize[7]=GetDlgItemInt(DM_P8,NULL,0);
  iBarSize[8]=GetDlgItemInt(DM_P9,NULL,0);
  iBarSize[9]=GetDlgItemInt(DM_P10,NULL,0);

  CModalDialog::OnOK();
}

void CMainWnd::OnBarData()
{
  CBarDataDialog dlgBarData(this);
  if (dlgBarData.DoModal()==IDOK)
  {
    InvalidateRect(NULL,TRUE);
    UpdateWindow();
  }
};

void CMainWnd::OnExit()
{
  DestroyWindow();
}

BEGIN_MESSAGE_MAP(CMainWnd,CFrameWnd)
  ON_WM_PAINT()
```

```
  ON_WM_SIZE()
  ON_WM_CREATE()
  ON_COMMAND(IDM_ABOUT,OnAbout)
  ON_COMMAND(IDM_INPUT,OnBarData)
  ON_COMMAND(IDM_EXIT,OnExit)
END_MESSAGE_MAP()

BOOL CTheApp::InitInstance()
{
  m_pMainWnd=new CMainWnd();
  m_pMainWnd->ShowWindow(m_nCmdShow);
  m_pMainWnd->UpdateWindow();

  return TRUE;
}
```

The MFCBAR.H Header File

CMainWnd now contains several function declarations and a message map. The member functions include **OnPaint()**, **OnSize()**, **OnCreate()**, **OnAbout()**, **OnData()**, and **OnExit()**. The **afx_msg** keyword is used instead of **virtual**. **OnPaint()** is a member function of the **CWnd** class that the **CMainWnd** class overrides. This allows the client area of the window to be altered.

```
  afx_msg void OnPaint();
  afx_msg void OnSize(UINT,int,int);
  afx_msg int  OnCreate(LPCREATESTRUCT cs);
  afx_msg void OnAbout();
  afx_msg void OnBarData();
  afx_msg void OnExit();

  DECLARE_MESSAGE_MAP()
```

The **OnPaint()** function is automatically called when a WM_PAINT message is sent to a **CMainWnd** object by Windows or the application. **OnSize()** is called whenever a WM_SIZE message is generated by changing the size of the window. This information will be useful in scaling graphics to the window size. **OnCreate()** points to a structure containing information about the window being created. This structure contains information on the size, style, and so on, of the window. **OnAbout()**, **OnBarData()**, and **OnExit()** are user-defined functions that respond to WM_COMMAND messages. WM_COMMAND messages are generated when the user selects an option from a menu or dialog box.

DECLARE_MESSAGE_MAP() is used again to state that the class overrides the handling of certain messages (see body of application). Recall that this technique is more space efficient than the use of virtual functions.

The MFC library supports regular and modal dialog boxes with the **CDialog** and **CModalDialog** classes. For very simple dialog boxes, such as about boxes, the foundation class can be used directly. For data entry dialog boxes, however, the class will have to be derived.

The dialog box for this example will permit the user to enter an integer for the number of harmonics to be drawn in the window and an optional graph title. The **CBarDataDialog** class is derived from the **CModalDialog** foundation class. Modal dialog boxes must be dismissed before other action can be taken in an application.

```
class CBarDataDialog : public CModalDialog
{
public:
  CBarDataDialog(CWnd* pParentWnd=NULL)
                : CModalDialog("BarDlgBox",pParentWnd)
                { }
  virtual void OnOK();
};
```

In a derived modal dialog class, member variables and functions can be added to specify the behavior of the dialog box. Member variables can also be used to save data entered by the user or to save data for display. Classes derived from **CModalDialog** require their own message maps, with the exception of the **OnInitDialog()**, **OnOK()**, and **OnCancel()** functions.

In this simple example, the **CBarDataDialog** constructor supplies the name of the dialog template (BarDlgBox) and the name of the parent window that owns the dialog. There is no owner for this modal dialog.

The dialog box will actually return data to the application when the user clicks on the OK dialog push button. If either the OK or Cancel push button is clicked, the dialog box closes and is removed from the screen. When the dialog box closes, its member variables are accessed through the member functions to retrieve information entered by the user. Dialog boxes requiring initialization can override the **OnInitDialog()** member function for this purpose.

Additional information on dialog box classes and their use can be found in the Microsoft Class Libraries User's Guide. Help is also available, on-line, from the QuickHelp utility.

The MFCBARR.H Resource Header, MFCBAR.RC Resource Script, and MFCBAR.DLG Dialog Script Files

These three files are combined by the Microsoft Resource Compiler into a single compiled Windows resource, MFCBAR.RES.

The MFCBAR.H resource header file contains three menu identification values: IDM_ABOUT, IDM_INPUT, and IDM_EXIT.

Thirteen identification values are also included for use by the modal dialog box. Three are for titles and labels: DM_TITLE, DM_XLABEL, and DM_YLABEL. The remaining ten values, DM_P1 to DM_P10, are for retrieving the height of the individual bars. They will be integer values.

The resource script file, MFCBAR.RC, contains a description of the application's menu, which is shown in Figure 4-3.

Compare the menu title and features to the text used in creating the menu in the resource file.

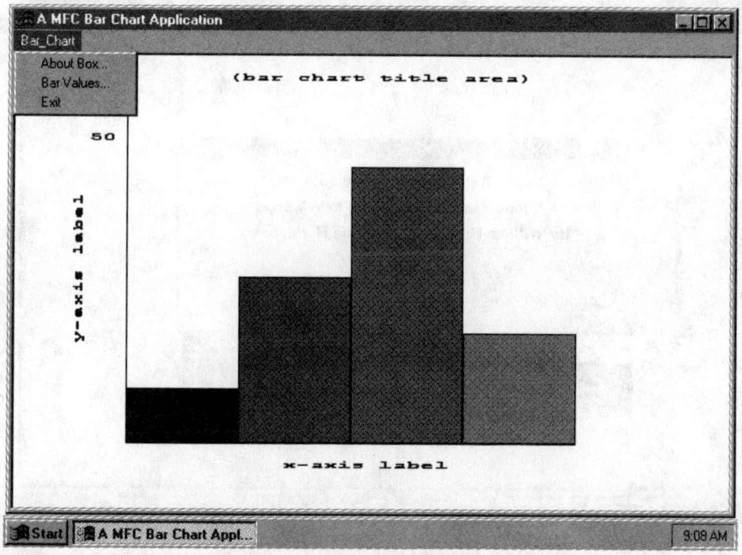

FIGURE 4-3. *A menu for the MFCBAR application*

The dialog script file, MFCBAR.DLG, contains a description of the application's about and data entry dialog boxes. The about dialog box is shown in Figure 4-4, while the data entry dialog box is shown in Figure 4-5.

The Dialog Editor, provided with the Visual C/C++ compiler, was used to construct both dialog boxes. The Dialog Editor automatically creates the dialog resource script file with the .DLG extension.

The MFCBAR.CPP Application File

The complexity of the application file for this example has increased greatly because of the inclusion of menus and dialog boxes. Other features have also been added, which you might want to include in your own programs. In the following sections, we'll show you how to select a new cursor, set the background color, determine the size of the current window, set a new viewport and origin for drawing, and draw and fill an object in the window. Let's examine these features as they appear in the program.

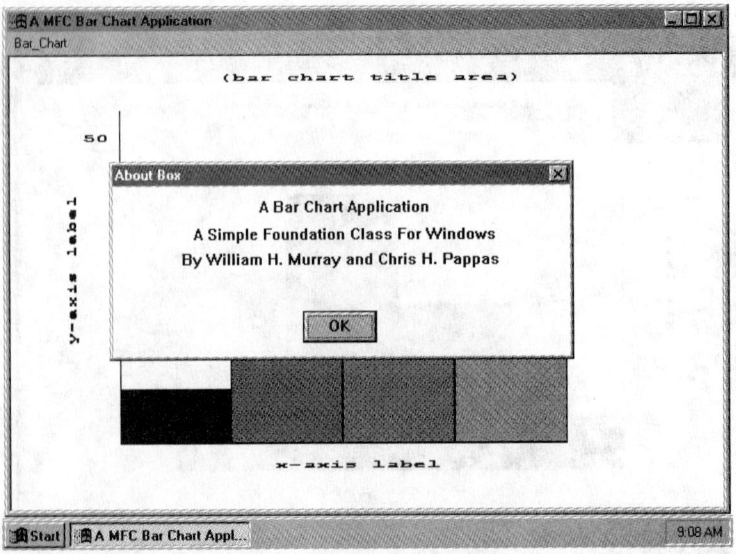

FIGURE 4-4. *An about dialog box for the MFCBAR application*

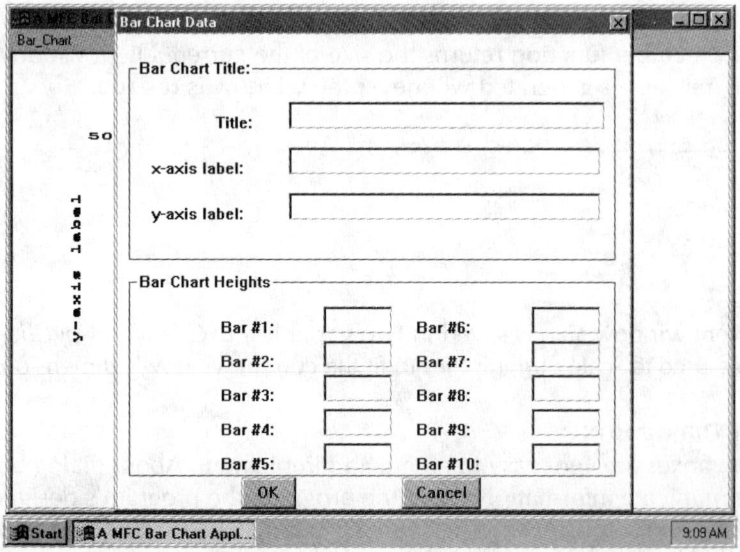

FIGURE 4-5. *The data entry dialog box for the MFCBAR application*

Creating a Custom CMainWnd Class

The **CMainWnd** class can be customized with the use of **AfxRegisterWndClass()** in creating a registration class. A registration class has many fields, but four are easily altered: style, cursor, background, and the minimize icon.

```
CMainWnd::CMainWnd()
{
  Create((AfxRegisterWndClass(CS_HREDRAW|CS_VREDRAW,
        LoadCursor(NULL,IDC_CROSS),
        (HBRUSH) GetStockObject(WHITE_BRUSH),NULL)),
        "A MFC Bar Chart Application",
        WS_OVERLAPPEDWINDOW,rectDefault,NULL,"BarMenu");
}
```

This small piece of code shows the syntax for changing the cursor to a stock cross shape (IDC_CROSS) and setting the brush, which paints the background, to a WHITE_BRUSH. Also note the menu name is identified in the **Create()** member function.

Determining the Window's Current Size

The **OnSize()** member function returns the size of the current client window. A WM_SIZE message is generated whenever the window is resized.

```
void CMainWnd::OnSize(UINT,int x,int y)
{
  m_cxClient=x;
  m_cyClient=y;
}
```

The current window size is saved in two variables, *cxClient* and *cyClient*. These values will be used to scale our graphics to fit the current window's dimensions.

The About Dialog Box

About dialog boxes are very easy to create and implement. About dialog boxes are used to communicate information about the program, the program's designers, copyright date, and so on.

A modal dialog box is created by selecting the Bar Chart About Box... option from the application's menu. The OnAbout command handler requires only a few lines of code.

```
void CMainWnd::OnAbout()
{
  CModalDialog about("AboutDlgBox",this);
  about.DoModal();
}
```

The constructor for **CModalDialog()** uses the current window at the parent window for the object. The **this** pointer is typically used here and refers to the currently used object. The **DoModal()** member function is responsible for drawing the about box in the client area. When the about box OK button is pushed, the box is removed and the client area is repainted.

The Data Entry Dialog Box

Dialog boxes that allow user input require a bit more programming than do simple about dialog boxes. A data input dialog box can be selected from the application's menu by selecting Bar_Chart.

A figure of this dialog box was shown earlier. The user is permitted to enter a chart title and an integer representing the bar values to draw. If the user selects the OK push button, the data entry dialog box is removed from the window and the client area is updated.

```
void CMainWnd::OnBarData()
{
  CBarDataDialog dlgBarData(this);
  if (dlgBarData.DoModal()==IDOK)
  {
    InvalidateRect(NULL,TRUE);
    UpdateWindow();
  }
};
```

CBarDataDialog was derived from **CModalDialog** in the header file, MFCBAR.H, and discussed earlier. Notice, however, that it is at this point in the application that data is retrieved. This data was entered in the dialog box by the user.

```
void CBarDataDialog::OnOK()
{
  GetDlgItemText(DM_TITLE,szTString,80);
  GetDlgItemText(DM_XLABEL,szXString,80);
  GetDlgItemText(DM_YLABEL,szYString,80);
  iBarSize[0]=GetDlgItemInt(DM_P1,NULL,0);
  iBarSize[1]=GetDlgItemInt(DM_P2,NULL,0);
  iBarSize[2]=GetDlgItemInt(DM_P3,NULL,0);
  iBarSize[3]=GetDlgItemInt(DM_P4,NULL,0);
  iBarSize[4]=GetDlgItemInt(DM_P5,NULL,0);
  iBarSize[5]=GetDlgItemInt(DM_P6,NULL,0);
  iBarSize[6]=GetDlgItemInt(DM_P7,NULL,0);
  iBarSize[7]=GetDlgItemInt(DM_P8,NULL,0);
  iBarSize[8]=GetDlgItemInt(DM_P9,NULL,0);
  iBarSize[9]=GetDlgItemInt(DM_P10,NULL,0);
```

The **GetDlgItemText()** function returns chart title information to *szTString* in the form of a string. The dialog box location for this information is identified by IDD_TITLE. Integer information can be processed in a similar manner with the **GetDlgItemInt()** function. Its dialog box identification value is IDD_TERMS, and the integer retrieved by the function is returned to *iBarSize[n]*. The second parameter is used to report translation errors, but is not used in this application. If the third parameter is nonzero, a check will be made for a signed number. In this application, only positive numbers are possible.

With the use of a modal dialog box, the user can specify a chart title, axes labels, and the height of up to ten bars. The chart will then be correctly scaled to the window, with each bar's color selected from an array of predefined values.

The maximum number of bars, **maxnumbar**, is set to ten at the start of the application.

```
#define maxnumbar 10
```

This value can be changed slightly, but remember a good bar chart doesn't crowd too many bars on a single chart.

Global data types hold initial bar chart values for titles, axes labels, and bar heights.

```
char szTString[80]="(bar chart title area)";
char szXString[80]="x-axis label";
char szYString[80]="y-axis label";
int iBarSize[maxnumbar]={20,10,40,50};
```

The size of the client area will also be saved as a global value. These are the same variable names used in the previous example.

```
int m_cxClient,m_cyClient;
```

By keeping track of the client area size, our bar chart can be scaled to fit the current window size.

Bar colors are selected from the *dwColor* array, in a sequential manner. If the bar chart has three bars, they will be black, red, and green. Colors can be exchanged if you so desire.

Responding to OnExit()

The final application menu option is Exit. Exit will destroy the client window by calling the **DestroyWindow** function.

```
void CMainWnd::OnExit()
{
  DestroyWindow();
}
```

This application menu option gives the user a method of exiting the application without using the system menu.

The Message Map

Again, two classes are specified in BEGIN_MESSAGE_MAP: **CMainWnd** and **CFrameWnd**. **CMainWnd** is the target class and **CFrameWnd** is a class based on **CWnd**. The **ON_WM_PAINT()** function handles all WM_PAINT messages and directs them to the **OnPaint()** member function. ON_WM_SIZE handles WM_SIZE messages and directs them to the **OnSize()** member function.

The ON_WM_CREATE function handles WM_CREATE messages and directs them to the **OnCreate()** member function. There is an ON_COMMAND function for each application menu item. Message information is processed on menu items, then returned to the appropriate member function for processing.

```
BEGIN_MESSAGE_MAP(CMainWnd,CFrameWnd)
  ON_WM_PAINT()
  ON_WM_SIZE()
  ON_WM_CREATE()
  ON_COMMAND(IDM_ABOUT,OnAbout)
  ON_COMMAND(IDM_INPUT,OnBarData)
  ON_COMMAND(IDM_EXIT,OnExit)
END_MESSAGE_MAP()
```

As we mentioned in an earlier example, the use of message maps has eliminated the need for the case/switch statements. These statements are typically a source of error in Windows applications.

In this section, we'll concentrate on those features that are new to the applications developed in this chapter. The MFCBAR.CPP application will allow the user to draw a presentation-quality bar chart in the client area of a window.

The **CFont** and **CBrush** classes permit the font or brush object to be passed to any **CDC** (base class for display context) member function. New fonts will be needed for drawing the chart title and axes. Brushes were discussed earlier in this chapter. Additional information for these classes is available in your Microsoft Class Libraries Reference manual. Here is the syntax we used to create a new font and brush object.

```
CFont newfont;
  CFont* oldfont;
  CBrush newbrush;
  CBrush* oldbrush;
```

Manipulating Bar Data

First you need to determine how many bar values are being held in the global array, *iBarSize*. This can be determined by counting values until the first zero value is encountered.

```
iNBars=0;
  for (i=0;i<maxnumbar;i++)
  {
    if(iBarSize[i]!=0) iNBars++;
  }
```

Data values are returned to this array whenever the data entry dialog box is closed.

The width of each bar drawn in the chart depends on the total number of bars. The chart will always be drawn to the same width. Bar width is determined with:

```
iBarWidth=400/iNBars;
```

The height of each bar is determined relative to the largest bar value entered by the user. The largest bar value is always drawn to the same chart height. The size of the largest bar value is easy to determine.

```
// Find bar with maximum height and scale
  iBarMax=iBarSize[0];
  for(i=0;i<iNBars;i++)
    if (iBarMax<iBarSize[i]) iBarMax=iBarSize[i];
```

This chart will also print the height of the largest bar value on the vertical axis. The **_itoa** function is used to convert this value to a string.

```
// Convert maximum y value to a string
  strptr=_itoa(iBarMax,sbuffer,10);
  ilenMaxLabel=strlen(sbuffer);
```

The remaining bars in the array are then scaled to the largest bar's value.

```
// Scale bars in array. Highest bar = 270
  for (i=0;i<iNBars;i++)
    iBarSizeScaled[i]=iBarSize[i]*(270/iBarMax);
```

Preparing the Window

Before we're ready to begin drawing in the window's client area, the mapping mode, window extent, viewport extent, and origin are set.

```
  // Create custom view port and map mode
  dc.SetMapMode(MM_ISOTROPIC);
  dc.SetWindowExt(640,400);
  dc.SetViewportExt(m_cxClient,m_cyClient);
  dc.SetViewportOrg(0,0);
```

This same action was taken for the previous example to ensure that as the window is sized, the chart will remain proportionally the same size. As a matter of fact, in this application the chart can be reduced to an icon, with all of the bars still clearly visible. See the last application for additional details on these function calls.

Drawing Text to the Window

This application needs several font sizes and orientations. Before continuing, let's look at how these can be created.

There are actually two ways to create and manipulate fonts in Windows. We will use the **CreateFont()** function in this example.

What Is a Font?

A font can be defined as a complete set of characters of the same typeface and size. Fonts include letters, punctuation marks, and additional symbols. The size of a font is measured in points. For example, a 12 point Arial font is different from 12 point Times New Roman, 14 point Times New Roman, or 12 point Lucida Bright. A *point* is the smallest unit of measure used in typography. There are 12 points in a pica and 72 points in an inch.

A *typeface* is a basic character design that is defined by a stroke width and a serif (a smaller line used to finish off a main stroke of a letter, as at the top and bottom of the uppercase letter *M*). A *font* represents a complete set of characters from one specific typeface, all with a certain size and style, for example, italics or bold. Usually the system owns all of the font resources and shares them with the application program. Fonts are not usually compiled into the final executable version of a program.

Applications, such as MFCBAR.CPP, treat fonts like other drawing objects. Windows supplies several fonts: System, Terminal, Courier, Helvetica, Modern, Roman, Script, and Times Roman as well as several new TrueType fonts. These are called *GDI-supplied fonts.*

The CreateFont Function Syntax

The **CreateFont()** function is defined in the WINDOWS.H header file. This function selects a logical font from the GDI's pool of physical fonts that most closely matches the characteristics specified by the developer in the function call. Once created, this logical font can be selected by any device. The syntax for **CreateFont()** is

```
CreateFont(Height,Width,Escapement,Orientation,Weight
           Italic,Underline,StrikeOut,CharSet,
           OutputPrecision,ClipPrecision,Quality,
           PitchAndFamily,Facename)
```

With 14 parameters, **CreateFont()** requires quite a bit of skill to use. Table 4-1 helps explain the CreateFont () parameters.

(int) Height	Desired font height in logical units
(int) Width	Average font width in logical units
(int) Escapement	Angle (tenths of a degree) for each line written in the font
(int) Orientation	Angle (tenths of a degree) for each character's baseline
(int) Weight	Weight of font (0 to 1000)—400 is normal, 700 is bold
(byte) Italic	Italic font
(byte) Underline	Underline font
(byte) StrikeOut	Struck-out fonts (redline)
(byte) CharSet	Character set (ANSI_CHARSET, OEM_CHARSET)
(byte) OutputPrecision	How closely output must match the requested specifications (OUT_CHARACTER_PRECIS, OUT_DEFAULT_PRECIS, OUT_STRING_PRECIS, OUT_STROKE_PRECIS)
(byte) ClipPrecision	How to clip characters outside of clipping range (CLIP_CHARACTER_PRECIS, CLIP_DEFAULT_PRECIS, CLIP_STROKE_PRECIS)
(byte) Quality	How carefully the logical attributes are mapped to the physical font (DEFAULT_QUALITY, DRAFT_QUALITY, PROOF_QUALITY)
(byte) PitchAndFamily	Pitch and family of font (DEFAULT_PITCH, FIXED_PITCH, PROOF_QUALITY, FF_DECORATIVE, FF_DONTCARE, FF_MODERN, FF_ROMAN, FF_SCRIPT, FF_SWISS)
(lpstr) Facename	A string pointing to the typeface name of the desired font

TABLE 4-1. ***CreateFont()*** *Parameters*

The first time **CreateFont()** is called, the parameters are set to the following values:

```
Height = 12
Width  = 12
Escapement = 0
Orientation = 0
Weight = FW_BOLD
Italic = FALSE
Underline = FALSE
StrikeOut = FALSE
CharSet = OEM_CHARSET
OutputPrecision = OUT_DEFAULT_PRECIS
ClipPrecision = CLIP_DEFAULT_PRECIS
Quality = DEFAULT_QUALITY
PitchAndFamily = VARIABLE_PITCH | FF_ROMAN
Facename = "Roman"
```

An attempt will be made to find a font to match the above specifications. This font will be used to print a horizontal string of text in the window. The next time **CreateFont()** is called, the parameters are set to the following values:

```
Height = 12
Width  = 12
Escapement = 900
Orientation = 900
Weight = FW_BOLD
Italic = FALSE
Underline = FALSE
StrikeOut = FALSE
CharSet = OEM_CHARSET
OutputPrecision = OUT_DEFAULT_PRECIS
ClipPrecision = CLIP_DEFAULT_PRECIS
Quality = DEFAULT_QUALITY
PitchAndFamily = VARIABLE_PITCH | FF_ROMAN
Facename = "Roman"
```

Again, an attempt will be made to find a match to the preceding specifications. Examine the listing and notice that only Escapement and Orientation are changed. Both parameters use angle values specified in tenths of a degree. Thus, 900 represents an angle of 90.0 degrees. The Escapement parameter rotates the line of text from horizontal to vertical. Orientation rotates each character, in this application, by 90.0 degrees. This font will be used to print a vertical axis label in the application.

Here is how we printed the vertical axis label in this application:

```
newfont.CreateFont(12,12,900,900,FW_BOLD,
                   FALSE,FALSE,FALSE,
                   OEM_CHARSET,
                   OUT_DEFAULT_PRECIS,
                   CLIP_DEFAULT_PRECIS,
                   DEFAULT_QUALITY,
                   VARIABLE_PITCH|FF_ROMAN,
                   "Roman");
oldfont=dc.SelectObject(&newfont);
dc.TextOut(50,200+(strlen(szXString)*10/2),
          szYString,strlen(szYString));
```

When developing your own applications, be sure to examine the documentation on the **CreateFont()** function and additional typefaces available for your use.

Drawing the Axes and Bars

You draw X- and Y-coordinate axes by using the **MoveTo** and **LineTo** functions.

```
// Draw coordinate axis
  dc.MoveTo(99,49);
  dc.LineTo(99,350);
  dc.LineTo(500,350);
  dc.MoveTo(99,350);
```

Then you prepare to draw each bar. The first bar always starts at position (100,350) on the chart, as defined by *x1* and *y1*. The width of the first bar, and all subsequent bars, is calculated from the last drawing position and the width of each bar. The second x value is defined by *x2*.

```
// Initial values
  x1=100;
  y1=350;
  x2=x1+iBarWidth;
```

Bars are drawn by retrieving the scaled bar height value from **iBarSizeScaled**. This scaled value, saved in *y2*, is used in the **Rectangle** function. Since the **Rectangle** function draws a closed figure, the figure will be filled with the current brush color. The color selected from the array is incremented during each pass through the loop.

```
// Draw Each Bar
  for(i=0;i<iNBars;i++)
  {
    newbrush.CreateSolidBrush(dwColor[i]);
    oldbrush=dc.SelectObject(&newbrush);
    y2=350-iBarSizeScaled[i];
    dc.Rectangle(x1,y1,x2,y2);
    x1=x2;
    x2+=iBarWidth;
  }
```

After each bar is drawn, the values in *x1* and *x2* are updated to point to the next bar's position. This process is repeated in the **for** loop until all bars are drawn.

Running MFCBAR

Compile the MFCBAR application from the command prompt or from within the integrated environment. When you execute the application, a default bar chart, similar to Figure 4-6, will be drawn in the window.

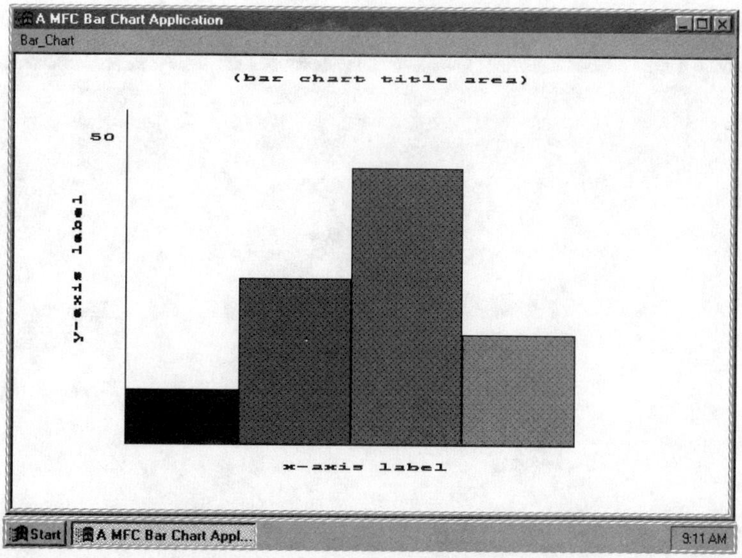

FIGURE 4-6. *The default bar chart for the MFCBAR application*

A custom bar chart, shown in Figure 4-7, can be created by entering a chart title, axes labels, and unique bar values.

You can continue the development of this application by adding axis tick marks, a legend, and so on. Customization is limited only by your imagination.

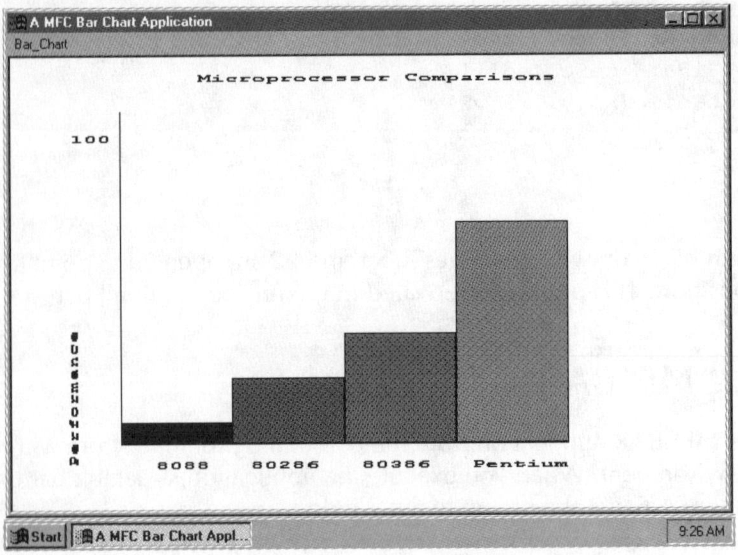

FIGURE 4-7. *A custom bar chart with chart title and labels*

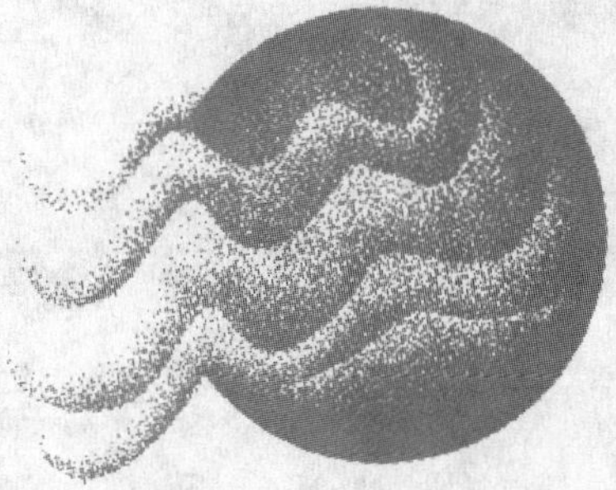

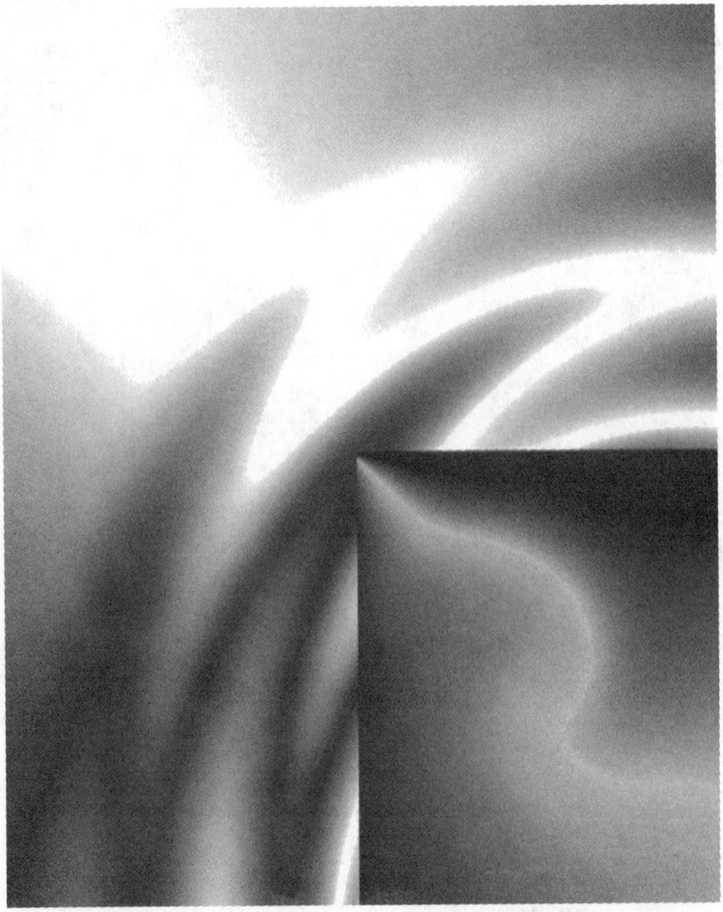

Chapter 5

OLE Concepts and Definitions

This chapter will introduce you to the concepts and definitions used with Microsoft's OLE 2 tools. OLE 2 is more than just an upgrade of the original OLE, version 1. OLE 2, which we'll refer to as simply "OLE" for the remainder of this chapter, enhances the work we've done to this point with object-oriented programming and the Microsoft Foundation Class library. The OLE tools provided with the Visual C++ compiler allow you to develop interconnected applications, called *compound documents,* that are dynamically linked. This dynamic linking allows one OLE application to incorporate data from another OLE application into its documents. OLE also allows *automation.* Automation allows one OLE application to issue commands to another OLE application. In this case the application receiving commands becomes the automation object, and the application sending commands becomes the automation controller.

Writing OLE applications from the ground up has been a difficult task even for the seasoned programmer. Fortunately, the code is redundant between applications, and hence lends itself to being packaged as a template. In the April 1994 issue of *Microsoft Systems Journal,* Paul DiLascia discussed his first OLE application. "After spending a month suffering in OLE hell, slogging through pre-release drafts ... I actually wrote enough code—just under five thousand lines ... [and converted an existing application] into an OLE server using totally generic classes." As you examine this article, you will find that DiLascia eventually found a better way of generating code equivalent to his first efforts. With the help of the MFC library and the AppWizard, the complex code for the OLE template can be generated automatically in approximately ten minutes!

In this chapter the AppWizard is used to automatically generate basic OLE template code, rather than developing this code from the ground up. The downside to automatic template generation is the possibility that you might never understand the purpose or use of OLE functions used in the template. If this is a concern, we suggest generating the template and then using it as a guide while you study each part of the application. You can then compare the placement and use of each OLE function by using the compiler's built-in help facility or with additional references such as *Osborne Windows Programming Series,* volumes 1-3, by Schildt, Pappas, and Murray.

The AppWizard is a great tool for developing applications with OLE features. The AppWizard lifts the program developer above the mundane tasks of repetitive programming code, with the use of dynamic templates. It also allows you to introduce features into your applications without having to worry about the details of the implementation. With the AppWizard, the difficulty of implementing OLE in an application has become very simple!

As an example of OLE development, the next two chapters of this book will contain OLE server and OLE container applications. These applications were developed with the AppWizard running under WIN 95 and Windows NT.

NOTE
If you build these applications under Windows 3.1, your windows will take on a slightly modified appearance over those shown in this chapter.

The AppWizard always generates object-oriented code that takes full advantage of the MFC library.

What is OLE?

When Microsoft introduced OLE, it stood for "Object Linking and Embedding." Today OLE has grown to mean more than just object linking and embedding, but the word "OLE" has been retained. In its simplest form, OLE allows two applications to be dynamically linked. In other words, these applications can share data between documents while both applications are still active. This dynamic or "hot" linking is desirable in cases where multiple documents such as spreadsheets, word processor files, and databases work on separate but related groups of files.

An important concept to appreciate immediately is that objects are linked and embedded. Object-oriented programming forms the foundation for OLE programming.

NOTE
OLE applications can be built using C structures, rather than C++ classes, but this approach is not directly supported by the AppWizard.

It should be no surprise then that the AppWizard generates object-oriented windows code and makes full use of the MFC library.

OLE 2 Features

OLE now offers additional features that are not directly related to compound documents. These features specify new methods for handling drag-and-drop, data transfer, files, and so on.

This section contains an overview of these concepts.

Objects

Procedure-oriented Windows programming makes extensive use of API function calls. Sometimes it is difficult to see the implementation language (C or C++) because these applications seem to contain nothing but function calls. You may wish to examine procedure-oriented Windows applications in books such as *Windows 3.1 Programming,* by Murray and Pappas, published by Osborne/McGraw-Hill.

Chapters 1 through 4 of this book present an object-oriented approach in developing applications. The Microsoft Foundation Class library (MFC) provides the necessary classes for developing these applications.

With the release of OLE 2 come additional tools for the object-oriented OLE programmer. The *Component Object Model* is a binary specification or standard that allows two unrelated applications to communicate with each other.

A *Component Object* can be instantiated through a component object library—a library that contains functions that support this instantiation. A Component Object is a Windows Object with a unique class ID. The object's functions, contained in the library and referred to as an *interface*, can be called via a returned pointer. This process allows objects to be created which are not dependent on the programming language. The library also marshals how function calls and function parameters are handled between processes.

Files

OLE allows the use of stream and storage objects, called *compound files*, that streamline file manipulation. The stream object most closely resembles a single file. The storage object resembles a file directory. This structured storage concept shields you from the actual location where data is stored on a disk.

Microsoft's long-range plans for OLE include a common file structure, so that all files can be browsed in an easy manner.

Data

Uniform data transfers are made through a *data object*. OLE uses pointers to a data object. This helps connect the data source to the data receiver. The data object, in turn, handles how data is actually exchanged. Thus, to the programmer, data transfers using the clipboard will be handled in the same manner as data transfers via drag-and-drop.

Embedding

Compound documents can hold information from a variety of unrelated sources. For example, a Word for Windows document may contain an Excel chart and a Paintbrush bitmap.

Before OLE, charts and bitmaps could be copied to another document via the clipboard. Once the objects were "pasted" into the receiving document, they retained no knowledge of their former life. They were static, dead images. If changes eventually had to be made in these objects, the user had to return to the application that originally generated the object and go through the cut-and-paste transfer process once again.

In this case, the Word for Windows document is called the *container*. Containers hold the objects created by other applications. Excel and Paintbrush are called *servers*. Servers are the source of new objects used by other applications.

Embedding Objects

To gain more experience with embedded objects, this section will show you how to embed a Paintbrush object in a Microsoft WordPad document. Microsoft WordPad will be the container, while Paintbrush will be the server.

Open the Microsoft WordPad application. Figure 5-1 shows a typical Microsoft WordPad screen with a small portion of text.

From the Microsoft WordPad Insert menu, select the Insert New Object... menu item, as shown in Figure 5-2.

Once the menu item is selected, the Insert Object dialog box will be opened, as shown in Figure 5-3.

From the Insert Object dialog box, choose Paintbrush Picture as the object to embed. Paintbrush will be opened automatically, as shown in Figure 5-4.

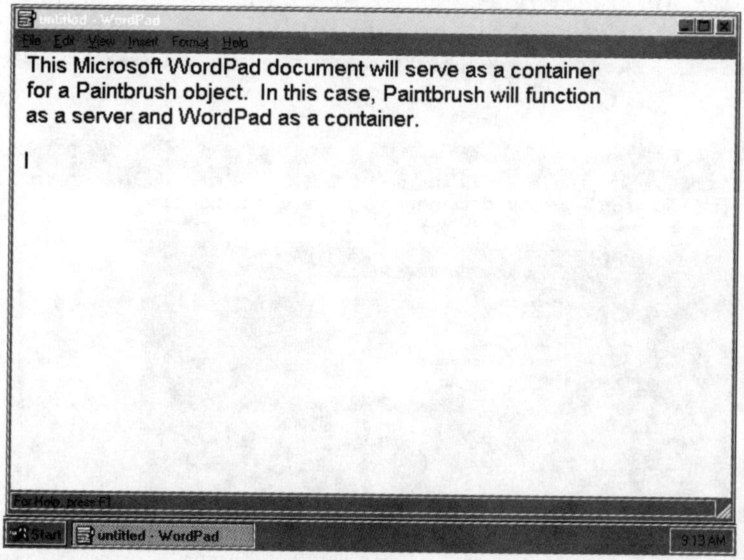

FIGURE 5-1. *Microsoft WordPad will serve as the container for the embedded object*

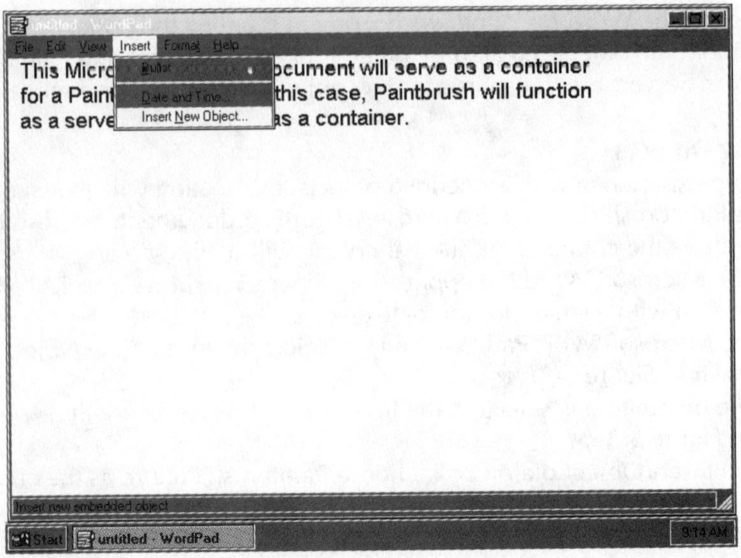

FIGURE 5-2. *Microsoft WordPad's Insert menu will allow an object to be inserted into the document*

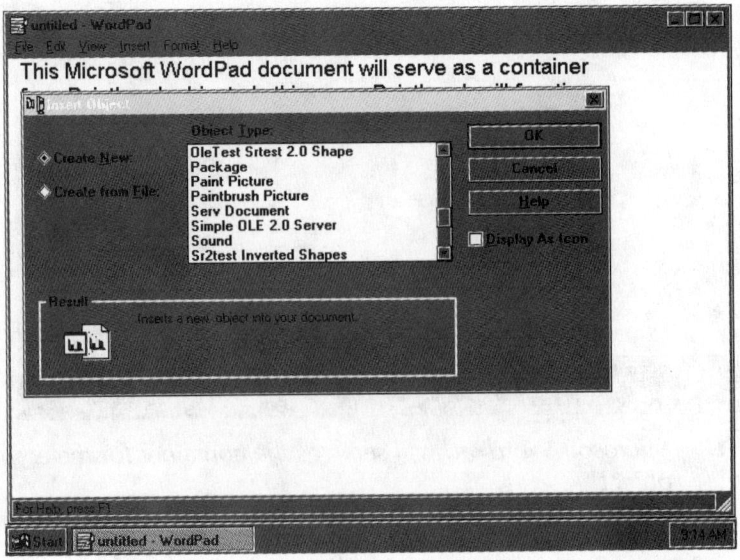

FIGURE 5-3. *The Insert Object dialog box will provide a list of object types that can be embedded within the Microsoft WordPad document*

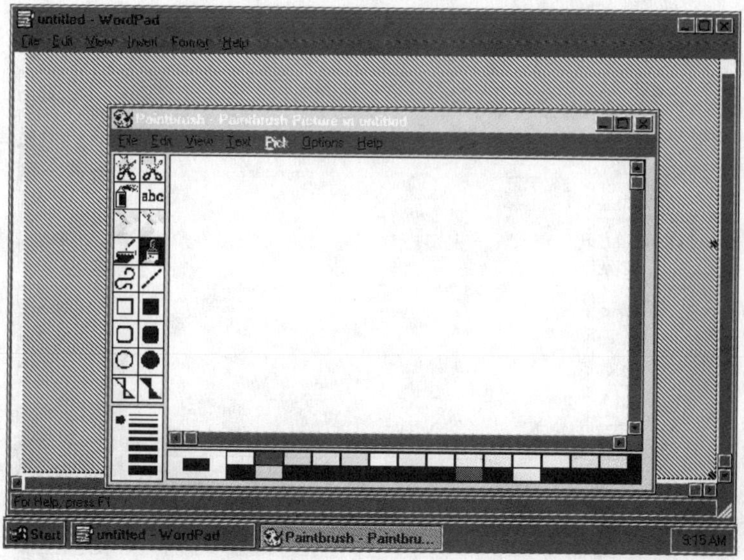

FIGURE 5-4. *When a Paintbrush Picture is selected from the Insert Object dialog box, Paintbrush is opened automatically*

The next step is to create the object, in Paintbrush, that you wish to embed in the Microsoft WordPad document. In this example, a simple graphic was drawn in the Paintbrush drawing area, as shown in Figure 5-5.

When the object is complete, select the Exit & Return to menu item in Paintbrush's File menu. Figure 5-6 shows this option.

The Paintbrush application terminates and the object is transferred to Microsoft WordPad, as shown in Figure 5-7.

Now, here is the magic. Suppose you decide that the object isn't exactly what you wanted. Under OLE, simply double-click on the object, as shown in Figure 5-8, to block it for editing.

When the object is selected in Microsoft WordPad by double-clicking the mouse on it, Paintbrush is immediately opened again with the currently selected object ready for editing. Figure 5-9 shows this process.

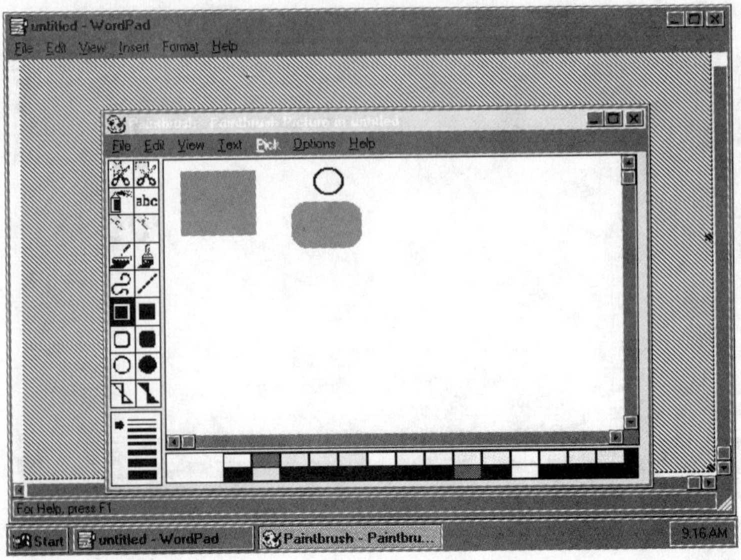

FIGURE 5-5. *The object to be embedded in Microsoft WordPad is drawn in Paintbrush*

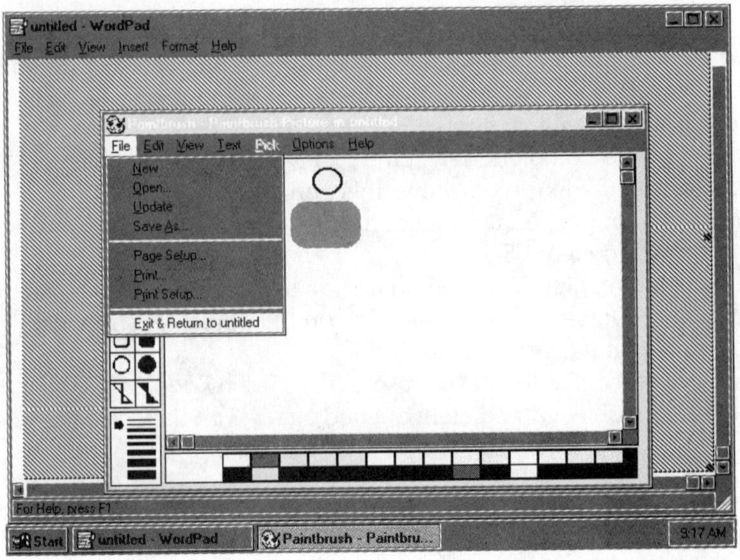

FIGURE 5-6. *The object can be embedded in Microsoft WordPad by selecting Paintbrush's Exit & Return to menu item*

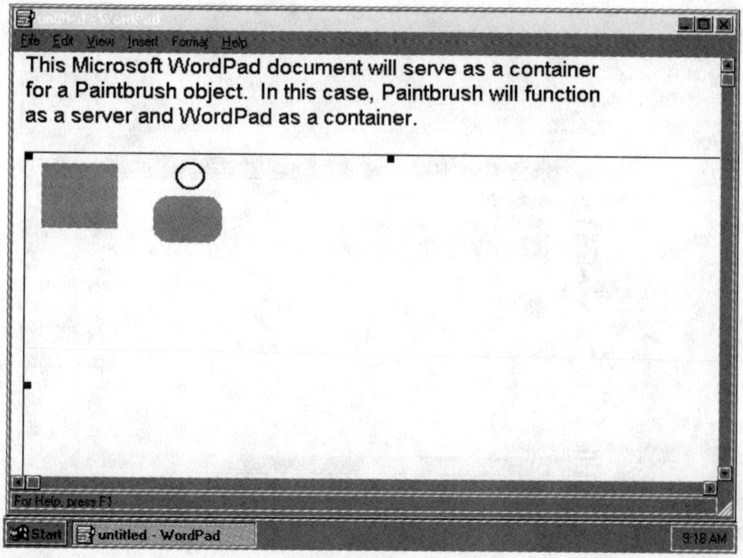

FIGURE 5-7. *The Paintbrush object is now embedded in the Microsoft WordPad document*

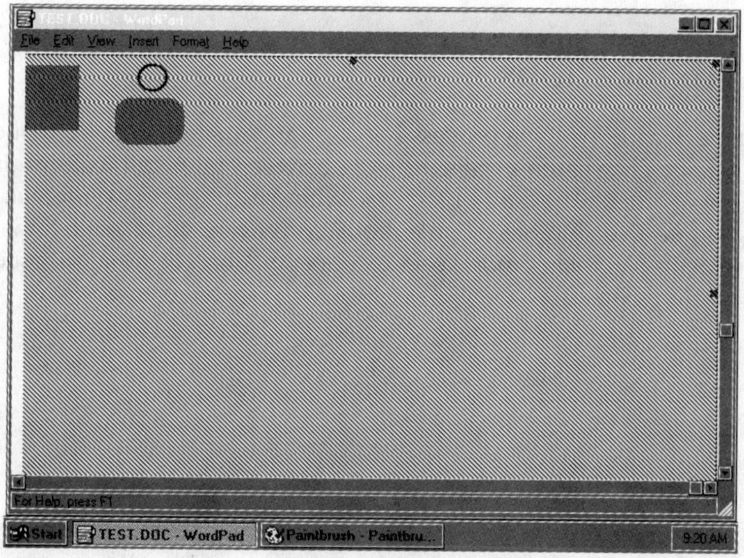

FIGURE 5-8. *The recently embedded object is selected in Microsoft WordPad for editing*

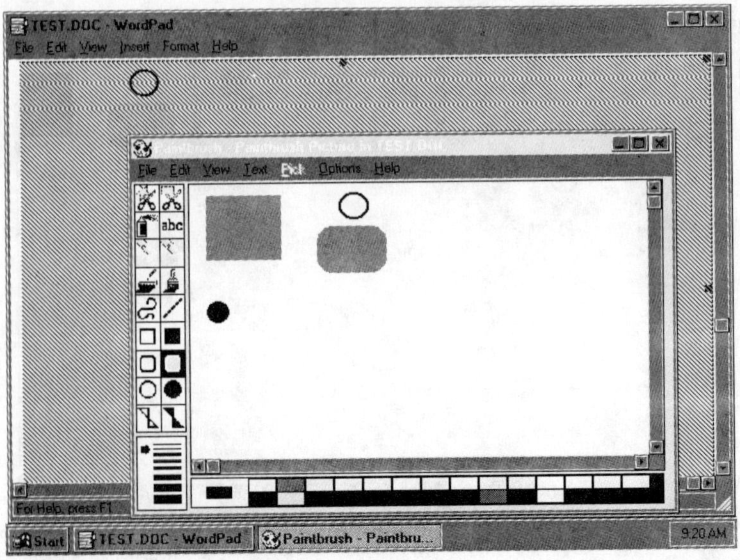

FIGURE 5-9. *When an OLE object is selected for editing, in the Microsoft WordPad container application, the Paintbrush server application is automatically opened*

Linked Applications

OLE supports a dynamic linking process between applications. When applications are linked, data can be shared instantaneously between both applications. In the past, linking was difficult because of the ease with which users could break the links. With the latest version of OLE, *file monikers* prevent most of the link breakage problems. An OLE 2 moniker is a conceptual handle to a link used in binding connecting objects.

Linking

In this section you will learn how to link two OLE applications. A Microsoft Word document will be linked to a Microsoft Excel chart. Through OLE linking, when data changes in the Excel application, the chart will automatically be updated in the Microsoft Word application.

Start this example by opening both Word and Excel, as shown in Figure 5-10.

Next, produce the chart in Microsoft Excel (functioning as the server document) that is to be linked to Microsoft Word (functioning as the container document). Figure 5-11 shows a simple pie chart that will be used for this example.

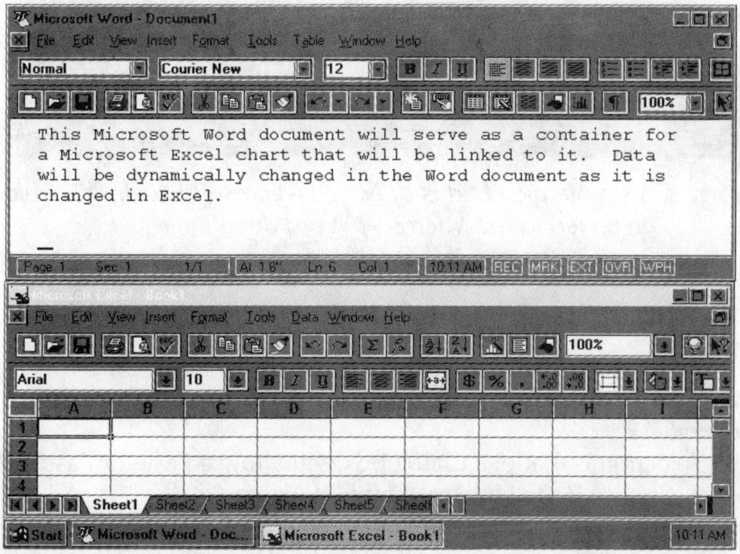

FIGURE 5-10. *To establish a link between two OLE applications, open both applications in the normal manner*

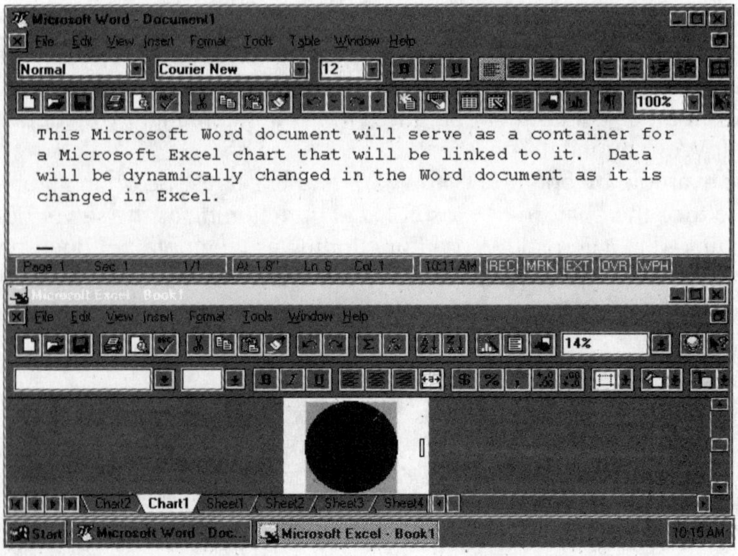

FIGURE 5-11. *A simple pie chart is drawn in Microsoft Excel. This object will be linked to the Microsoft Word document*

From Microsoft Word's Edit menu, select the Paste Special... menu item, as shown in Figure 5-12.

When this selection is made, a dialog box will allow a Paste or Paste Link option to be set. Choose Paste Link, as shown in Figure 5-13.

Instantly, the Excel object is inserted in the Microsoft Word document. Figure 5-14 shows a portion of the chart contained in the document.

If the chart's data is now changed in Microsoft Excel, the chart that is linked in Microsoft Word will change instantly. Figure 5-15 shows a change in Excel's data and a corresponding change in the Microsoft Word chart.

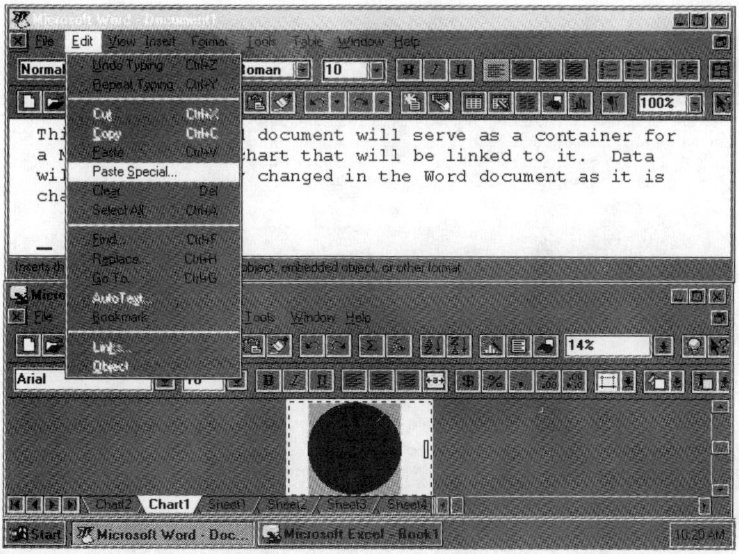

FIGURE 5-12. *To establish a link between Word and Excel, select Paste Special... from Word's Edit menu*

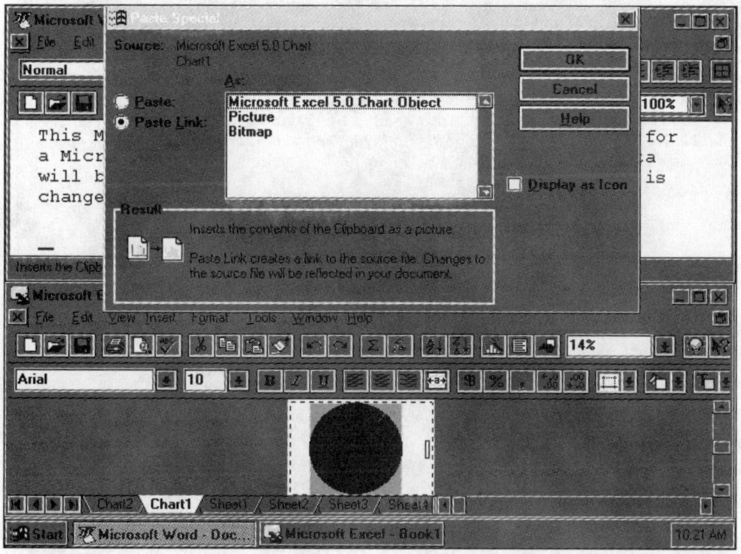

FIGURE 5-13. *Select Paste Link, to dynamically link the Excel chart to the Word document*

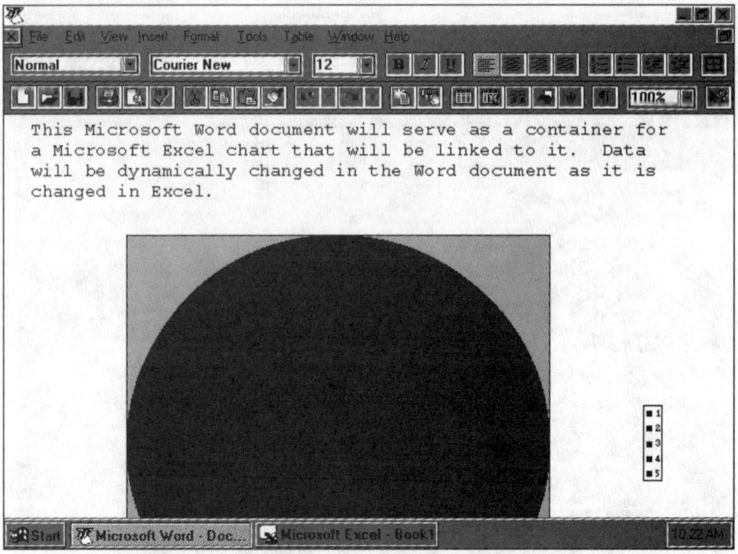

FIGURE 5-14. *A portion of the Microsoft Excel chart linked and inserted in the Microsoft Word document*

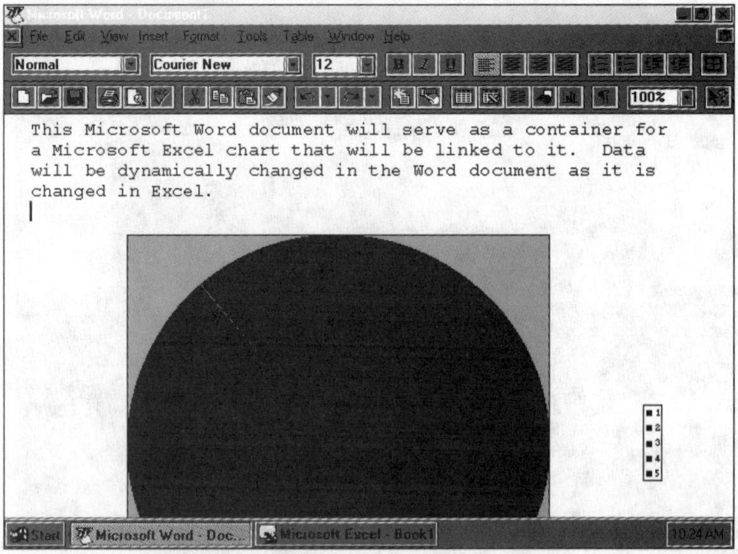

FIGURE 5-15. *When OLE applications are linked, changes in one application are automatically and instantaneously changed in the other application*

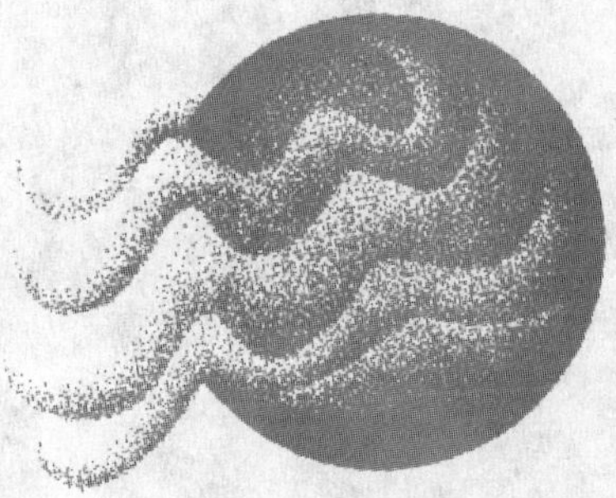

CHAPTER 6

Developing OLE Container Applications

This chapter will introduce you to Microsoft's Wizards for application development and then show you how to create a simple container application. Microsoft's Wizards are dynamic code generators. The first programming example, using Wizards, is a simple programming application that does not use OLE features. This application is named *graph* and will illustrate the six-step process for automatically developing all applications. Next, an OLE container application, named *cnt*, will be designed and patterned closely after the graph example.

As you examine the code in this chapter, you might be taken aback by the fact that each example uses several source code files. Do not be alarmed; this is essentially the same code you saw in Chapter 4, broken into several pieces. Microsoft decided to break application code into functioning units. For example, if an application is named app, you might find these four files: APP.CPP, MAINFRM.CPP, APPDOC.CPP, and APPVIEW.CPP. The APP.CPP is the main source code file for the application. The MAINFRM.CPP file is used to describe the document interface for the application. The APPDOC.CPP file is used to describe the document data. The APPVIEW.CPP file is used for viewing objects. These source code files are combined, by the linker, into a single executable application. In this case, the file would be named APP.EXE.

A First Look at Application and Class Wizards

In Chapters 3 and 4 you learned how to develop Windows applications with an object-oriented approach using the Microsoft Foundation Class (MFC) library. These chapters rely heavily on the use of templates for code development. Templates allow you, the programmer, to use redundant code over and over again, freeing you to concentrate on the new features of a particular application. These templates were static templates that you merely copied and reused from one application to another.

Sometimes, however, simple static templates are not enough. Imagine an application where you want to incorporate file I/O capabilities, such as New, Open, and Save, or editing capabilities, such as Cut, Copy, and Paste. While these features often use a familiar menu style, that style was not part of our static templates. Now, extend your thinking a little further, and imagine creating applications with a Multiple Document Interface (MDI) and OLE features. No single static template will allow us to easily pick and choose from this list of programming features.

Microsoft's solution to this problem was to create a dynamic template generator named AppWizard. The AppWizard depends heavily on the MFC library and generates object-oriented code. The AppWizard can be selected from the C++ compiler's Project menu. The AppWizard generates, in a six-step process, a code template that will allow you to select just those features needed for your application. However, as was the case for earlier static templates in this book, it is still up to you to write the code for your unique application.

A close relative of the AppWizard is the ClassWizard. The ClassWizard allows you to add classes or customize existing classes. The ClassWizard is used after the template code is created by the AppWizard. The ClassWizard can be selected from the Project pop-up menu once the template is created.

This chapter will explore the use of these two Wizards and help you understand how they can be put to work for you. As mentioned earlier, two applications will be developed, as examples. One application, called graph, will use the bare minimum AppWizard code and create an application with a client area containing simple GDI (Graphic Device Interface) graphics shapes. This initial application does not use any MFC library OLE classes. The second application will be a simple container application, cnt, which can accept objects from other OLE servers. You'll discover that the MFC library allows you to access over 20,000 programming lines of OLE code—code that you'll never have to write!

Be warned, however, that there is a learning curve that must be overcome before you will become comfortable using these new tools. We strongly recommend that you review Chapters 3 and 4. These are the chapters that deal with the MFC library.

Using Wizards

In this section, you will learn all of the steps necessary to create a simple application named graph, by using the AppWizard and ClassWizard tools. The six steps discussed will take you through the development of code that will later be used to create our first OLE container program.

If your compiler is up and running, why not follow along with us as we create this application with a step-by-step approach.

The AppWizard

From The Microsoft Visual C++ menu bar, select the File menu and then the New menu item from the menu list. A dialog box will now appear that will allow you to select a new project, as shown in Figure 6-1.

Once Project is selected, another dialog box will appear that will allow you to name the project and select a directory. Name this new project **graph**, as shown in Figure 6-2.

Once the project is named, the development using the AppWizard can be started. Notice the default project type (.EXE) in this dialog box, as shown in the previous figure. The first step in generating a project with the AppWizard is to decide how the project will handle single, multiple, or dialog-based documents. For this example, a single-document interface was desired, as shown in Figure 6-3.

To continue to the next step in AppWizard, select Next>. The second step is used only when database support is to be included. In this case, None is selected, as shown in Figure 6-4.

The third step allows the developer to specify the type of OLE support. In this example, None is selected, as shown in Figure 6-5.

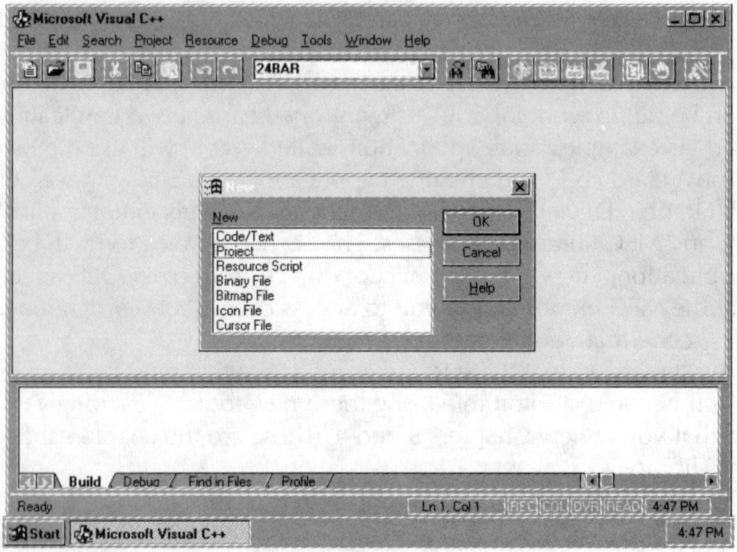

FIGURE 6-1. *Select Project from the New dialog box*

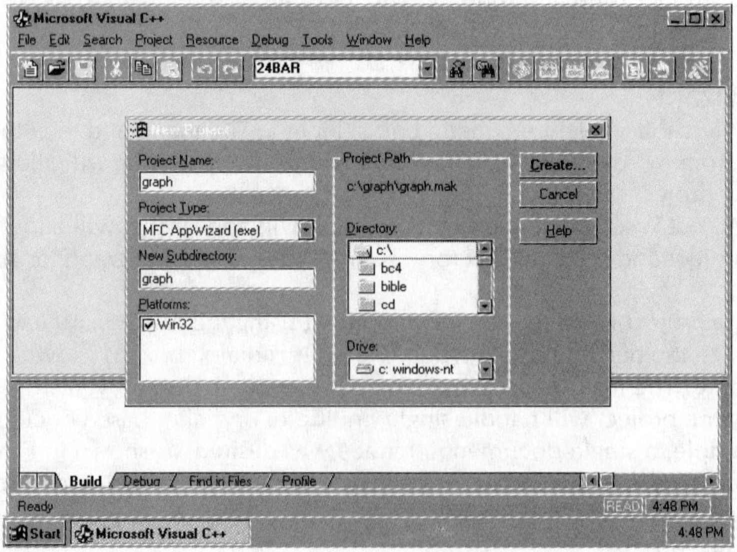

FIGURE 6-2. *Creating a new project named graph*

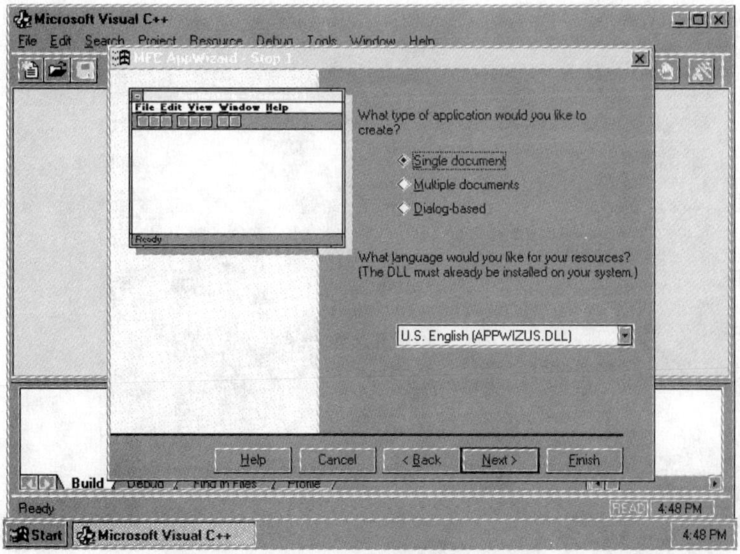

FIGURE 6-3. *Step 1: Selecting a single document interface from within the AppWizard*

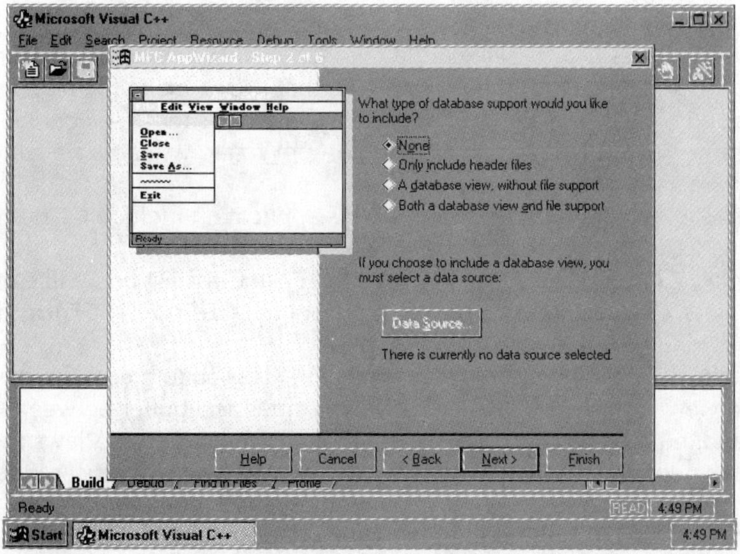

FIGURE 6-4. *Step 2: Selecting database support from within the AppWizard*

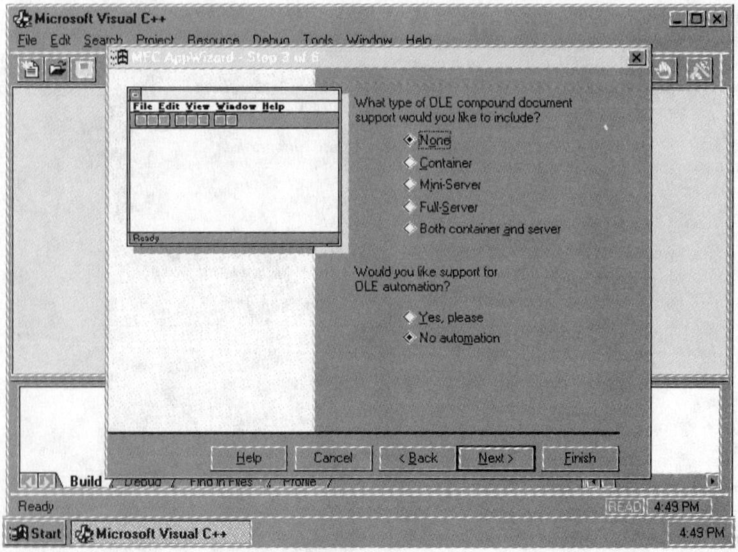

FIGURE 6-5. *Step 3: Selecting OLE support from within the AppWizard*

The fourth step allows programmers to add special features to the project. For example, a toolbox or status bar could be added at this point. In the example, however, no special features are added, as shown by Figure 6-6.

Additional features can be selected in the fifth step. For example, we'll request that comments be generated for the source file, that a C++ make file be generated, and that a static MFC library be used. Figure 6-7 illustrates these selections.

The sixth step lists the new classes that the AppWizard will automatically generate. These are shown in Figure 6-8.

The four classes that will be created for this application include **CGraphApp**, **CMainFrame**, **CGraphDoc**, and **CGraphView**.

If you select **CGraphView** in the list box, the Base Class list box will expand to allow your class, **CGraphView**, to be derived from the **CEditView**, **CFormView**, **CScrollView**, or **CView** base classes.

The **CView** class, derived from the **CWnd** class, is used to create the base for user-defined view classes. A view class ("view") serves as a buffer between the document and the user and is actually a child of a frame window. Views produce an image of the document (such as screen, printer, and so on) and user input (such as keyboard, mouse, and so on) as an operation on the document.

Two other classes, just mentioned, are derived from the **CView** base class. They are **CFormView** and **CEditView**. **CFormView** describes a scrollable view. This view

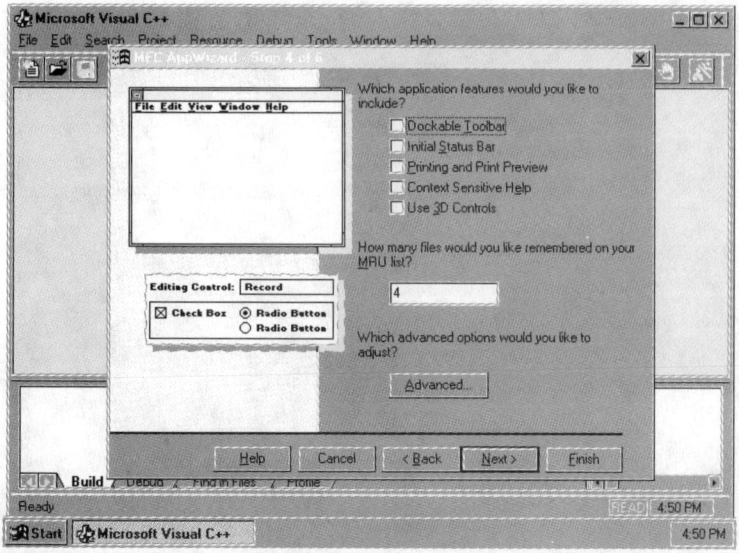

FIGURE 6-6. *Step 4: Selecting application features from within the AppWizard*

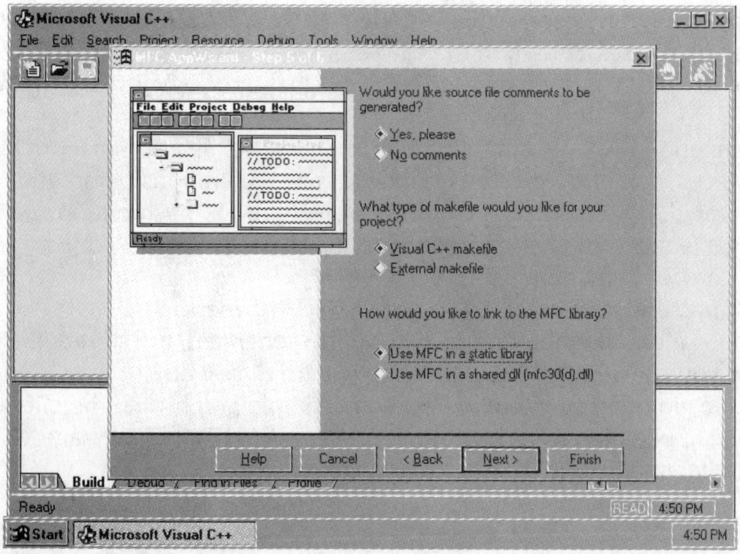

FIGURE 6-7. *Step 5: Selecting additional features for the project from within the AppWizard*

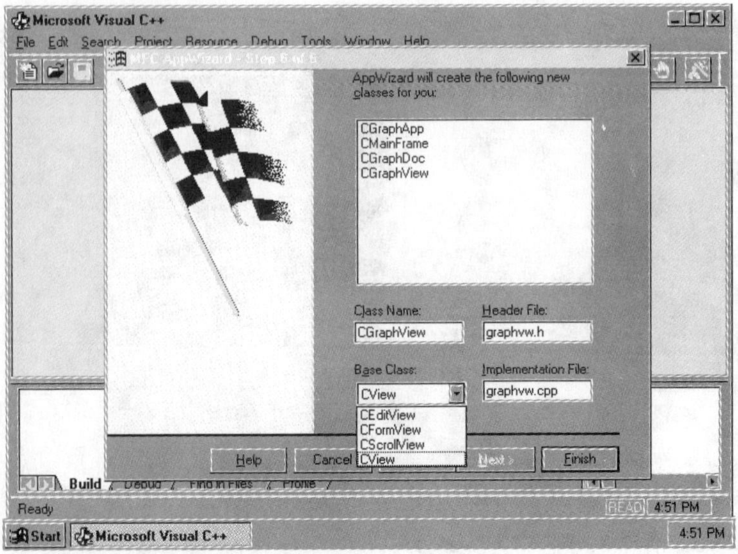

FIGURE 6-8. *Step 6: Lists the classes that will be generated using the AppWizard*

is based upon a dialog template resource and includes dialog box controls. **CEditView** describes a simple text editor. This class will be used in the next chapter.

This application, however, will use **CView** as the base class. As a matter of fact, all of the default classes, shown in the Classes dialog box, are acceptable. Select the Finish push button and see a description of what the AppWizard will create for this project. Figure 6-9 shows this information.

The information displayed in the previous dialog box is a summary of your previous choices, and also your last chance to make alterations before the template code is generated. If the options are correct, select the OK push button.

Additional features can now be added to the skeleton project code by selecting the ClassWizard, as shown in Figure 6-10.

For example, this project will process WM_PAINT messages.

The various files, and there are many, will be generated and stored in the subdirectory you specified in the initial AppWizard dialog box.

This application will eventually draw some simple graphics to the client area. Therefore, the application must be able to process WM_PAINT messages. The message handler can be added with ClassWizard.

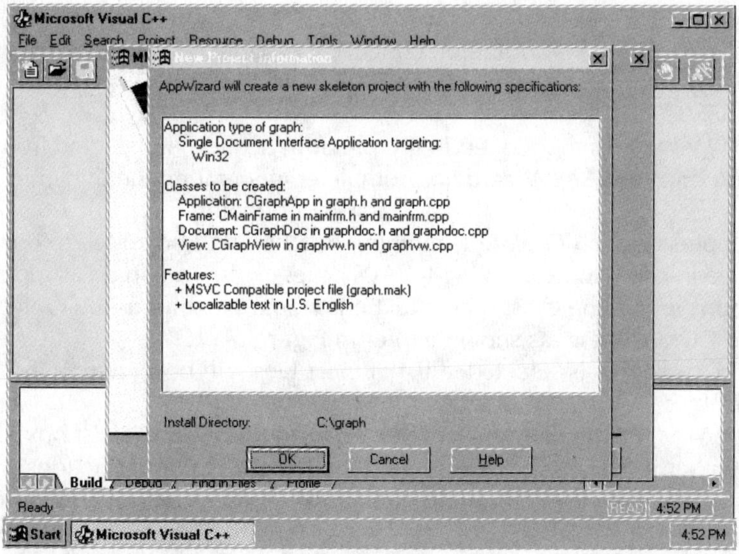

FIGURE 6-9. *The skeleton project description of the new AppWizard project*

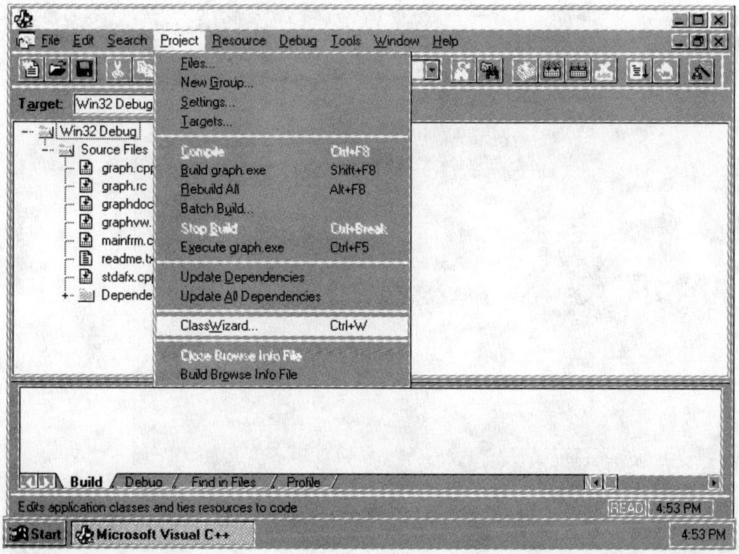

FIGURE 6-10. *Additional project features can be added by the ClassWizard*

The ClassWizard

The ClassWizard generates additional code for the application. This code can be used to support the processing of messages such as WM_PAINT and WM_MOUSEMOVE.

The ClassWizard, as mentioned in the previous section, is selected from the Project menu once the AppWizard has completed generating the dynamic code template. Figure 6-11 shows the initial ClassWizard dialog box.

In this application, an **OnPaint()** member function will be added to our program code in order to process WM_PAINT messages. To add this support code, select **CGraphView** in the Class Name text entry box. Next, from the Object IDs list box, choose **CGraphView**, as shown earlier in Figure 6-11.

When **CGraphView** is selected, a list of messages will be shown in the Messages list box.

Once the WM_PAINT message is selected from the Messages list box, the **OnPaint** member function will be shown in the list of Member Functions. You now have to select **Add Function** or double-click on **WM_Paint** before **OnPaint()** is added.

The GRAPHVW.CPP file will now contain this newly inserted code, as shown in Figure 6-12.

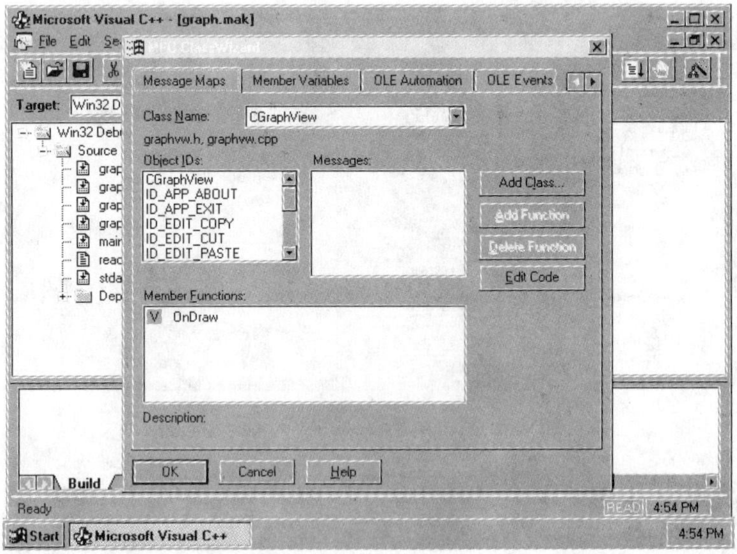

FIGURE 6-11. *The initial dialog box for the ClassWizard*

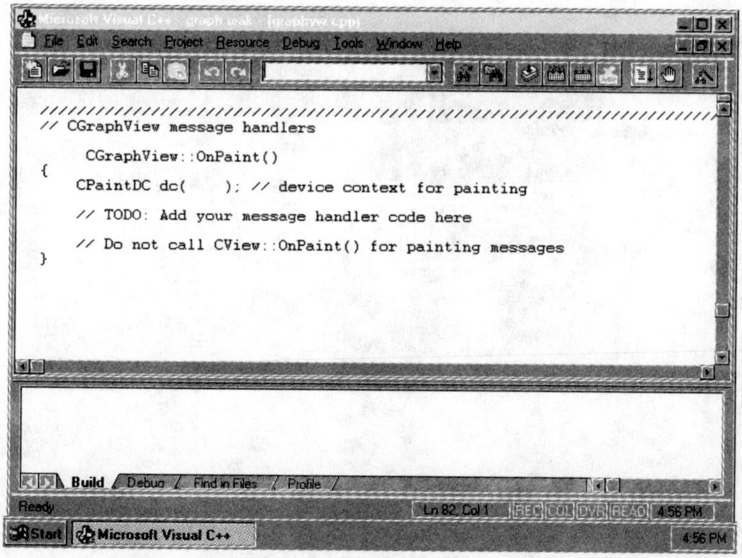

FIGURE 6-12. *Editing the ClassWizard's WM_PAINT message handler code*

It is at this point that you can add various graphics functions to make this application unique. You'll see how this is done when the first application is discussed in more detail.

However, the next step is to compile the application.

Building the Application

When all of the message handlers are added to the program's code, via the ClassWizard, the application can be compiled and linked.

Select the Rebuild All menu item from the compiler's Project menu, as shown in Figure 6-13.

During the build operation, details of the compile-and-link operation are displayed on the screen. Figure 6-14 shows the steps performed in this process.

Notice, in particular, that four files will be compiled and then linked: GRAPH.CPP, MAINFRM.CPP, GRAPHDOC.CPP, and GRAPHVW.CPP. These files are just the tip of the iceberg. When compilation is complete, examine the subdirectory where these files are stored. There are over 35 files stored here. Automation has its price!

An executable file should also be present in this subdirectory. Execute the program. You should see a figure similar to Figure 6-15 on your screen.

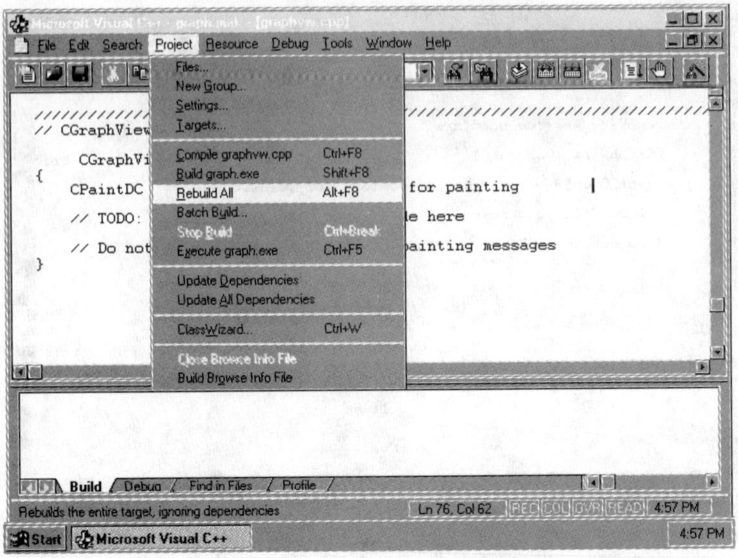

FIGURE 6-13. *Select Rebuild All to compile and link this application*

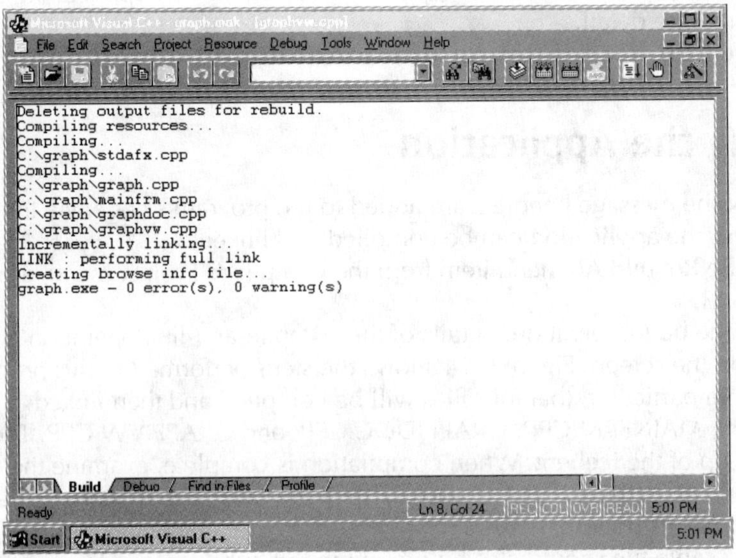

FIGURE 6-14. *Details of the compile-and-link process for this application*

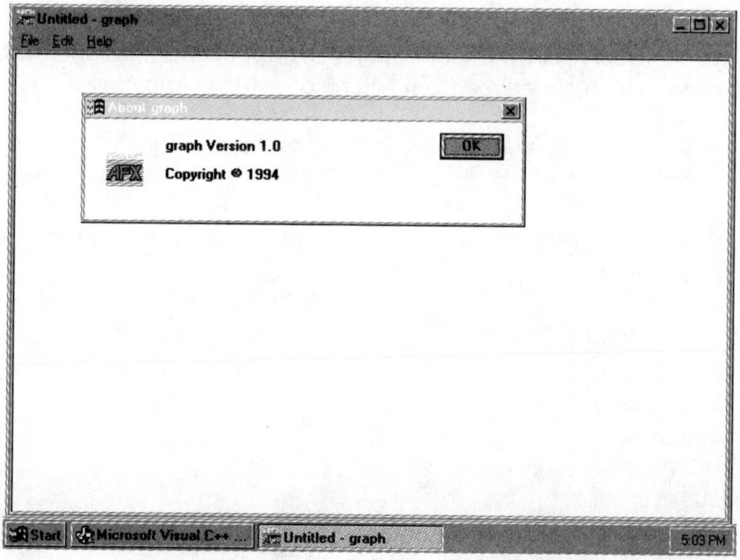

FIGURE 6-15. *The window for the graph application generated by the AppWizard and enhanced with the ClassWizard*

The initial screen is empty because no graphics functions have been added at this point. Worse yet, none of the pop-up menu items work, except the About box from the Help menu. This is because code for processing these messages must be added by you—it is not automatically generated. However, if you have gained a good understanding of the MFC library, this will not be too difficult.

Understanding the AppWizard's Code

The AppWizard, with a little additional help from the ClassWizard, generated four important C++ files for the initial graph application. These files were named GRAPH.CPP, MAINFRM.CPP, GRAPHDOC.CPP, and GRAPHVW.CPP. Each of these C++ files has an associated header file: GRAPH.H, MAINFRM.H, GRAPHDOC.H, and GRAPHVW.H. The header files contain the declarations of the specific classes in each C++ file. The purpose of each C++ file will be examined in the following sections. The "GRAPH.MAK" window can be used to easily browse and open files in the project.

The GRAPH.CPP File

The GRAPH.CPP file serves as the main file for the application. It contains our **CGraphApp** class, which is derived from Microsoft's **CWinApp** class.

```
// graph.cpp : Defines the class behaviors
// for the application.
//

#include "stdafx.h"
#include "graph.h"

#include "mainfrm.h"
#include "graphdoc.h"
#include "graphvw.h"

#ifdef _DEBUG
#undef THIS_FILE
static char BASED_CODE THIS_FILE[] = __FILE;
#endif

/////////////////////////////////////////////////////////////
// CGraphApp

BEGIN_MESSAGE_MAP(CGraphApp, CWinApp)
  //{{AFX_MSG_MAP(CGraphApp)
  ON_COMMAND(ID_APP_ABOUT, OnAppAbout)
    // NOTE - the ClassWizard will add and remove
    // mapping macros here.
    //    DO NOT EDIT what you see in these blocks
    // of generated code!
  //}}AFX_MSG_MAP
  // Standard file based document commands
  ON_COMMAND(ID_FILE_NEW, CWinApp::OnFileNew)
  ON_COMMAND(ID_FILE_OPEN, CWinApp::OnFileOpen)
END_MESSAGE_MAP()

/////////////////////////////////////////////////////////////
// CGraphApp construction

CGraphApp::CGraphApp()
{
  // TODO: add construction code here,
  // Place all significant initialization in InitInstance
```

```
}

/////////////////////////////////////////////////////////////////////////////
// The one and only CGraphApp object

CGraphApp NEAR theApp;

/////////////////////////////////////////////////////////////////////////////
// CGraphApp initialization

BOOL CGraphApp::InitInstance()
{
  // Standard initialization
  // If you are not using these features and wish to reduce
  // the size of your final executable, you should remove
  // from the following the specific initialization routines
  // you do not need.

  SetDialogBkColor();  //Set dialog background color to gray
  LoadStdProfileSettings();  //Load standard INI file options

  // Register the application's document templates.
  // Document templates serve as the connection between
  // documents, frame windows and views.

  CSingleDocTemplate* pDocTemplate;
  pDocTemplate = new CSingleDocTemplate(
    IDR_MAINFRAME,
    RUNTIME_CLASS(CGraphDoc),
    RUNTIME_CLASS(CMainFrame),     // main SDI frame window
    RUNTIME_CLASS(CGraphView));
  AddDocTemplate(pDocTemplate);

  // create a new (empty) document
  OnFileNew();

  if (m_lpCmdLine[0] != '\0')
  {
    // TODO: add command line processing here
  }
```

```
  return TRUE;
}

/////////////////////////////////////////////////////////////////////////////
// CAboutDlg dialog used for App About

class CAboutDlg : public CDialog
{
public:
  CAboutDlg();

// Dialog Data
  //{{AFX_DATA(CAboutDlg)
  enum { IDD = IDD_ABOUTBOX };
  //}}AFX_DATA

// Implementation
protected:
  virtual void DoDataExchange(CDataExchange* pDX); //DDX/DDV
  //{{AFX_MSG(CAboutDlg)
    // No message handlers
  //}}AFX_MSG
  DECLARE_MESSAGE_MAP()
};

CAboutDlg::CAboutDlg() : CDialog(CAboutDlg::IDD)
{
  //{{AFX_DATA_INIT(CAboutDlg)
  //}}AFX_DATA_INIT
}

void CAboutDlg::DoDataExchange(CDataExchange* pDX)
{
  CDialog::DoDataExchange(pDX);
  //{{AFX_DATA_MAP(CAboutDlg)
  //}}AFX_DATA_MAP
}

BEGIN_MESSAGE_MAP(CAboutDlg, CDialog)
  //{{AFX_MSG_MAP(CAboutDlg)
    // No message handlers
  //}}AFX_MSG_MAP
```

```
END_MESSAGE_MAP()

// App command to run the dialog
void CGraphApp::OnAppAbout()
{
  CAboutDlg aboutDlg;
  aboutDlg.DoModal();
}

//////////////////////////////////////////////////////////////////////
// CGraphApp commands
```

Our class **CGraphApp** is derived from Microsoft's **CWinApp** class. The **CWinApp** class holds the code that initializes, runs, and terminates the application. **CWinApp**, itself, is derived from several other classes:

```
CObject—
        CCmdtarget—
                    CWinThread—
                                CWinApp
```

The message map, near the top of the listing, belongs to the **CGraphApp** class. This message map specifically links the ID_APP_ABOUT, ID_FILE_NEW, and ID_FILE_OPEN messages with their member functions, **OnAppAbout()**, **CWinApp::OnFileNew()**, and **CWinApp::OnFileOpen()**. Also notice in the listing that a constructor (**InitInstance()**), and a member function (**OnAppAbout()**) are implemented. In this section you will also notice the use of a template for single documents. **CSingleDocTemplate** is responsible for constructing the object.

CSingleDocTemplate is derived from several other classes:

```
CObject—
        CCmdtarget—
                    CDocTemplate—
                                  CSingleDocTemplate
```

The about dialog box is derived from the **CDialog** class. **CDialog** serves as the base class for all dialog boxes. **CDialog** is derived from several other classes:

```
CObject—
        CCmdtarget—
                    CWnd—
                         CDialog
```

Finally, examine the lower portion of code and notice a message map, constructor, and a member function, **CDialog::DoDataExchange()**, for this derived dialog class.

This listing contains several placeholders for user entries. Examine the listing again, and find the occurrence of statements such as // To Do: and // No message handlers.

Examine the listing and notice that there are no initial **CGraphApp** commands, as you can see from the end of the listing.

The MAINFRM.CPP File

This file contains our frame class **CMainFrame**. This class is derived from Microsoft's **CFrameWnd** class and serves as the base class used to control all single document interface (SDI) frame features. You'll recall the use of this class from examples in Chapters 3 and 4.

```
// mainfrm.cpp : implementation of the CMainFrame class
//

#include "stdafx.h"
#include "graph.h"

#include "mainfrm.h"

#ifdef _DEBUG
#undef THIS_FILE
static char BASED_CODE THIS_FILE[] = __FILE;
#endif

/////////////////////////////////////////////////////////////////
// CMainFrame

IMPLEMENT_DYNCREATE(CMainFrame, CFrameWnd)

BEGIN_MESSAGE_MAP(CMainFrame, CFrameWnd)
  //{{AFX_MSG_MAP(CMainFrame)
    // NOTE - the ClassWizard will add and remove mapping
    // macros here. DO NOT EDIT what you see in these blocks
    // of generated code !
  //}}AFX_MSG_MAP
END_MESSAGE_MAP()

/////////////////////////////////////////////////////////////////
// CMainFrame construction/destruction
```

```
CMainFrame::CMainFrame()
{
  // TODO: add member initialization code here
}

CMainFrame::~CMainFrame()
{
}

/////////////////////////////////////////////////////////////////////////////
// CMainFrame diagnostics

#ifdef _DEBUG
void CMainFrame::AssertValid() const
{
  CFrameWnd::AssertValid();
}

void CMainFrame::Dump(CDumpContext& dc) const
{
  CFrameWnd::Dump(dc);
}

#endif //_DEBUG

/////////////////////////////////////////////////////////////////////////////
// CMainFrame message handlers
```

CFrameWnd is derived from several other classes:

```
CObject-
      CCmdtarget-
               CWnd-
                   CFrameWnd
```

Next, examine this listing and notice that the message map, constructor, and destructor initially contain no code. The member functions, **AssertValid()** and **Dump()**, use definitions contained in the parent class. Also note that **CMainFrame** initially contains no message handlers.

The GRAPHDOC.CPP File

The GRAPHDOC.CPP file contains our **CGraphDoc** class. This class will contain code unique to your application when the application is designed to hold document data and for file loading and saving. **CGraphDoc** is derived from Microsoft's **CDocument** class. The **CDocument** class serves as the base class for all application-specific documents.

```
// graphdoc.cpp : implementation of the CGraphDoc class
//

#include "stdafx.h"
#include "graph.h"

#include "graphdoc.h"

#ifdef _DEBUG
#undef THIS_FILE
static char BASED_CODE THIS_FILE[] = __FILE__;
#endif

/////////////////////////////////////////////////////////////////
// CGraphDoc

IMPLEMENT_DYNCREATE(CGraphDoc, CDocument)

BEGIN_MESSAGE_MAP(CGraphDoc, CDocument)
  //{{AFX_MSG_MAP(CGraphDoc)
    // NOTE - the ClassWizard will add and remove mapping
    // macros here. DO NOT EDIT what you see in these blocks
    // of generated code!
  //}}AFX_MSG_MAP
END_MESSAGE_MAP()

/////////////////////////////////////////////////////////////////
// CGraphDoc construction/destruction

CGraphDoc::CGraphDoc()
{
  // TODO: add one-time construction code here
}

CGraphDoc::~CGraphDoc()
{
```

```
}

BOOL CGraphDoc::OnNewDocument()
{
  if (!CDocument::OnNewDocument())
    return FALSE;

  // TODO: add reinitialization code here
  // (SDI documents will reuse this document)

  return TRUE;
}

/////////////////////////////////////////////////////////////////////////////
// CGraphDoc serialization

void CGraphDoc::Serialize(CArchive& ar)
{
  if (ar.IsStoring())
  {
    // TODO: add storing code here
  }
  else
  {
    // TODO: add loading code here
  }
}

/////////////////////////////////////////////////////////////////////////////
// CGraphDoc diagnostics

#ifdef _DEBUG
void CGraphDoc::AssertValid() const
{
  CDocument::AssertValid();
}

void CGraphDoc::Dump(CDumpContext& dc) const
{
  CDocument::Dump(dc);
}
#endif //_DEBUG
```

```
/////////////////////////////////////////////////////////////////
// CGraphDoc commands
```

CDocument is derived from several other classes:

```
CObject–
      CCmdtarget–
               CDocument
```

You'll notice as you examine this listing that once again the message map, constructor, and destructor contain no code. Several member functions can be used to provide vital document support. For example, **OnNewDocument()** uses the definition provided by the parent class to create a new document. **Serialize()** supports persistent objects. This member function is used to aid in file I/O. The member functions, **AssertValid()** and **Dump()**, use definitions contained in the parent class. There are no initial **CGraphDoc** commands.

The GRAPHVW.CPP File

The GRAPHVW.CPP file provides the view of the document. In this implementation, our **CGraphView** class is derived from Microsoft's **CView** class. **CView** is derived from several other classes:

```
CObject–
      CCmdtarget–
               CWnd–
                  CView
```

CView serves as the base, or parent, class for all specific views of the document's data. In other words, **CGraphView** objects are used to view **CGraphDoc** objects.

```
// graphvw.cpp : implementation of the CGraphView class
//

#include "stdafx.h"
#include "graph.h"

#include "graphdoc.h"
#include "graphvw.h"

#ifdef _DEBUG
#undef THIS_FILE
```

```
static char BASED_CODE THIS_FILE[] = _FILE;
#endif

/////////////////////////////////////////////////////////////////
// CGraphView

IMPLEMENT_DYNCREATE(CGraphView, CView)

BEGIN_MESSAGE_MAP(CGraphView, CView)
  //{{AFX_MSG_MAP(CGraphView)
  ON_WM_PAINT()
  //}}AFX_MSG_MAP
END_MESSAGE_MAP()

/////////////////////////////////////////////////////////////////
// CGraphView construction/destruction

CGraphView::CGraphView()
{
  // TODO: add construction code here
}

CGraphView::~CGraphView()
{
}

/////////////////////////////////////////////////////////////////
// CGraphView drawing

void CGraphView::OnDraw(CDC* pDC)
{
  CGraphDoc* pDoc = GetDocument();
  ASSERT_VALID(pDoc);

  // TODO: add draw code for native data here
}

/////////////////////////////////////////////////////////////////
// CGraphView diagnostics

#ifdef _DEBUG
void CGraphView::AssertValid() const
```

```
{
  CView::AssertValid();
}

void CGraphView::Dump(CDumpContext& dc) const
{
  CView::Dump(dc);
}

CGraphDoc* CGraphView::GetDocument() // non-debug version is inline
{
  ASSERT(m_pDocument->IsKindOf(RUNTIME_CLASS(CGraphDoc)));
  return (CGraphDoc*)m_pDocument;
}
#endif //_DEBUG

/////////////////////////////////////////////////////////////////////////////
// CGraphView message handlers

void CGraphView::OnPaint()
{
  CPaintDC dc(this); // device context for painting

  // TODO: Add your message handler code here

  // Do not call CView::OnPaint() for painting messages
}
```

The **OnDraw()** member function uses the pointer, *pDoc*, to point to the document. The member functions, **AssertValid()** and **Dump()**, use definitions contained in the parent class.

Normally, the **CGraphView** message handler area would be empty (for a template). However, remember that we used the ClassWizard to add ON_WM_PAINT message handling abilities. Simple graphics commands such as those shown in Chapters 3 and 4 can be inserted here.

Drawing in the Client Area

In the first walk-through, using the AppWizard and ClassWizard, a single document interface (SDI) application was created. The view class was derived from the parent class, **CView**. Recall that the ClassWizard allowed us to add the WM_PAINT message handler to this code.

This code is exactly the platform from which simple graphics can be drawn to the client area, with very little additional work.

To show you how easy this can be, add the following code to the **OnPaint()** message handler shown in the previous listing.

```
// CGraphView message handlers

void CGraphView::OnPaint()
{
  static DWORD dwColor[9]={RGB(0,0,0),          //black
                           RGB(255,0,0),        //red
                           RGB(0,255,0),        //green
                           RGB(0,0,255),        //blue
                           RGB(255,255,0),      //yellow
                           RGB(255,0,255),      //magenta
                           RGB(0,255,255),      //cyan
                           RGB(127,127,127),    //gray
                           RGB(255,255,255)};   //white

  POINT polylpts[4],polygpts[5];
  int xcoord;

  CBrush newbrush;
  CBrush* oldbrush;
  CPen  newpen;
  CPen* oldpen;

  CPaintDC dc(this); // device context for painting

  // draws and fills a red ellipse
  newpen.CreatePen(PS_SOLID,1,dwColor[1]);
  oldpen=dc.SelectObject(&newpen);
  newbrush.CreateSolidBrush(dwColor[1]);
  oldbrush=dc.SelectObject(&newbrush);
  dc.Ellipse(275,300,200,250);
  dc.TextOut(220,265,"ellipse",7);
  dc.SelectObject(oldbrush);
  newbrush.DeleteObject();
  dc.SelectObject(oldpen);
  newpen.DeleteObject();
```

```
// draws and fills a blue circle with ellipse function
newpen.CreatePen(PS_SOLID,1,dwColor[3]);
oldpen=dc.SelectObject(&newpen);
newbrush.CreateSolidBrush(dwColor[3]);
oldbrush=dc.SelectObject(&newbrush);
dc.Ellipse(375,75,525,225);
dc.TextOut(435,190,"circle",6);
dc.SelectObject(oldbrush);
newbrush.DeleteObject();
dc.SelectObject(oldpen);
newpen.DeleteObject();

// draws several green pixels
for(xcoord=400;xcoord<450;xcoord+=5)
  dc.SetPixel(xcoord,350,0L);
dc.TextOut(460,345,"<- pixels",9);

// draws a wide black diagonal line
newpen.CreatePen(PS_SOLID,6,dwColor[0]);
oldpen=dc.SelectObject(&newpen);
dc.MoveTo(20,20);
dc.LineTo(100,100);
dc.TextOut(60,20,"<- diagonal line",16);
dc.SelectObject(oldpen);
newpen.DeleteObject();

// draws a blue arc
newpen.CreatePen(PS_DASH,1,dwColor[3]);
oldpen=dc.SelectObject(&newpen);
dc.Arc(25,125,175,225,175,225,100,125);
dc.TextOut(50,150,"small arc ->",12);
dc.SelectObject(oldpen);
newpen.DeleteObject();

// draws a wide green chord
newpen.CreatePen(PS_SOLID,8,dwColor[2]);
oldpen=dc.SelectObject(&newpen);
dc.Chord(125,125,275,225,275,225,200,125);
dc.TextOut(280,150,"<- chord",8);
dc.SelectObject(oldpen);
newpen.DeleteObject();
```

```
// draws a black pie slice and fills with green
newpen.CreatePen(PS_SOLID,1,dwColor[0]);
oldpen=dc.SelectObject(&newpen);
newbrush.CreateSolidBrush(dwColor[2]);
oldbrush=dc.SelectObject(&newbrush);
dc.Pie(200,0,300,100,200,50,250,100);
dc.TextOut(260,80,"<- pie wedge",12);
dc.SelectObject(oldbrush);
newbrush.DeleteObject();
dc.SelectObject(oldpen);
newpen.DeleteObject();

// draws a black rectangle and fills with gray
newbrush.CreateSolidBrush(dwColor[7]);
oldbrush=dc.SelectObject(&newbrush);
dc.Rectangle(25,300,150,375);
dc.TextOut(50,325,"rectangle",9);
dc.SelectObject(oldbrush);
newbrush.DeleteObject();

// draws a black rounded rectangle and fills with blue
newbrush.CreateHatchBrush(HS_CROSS,dwColor[3]);
oldbrush=dc.SelectObject(&newbrush);
dc.RoundRect(350,250,400,290,20,20);
dc.TextOut(410,270,"<—rounded rectangle",20);
dc.SelectObject(oldbrush);
newbrush.DeleteObject();

// draws several wide magenta lines with polyline
newpen.CreatePen(PS_SOLID,3,dwColor[5]);
oldpen=dc.SelectObject(&newpen);
polylpts[0].x=10;
polylpts[0].y=30;
polylpts[1].x=10;
polylpts[1].y=100;
polylpts[2].x=50;
polylpts[2].y=100;
polylpts[3].x=10;
polylpts[3].y=30;
dc.Polyline(polylpts,4);
dc.TextOut(10,110,"polyline",8);
```

```
    dc.SelectObject(oldpen);
    newpen.DeleteObject();

    // draws a wide cyan polygon and
    // fills with diagonal yellow
    newpen.CreatePen(PS_SOLID,4,dwColor[6]);
    oldpen=dc.SelectObject(&newpen);
    newbrush.CreateHatchBrush(HS_FDIAGONAL,dwColor[4]);
    oldbrush=dc.SelectObject(&newbrush);
    polygpts[0].x=40;
    polygpts[0].y=200;
    polygpts[1].x=100;
    polygpts[1].y=270;
    polygpts[2].x=80;
    polygpts[2].y=290;
    polygpts[3].x=20;
    polygpts[3].y=220;
    polygpts[4].x=40;
    polygpts[4].y=200;
    dc.Polygon(polygpts,5);
    dc.TextOut(80,230,"<- polygon",10);
    dc.SelectObject(oldbrush);
    newbrush.DeleteObject();
    dc.SelectObject(oldpen);
    newpen.DeleteObject();

  // Do not call CView::OnPaint() for painting messages
}
```

This should be familiar code, since it employs simple GDI graphics functions.

Compile and execute the revised version of this application. Your screen should be similar to Figure 6-16.

The AppWizard generated a template with a menu bar containing File, Edit, and Help menus. Select the about option from the Help menu to view the About graph dialog box shown in Figure 6-17.

Note that most of the other menus or menu items are not functional. Why? They are not functional because no additional code was added to the template to handle those responses.

If you diligently went through the template removing code not used by this application, you would arrive at a template very similar to the static templates we created and used in Chapter 4.

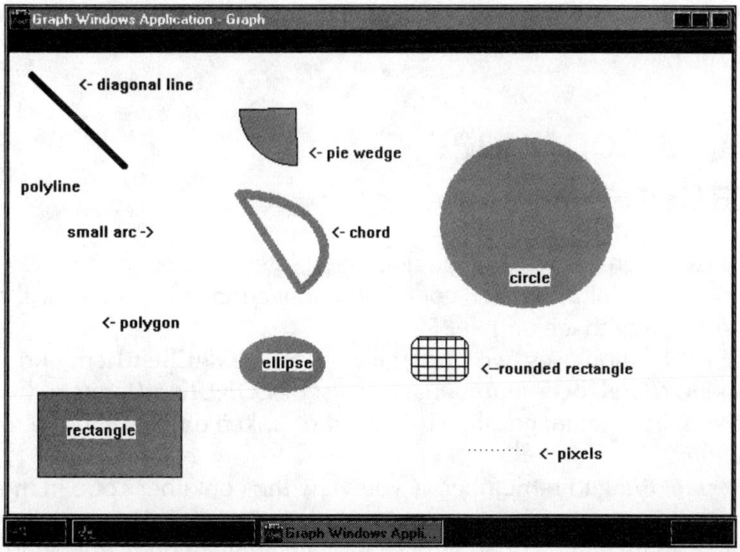

FIGURE 6-16. *Minor additions to the AppWizard code allow simple graphics shapes to be drawn*

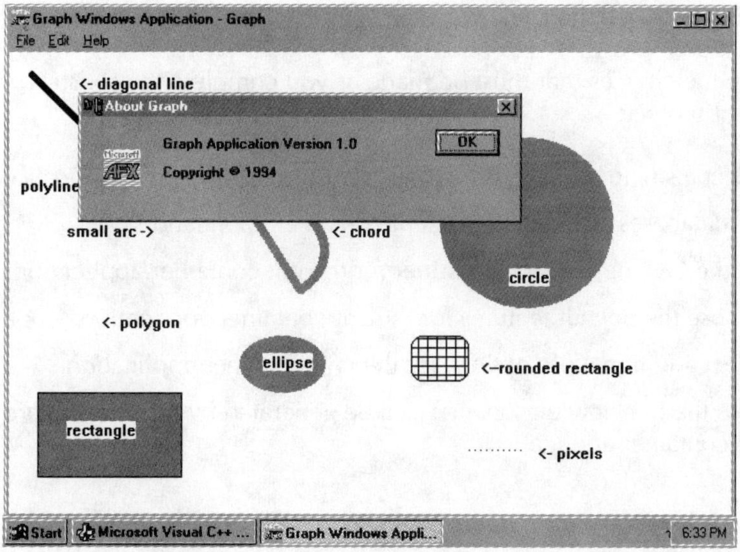

FIGURE 6-17. *An About box generated by the AppWizard*

The next example will use a new AppWizard template to generate a simple OLE container application.

Building a Container Application

In the previous section a simple single document interface application was developed, named graph. The OLE container application, named cnt, will be patterned closely after that example.

This OLE application uses two important classes, **COleClientItem** and **COleDocument**. **COleDocument** manages a list of **COleClientItem(s)** while **COleClientItem**, itself, manages the embedded or linked objects and the required communications.

The important thing to remember as you view the container code in the next sections, is that it is completely generated by the AppWizard. This container template code can be enhanced with your specific application features into a full-blown product. However, for simplicity, nothing was added to the basic template developed in this section.

Using the AppWizard

The AppWizard is used the same way it was used to create the application in the previous section.

Here are the choices that must be made as you complete the six-step process to create the cnt project:

1. Select a single document interface for the cnt container application.
2. No databases are used by the cnt container application.
3. Set the OLE options to **Container** for the cnt container application.
4. Choose the default features for the cnt container application.
5. Select additional file options for the cnt container application.
6. Note the five new classes that will be generated by the AppWizard for the cnt container application.

These options reflect the entire six-step design process of the AppWizard and will produce an application with a single document interface, no database options, a container option, default applications features, and detailed file comments. The additional class, **CCntCntritem**, will be described shortly.When all selections are completed, click on the AppWizard's Finish push button. This will start the file-creation process and present you with the details you have selected.

Finally, build the executable file by selecting the Build All option from the C/C++ compiler's Project menu. When complete, you will have an executable file named CNT.EXE.

AppWizard Files

The files generated by the AppWizard produce a fully working container application named cnt. When the files are generated by the AppWizard, your subdirectory will contain the following C++ files: CNT.CPP, MAINFRM.CPP, CNTDOC.CPP, CNTVIEW.CPP, and CNTRITEM.CPP. Also in this subdirectory will be a whole host of supporting header files, resource files, and so on, as there were for the previous example.

The Container CNT.CPP File

The code used in the OLE container file, CNT.CPP, is almost identical to the code used in the GRAPH.CPP file in the graph application.

The file is listed here, so this section will contain the complete code for the application.

```
// cnt.cpp : Defines the class behaviors for the application.
//

#include "stdafx.h"
#include "cnt.h"

#include "mainfrm.h"
#include "cntdoc.h"
#include "cntview.h"

#ifdef _DEBUG
#undef THIS_FILE
static char BASED_CODE THIS_FILE[] = __FILE__;
#endif

/////////////////////////////////////////////////////////////////////////////
```

```
// CCntApp

BEGIN_MESSAGE_MAP(CCntApp, CWinApp)
  //{{AFX_MSG_MAP(CCntApp)
  ON_COMMAND(ID_APP_ABOUT, OnAppAbout)
  //}}AFX_MSG_MAP
  // Standard file based document commands
  ON_COMMAND(ID_FILE_NEW, CWinApp::OnFileNew)
  ON_COMMAND(ID_FILE_OPEN, CWinApp::OnFileOpen)
END_MESSAGE_MAP()

/////////////////////////////////////////////////////////////////
// CCntApp construction

CCntApp::CCntApp()
{
}

/////////////////////////////////////////////////////////////////
// The one and only CCntApp object

CCntApp NEAR theApp;

/////////////////////////////////////////////////////////////////
// CCntApp initialization

BOOL CCntApp::InitInstance()
{
  // Initialize OLE 2.0 libraries
  if (!AfxOleInit())
  {
    AfxMessageBox(IDP_OLE_INIT_FAILED);
    return FALSE;
  }

  // Standard initialization

  SetDialogBkColor();        // dialog background to gray
  LoadStdProfileSettings();  // standard INI file options

  // Register document templates
```

```
    CSingleDocTemplate* pDocTemplate;
    pDocTemplate = new CSingleDocTemplate(
        IDR_MAINFRAME,
        RUNTIME_CLASS(CCntDoc),
        RUNTIME_CLASS(CMainFrame),      // main SDI frame window
        RUNTIME_CLASS(CCntView));
    pDocTemplate->SetContainerInfo(IDR_CNTR_INPLACE);
    AddDocTemplate(pDocTemplate);

    // create a new (empty) document
    OnFileNew();

    if (m_lpCmdLine[0] != '\0')
    {
    }


    return TRUE;
}

/////////////////////////////////////////////////////////////////////////////
// CAboutDlg dialog used for App About

class CAboutDlg : public CDialog
{
public:
    CAboutDlg();

// Dialog Data
    //{{AFX_DATA(CAboutDlg)
    enum { IDD = IDD_ABOUTBOX };
    //}}AFX_DATA

// Implementation
protected:
    virtual void DoDataExchange(CDataExchange* pDX); // DDX/DDV
    //{{AFX_MSG(CAboutDlg)
        // No message handlers
    //}}AFX_MSG
    DECLARE_MESSAGE_MAP()
};
```

```
CAboutDlg::CAboutDlg() : CDialog(CAboutDlg::IDD)
{
  //{{AFX_DATA_INIT(CAboutDlg)
  //}}AFX_DATA_INIT
}

void CAboutDlg::DoDataExchange(CDataExchange* pDX)
{
  CDialog::DoDataExchange(pDX);
  //{{AFX_DATA_MAP(CAboutDlg)
  //}}AFX_DATA_MAP
}

BEGIN_MESSAGE_MAP(CAboutDlg, CDialog)
  //{{AFX_MSG_MAP(CAboutDlg)
    // No message handlers
  //}}AFX_MSG_MAP
END_MESSAGE_MAP()

// App command to run the dialog
void CCntApp::OnAppAbout()
{
  CAboutDlg aboutDlg;
  aboutDlg.DoModal();
}

/////////////////////////////////////////////////////////////////////////////
// CCntApp commands
```

The only real change in this file, from the previous example, is the insertion of this portion of OLE code:

```
// Initialize OLE 2.0 libraries
  if (!AfxOleInit())
  {
    AfxMessageBox(IDP_OLE_INIT_FAILED);
    return FALSE;
  }
```

As indicated, this code is responsible for initializing OLE libraries for your use.

There is an interesting section of code in this file that should be mentioned. Under OLE, *in-place editing* is supported. In-place editing means that when an object is embedded in a container, such as this cnt application, its menu replaces the container's menu. For example, if an Excel (the server) spreadsheet object is embedded in cnt (the container), the cnt menu will change to that of Excel's!

This menu change is handled by the MFC library almost automatically. This is achieved by having three menu sources available: IDR_MAINFRAME, IDR_DOCTYPE, and IDR_CNTR_INPLACE (the name is specific to your application). When no object is embedded in the container application, IDR_MAINFRAME is used. When a document is opened, IDR_DOCTYPE is used. Finally, IDR_CNTR_INPLACE is used when an object has been embedded in the container.

The Container MAINFRM.CPP File

The code used in the container file, MAINFRM.CPP, is the same as the code used in the first application in this chapter. Return to this example if you need more details on the message map and classes used in this file.

Again, this file is listed here, so the example code will be complete.

```
// mainfrm.cpp : implementation of the CMainFrame class
//

#include "stdafx.h"
#include "cnt.h"

#include "mainfrm.h"

#ifdef _DEBUG
#undef THIS_FILE
static char BASED_CODE THIS_FILE[] = __FILE__;
#endif

/////////////////////////////////////////////////////////////////////////////
// CMainFrame

IMPLEMENT_DYNCREATE(CMainFrame, CFrameWnd)

BEGIN_MESSAGE_MAP(CMainFrame, CFrameWnd)
    //{{AFX_MSG_MAP(CMainFrame)
    //}}AFX_MSG_MAP
END_MESSAGE_MAP()

/////////////////////////////////////////////////////////////////////////////
// CMainFrame construction/destruction
```

```
CMainFrame::CMainFrame()
{
}

CMainFrame::~CMainFrame()
{
}

/////////////////////////////////////////////////////////////////////////////
// CMainFrame diagnostics

#ifdef _DEBUG
void CMainFrame::AssertValid() const
{
    CFrameWnd::AssertValid();
}

void CMainFrame::Dump(CDumpContext& dc) const
{
    CFrameWnd::Dump(dc);
}

#endif //_DEBUG

/////////////////////////////////////////////////////////////////////////////
// CMainFrame message handlers
```

The Container CNTDOC.CPP File

The code used in the container file, CNTDOC.CPP, contains additional code, over its equivalent file used in the previous graph application. Compare the two files and see if you can spot the differences.

```
// cntdoc.cpp : implementation of the CCntDoc class
//

#include "stdafx.h"
#include "cnt.h"

#include "cntdoc.h"
#include "cntritem.h"

#ifdef _DEBUG
```

```
#undef THIS_FILE
static char BASED_CODE THIS_FILE[] = __FILE__;
#endif

/////////////////////////////////////////////////////////////////////////////
// CCntDoc

IMPLEMENT_DYNCREATE(CCntDoc, COleDocument)

BEGIN_MESSAGE_MAP(CCntDoc, COleDocument)
    //{{AFX_MSG_MAP(CCntDoc)
    //}}AFX_MSG_MAP
    // Enable default OLE container implementation
    ON_UPDATE_COMMAND_UI(ID_EDIT_PASTE,
                         COleDocument::OnUpdatePasteMenu)
    ON_UPDATE_COMMAND_UI(ID_EDIT_PASTE_LINK,
                         COleDocument::OnUpdatePasteLinkMenu)
    ON_UPDATE_COMMAND_UI(ID_OLE_EDIT_LINKS,
                         COleDocument::OnUpdateEditLinksMenu)
    ON_COMMAND(ID_OLE_EDIT_LINKS,
                         COleDocument::OnEditLinks)
    ON_UPDATE_COMMAND_UI(ID_OLE_VERB_FIRST,
                         COleDocument::OnUpdateObjectVerbMenu)
    ON_UPDATE_COMMAND_UI(ID_OLE_EDIT_CONVERT,
                         COleDocument::OnUpdateObjectVerbMenu)
    ON_COMMAND(ID_OLE_EDIT_CONVERT,
                         COleDocument::OnEditConvert)
END_MESSAGE_MAP()

/////////////////////////////////////////////////////////////////////////////
// CCntDoc construction/destruction

CCntDoc::CCntDoc()
{
    EnableCompoundFile();

}

CCntDoc::~CCntDoc()
{
}
```

```
BOOL CCntDoc::OnNewDocument()
{
    if (!COleDocument::OnNewDocument())
        return FALSE;

    return TRUE;
}

//////////////////////////////////////////////////////////////
// CCntDoc serialization

void CCntDoc::Serialize(CArchive& ar)
{
    if (ar.IsStoring())
    {
    }
    else
    {
    }
    COleDocument::Serialize(ar);
}

//////////////////////////////////////////////////////////////
// CCntDoc diagnostics

#ifdef _DEBUG
void CCntDoc::AssertValid() const
{
    COleDocument::AssertValid();
}

void CCntDoc::Dump(CDumpContext& dc) const
{
    COleDocument::Dump(dc);
}
#endif //_DEBUG

//////////////////////////////////////////////////////////////
// CCntDoc commands
```

You may have observed that the most significant change in this file comes with the expansion of the message map.

```
BEGIN_MESSAGE_MAP(CCntDoc, COleDocument)
    //{{AFX_MSG_MAP(CCntDoc)
    //}}AFX_MSG_MAP
    // Enable default OLE container implementation
    ON_UPDATE_COMMAND_UI(ID_EDIT_PASTE,
                         COleDocument::OnUpdatePasteMenu)
    ON_UPDATE_COMMAND_UI(ID_EDIT_PASTE_LINK,
                         COleDocument::OnUpdatePasteLinkMenu)
    ON_UPDATE_COMMAND_UI(ID_OLE_EDIT_LINKS,
                         COleDocument::OnUpdateEditLinksMenu)
    ON_COMMAND(ID_OLE_EDIT_LINKS,
                         COleDocument::OnEditLinks)
    ON_UPDATE_COMMAND_UI(ID_OLE_VERB_FIRST,
                         COleDocument::OnUpdateObjectVerbMenu)
    ON_UPDATE_COMMAND_UI(ID_OLE_EDIT_CONVERT,
                         COleDocument::OnUpdateObjectVerbMenu)
    ON_COMMAND(ID_OLE_EDIT_CONVERT,
                         COleDocument::OnEditConvert)
END_MESSAGE_MAP()
```

The message map will now allow the implementation of the default OLE container. You can also see that the constructor calls the **EnableCompoundFile()** function. This is required for a container application.

The Container CNTVIEW.CPP File

The container file, cntview.cpp, has some major changes for this OLE implementation. Examine the following file and first note the additions to the message map.

```
// cntview.cpp : implementation of the CCntView class
//

#include "stdafx.h"
#include "cnt.h"

#include "cntdoc.h"
#include "cntritem.h"
#include "cntview.h"

#ifdef _DEBUG
#undef THIS_FILE
static char BASED_CODE THIS_FILE[] = __FILE__;
#endif
```

```
/////////////////////////////////////////////////////////////////////////////
// CCntView

IMPLEMENT_DYNCREATE(CCntView, CView)

BEGIN_MESSAGE_MAP(CCntView, CView)
    //{{AFX_MSG_MAP(CCntView)
    ON_WM_SETFOCUS()
    ON_WM_SIZE()
    ON_COMMAND(ID_OLE_INSERT_NEW, OnInsertObject)
    ON_COMMAND(ID_CANCEL_EDIT, OnCancelEdit)
    //}}AFX_MSG_MAP
END_MESSAGE_MAP()

/////////////////////////////////////////////////////////////////////////////
// CCntView construction/destruction

CCntView::~CCntView()
{
}

CCntView::CCntView()
{
}

/////////////////////////////////////////////////////////////////////////////
// CCntView drawing

void CCntView::OnDraw(CDC* pDC)
{
    CCntDoc* pDoc = GetDocument();
    ASSERT_VALID(pDoc);

    // Draw the selection at an arbitrary position.
    // This code should be removed once your real drawing code
    // is implemented.  This position corresponds exactly to
    // the rectangle returned by CCntCntrItem, to give the
    // effect of in-place editing.

    // TODO: remove this code when final draw code is complete.
```

```
    if (m_pSelection == NULL)
    {
        POSITION pos = pDoc->GetStartPosition();
        m_pSelection = (CCntCntrItem*)pDoc->
                            GetNextClientItem(pos);
    }
    if (m_pSelection != NULL)
        m_pSelection->Draw(pDC, CRect(10, 10, 210, 210));
}

void CCntView::OnInitialUpdate()
{
    CView::OnInitialUpdate();

    m_pSelection = NULL;    // initialize selection

}

//////////////////////////////////////////////////////////////
// OLE Client support and commands

BOOL CCntView::IsSelected(const CObject* pDocItem) const
{
    return pDocItem == m_pSelection;
}

void CCntView::OnInsertObject()
{
    COleInsertDialog dlg;
    if (dlg.DoModal() != IDOK)
        return;

    BeginWaitCursor();

    CCntCntrItem* pItem = NULL;
    TRY
    {
        CCntDoc* pDoc = GetDocument();
        ASSERT_VALID(pDoc);
        pItem = new CCntCntrItem(pDoc);
        ASSERT_VALID(pItem);
```

```
        if (!dlg.CreateItem(pItem))
            AfxThrowMemoryException();  // any exception
        ASSERT_VALID(pItem);

        if (dlg.GetSelectionType() ==
            COleInsertDialog::createNewItem)
            pItem->DoVerb(OLEIVERB_SHOW, this);

        ASSERT_VALID(pItem);

        m_pSelection = pItem; // set to last inserted item
        pDoc->UpdateAllViews(NULL);
    }
    CATCH(CException, e)
    {
        if (pItem != NULL)
        {
            ASSERT_VALID(pItem);
            pItem->Delete();
        }
        AfxMessageBox(IDP_FAILED_TO_CREATE);
    }
    END_CATCH

    EndWaitCursor();
}

void CCntView::OnCancelEdit()
{
    // Close any in-place active item on this view.
    COleClientItem* pActiveItem = GetDocument()->
                                  GetInPlaceActiveItem(this);
    if (pActiveItem != NULL)
    {
        pActiveItem->Close();
    }
    ASSERT(GetDocument()->GetInPlaceActiveItem(this) == NULL);
}

void CCntView::OnSetFocus(CWnd* pOldWnd)
{
    COleClientItem* pActiveItem = GetDocument()->
```

```
                                    GetInPlaceActiveItem(this);
    if (pActiveItem != NULL &&
        pActiveItem->GetItemState() ==
                     COleClientItem::activeUIState)
    {
        // set focus to this item if it is in same view
        CWnd* pWnd = pActiveItem->GetInPlaceWindow();
        if (pWnd != NULL)
        {
            pWnd->SetFocus();   // don't call the base class
            return;
        }
    }

    CView::OnSetFocus(pOldWnd);
}

void CCntView::OnSize(UINT nType, int cx, int cy)
{
    CView::OnSize(nType, cx, cy);
    COleClientItem* pActiveItem = GetDocument()->
                                    GetInPlaceActiveItem(this);
    if (pActiveItem != NULL)
        pActiveItem->SetItemRects();
}

/////////////////////////////////////////////////////////////////////////////
// CCntView diagnostics

#ifdef _DEBUG
void CCntView::AssertValid() const
{
    CView::AssertValid();
}

void CCntView::Dump(CDumpContext& dc) const
{
    CView::Dump(dc);
}

CCntDoc* CCntView::GetDocument() // non-debug version inline
{
```

```
    ASSERT(m_pDocument->IsKindOf(RUNTIME_CLASS(CCntDoc)));
    return (CCntDoc*)m_pDocument;
}
#endif //_DEBUG

/////////////////////////////////////////////////////////////
// CCntView message handlers
```

To handle drawing (that is, inserted objects) for the **CCntView** container, **OnDraw()** has been altered by the AppWizard.

```
void CCntView::OnDraw(CDC* pDC)
{
    CCntDoc* pDoc = GetDocument();
    ASSERT_VALID(pDoc);

    // Draw the selection at an arbitrary position.
    // This code should be removed once your real drawing code
    // is implemented.  This position corresponds exactly to
    // the rectangle returned by CCntCntrItem, to give the
    // effect of in-place editing.

    // TODO: remove this code when final draw code is complete.

    if (m_pSelection == NULL)
    {
        POSITION pos = pDoc->GetStartPosition();
        m_pSelection = (CCntCntrItem*)pDoc->
                        GetNextClientItem(pos);
    }
    if (m_pSelection != NULL)
        m_pSelection->Draw(pDC, CRect(10, 10, 210, 210));
}
```

This code places the object at a predetermined location designated by **Crect()**: 10,10 and 210,210. These values can be changed manually or automatically as suggested in the listing's comments.

Other additions include **OnInitialUpdate()**, **IsSelected()**, **OnInsertObject()**, **OnCancelEdit()**, **OnSetFocus()**, and **OnSize()**. These implementations allow selecting, inserting, canceling, and sizing of OLE objects. Any additional code for these functions must be supplied by you, the programmer.

The Container CNTRITEM.CPP File

The container file, CNTRITEM.CPP, is responsible for the implementation of our **CCntCntrItem** class from Microsoft's **COleClientItem** class.

```
// cntritem.cpp : implementation of the CCntCntrItem class
//

#include "stdafx.h"
#include "cnt.h"

#include "cntdoc.h"
#include "cntritem.h"

#ifdef _DEBUG
#undef THIS_FILE
static char BASED_CODE THIS_FILE[] = __FILE__;
#endif

/////////////////////////////////////////////////////////////////////////////
// CCntCntrItem implementation

IMPLEMENT_SERIAL(CCntCntrItem, COleClientItem, 0)

CCntCntrItem::CCntCntrItem(CCntDoc* pContainer)
    : COleClientItem(pContainer)
{
}

CCntCntrItem::~CCntCntrItem()
{
}

void CCntCntrItem::OnChange(OLE_NOTIFICATION nCode,
                            DWORD dwParam)
{
    ASSERT_VALID(this);

    COleClientItem::OnChange(nCode, dwParam);
}

BOOL CCntCntrItem::OnChangeItemPosition(const CRect& rectPos)
{
    ASSERT_VALID(this);
```

```
    if (!COleClientItem::OnChangeItemPosition(rectPos))
        return FALSE;

    return TRUE;
}

void CCntCntrItem::OnGetItemPosition(CRect& rPosition)
{
    ASSERT_VALID(this);

    rPosition.SetRect(10, 10, 210, 210);
}

void CCntCntrItem::OnDeactivateUI(BOOL bUndoable)
{
    COleClientItem::OnDeactivateUI(bUndoable);

    // Close an in-place active item whenever it removes the
    // user interface.  The action here should match as
    // closely as possible to the handling of the escape key
    // in the view.
    Deactivate();   // deactivate the object
}

void CCntCntrItem::Serialize(CArchive& ar)
{
    ASSERT_VALID(this);

    COleClientItem::Serialize(ar);

    if (ar.IsStoring())
    {
    }
    else
    {
    }
}

/////////////////////////////////////////////////////////////////
// CCntCntrItem diagnostics
```

```
#ifdef _DEBUG
void CCntCntrItem::AssertValid() const
{
    COleClientItem::AssertValid();
}

void CCntCntrItem::Dump(CDumpContext& dc) const
{
    COleClientItem::Dump(dc);
}
#endif

/////////////////////////////////////////////////////////////////
```

COleClientItem is derived from other classes in the following manner:

```
CObject—
        CCmdTarget—
                   CDocItem—
                            COleClientItem
```

COleClientItem is a class used to represent the client's portion of a connection to an embedded OLE object.

There are 19 member functions that can be overridden for this class. In the previous listing you'll see that four of them are implemented. These four member functions include **OnChange()**, **OnGetItemPosition()**, **OnDeactivateUI()**, and **OnChangeItemPosition()**.

OnChange() responds to changes brought about when the server changes this item. *nCode* can take on the following values: OLE_CHANGED (if the item's appearance has changed), OLE_SAVED (if the OLE item has been saved), OLE_CLOSED (if the OLE item has been closed), and OLE_CHANGED_STATE (if the item has changed from one state to another). **OnDeactivateUI()** is used to specify if current editing changes cannot be undone. The parameter for this function is a Boolean value. Examine the next portion of code, taken from the previous listing, to see how **OnGetItemPosition()** and **OnChangeItemPosition()** are used.

```
BOOL CCntCntrItem::OnChangeItemPosition(const CRect& rectPos)
{
    ASSERT_VALID(this);
```

```
    if (!COleClientItem::OnChangeItemPosition(rectPos))
        return FALSE;

    return TRUE;
}

void CCntCntrItem::OnGetItemPosition(CRect& rPosition)
{
    ASSERT_VALID(this);

    rPosition.SetRect(10, 10, 210, 210);
}
```

OnGetItemPosition() references **CRect**, which in turn contains the item's position coordinates. In this instance, they are set to 10, 10, 210, and 210. **OnChangeItemPosition()** gives the item's position relative to the client area in the container.

Working with the Container and Server Applications

The previously described files contain the minimum code necessary to implement a container application. However, this container application is functional as shown.

Compile and link this application to produce an executable file. To execute the application, use Window's Run command or type **cnt** from the command line prompt. Figure 6-18 shows the initial container window.

This container can utilize an object from any server. For this case let Microsoft's Excel be the server application. To select Excel, choose the container's Edit menu, as shown in Figure 6-19.

Select the Insert New Object... menu item to open the Insert Object dialog box, shown in Figure 6-20.

From the Insert Object dialog box, choose an Excel Document as the object to embed in the container.

Figure 6-21 shows the initial insertion of the Excel object into the container document.

Notice that the window caption now reads "Excel Document in Cnt." This indicates that the server object has been properly embedded.

Figure 6-22 shows that data can be entered in the embedded object, which is now part of the container.

In the next chapter, you'll learn how to use the AppWizard to build a simple server application.

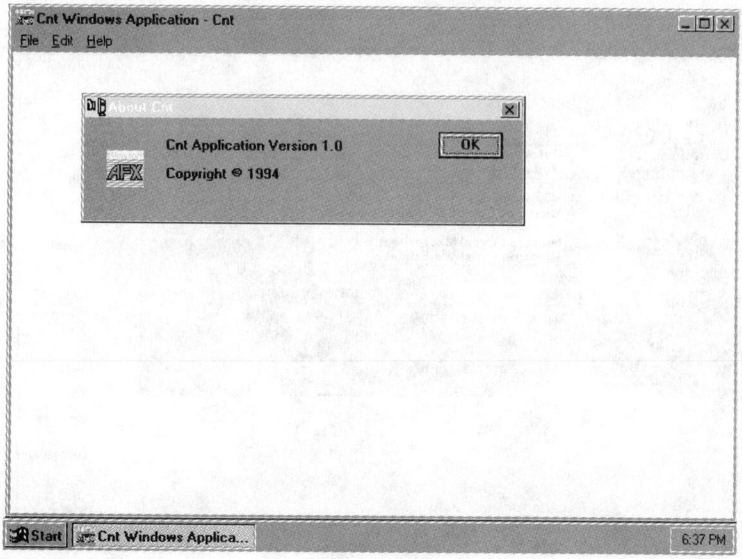

FIGURE 6-18. *The container's initial window*

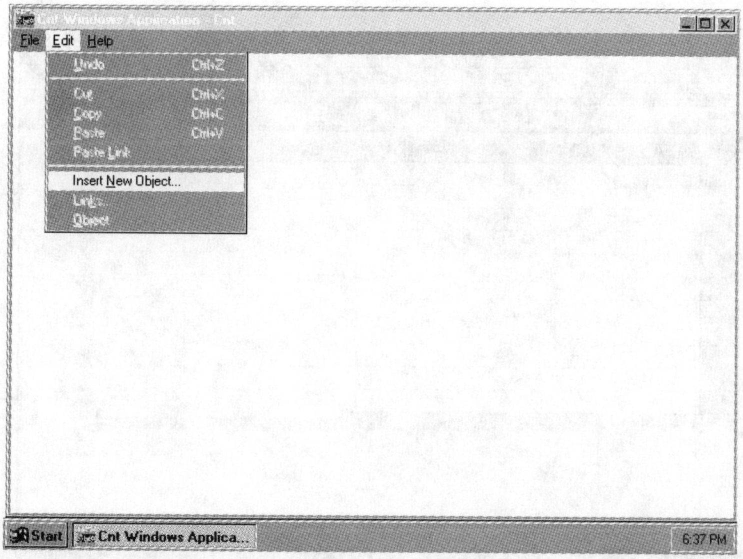

FIGURE 6-19. *The container's Edit menu will allow the user to insert an object*

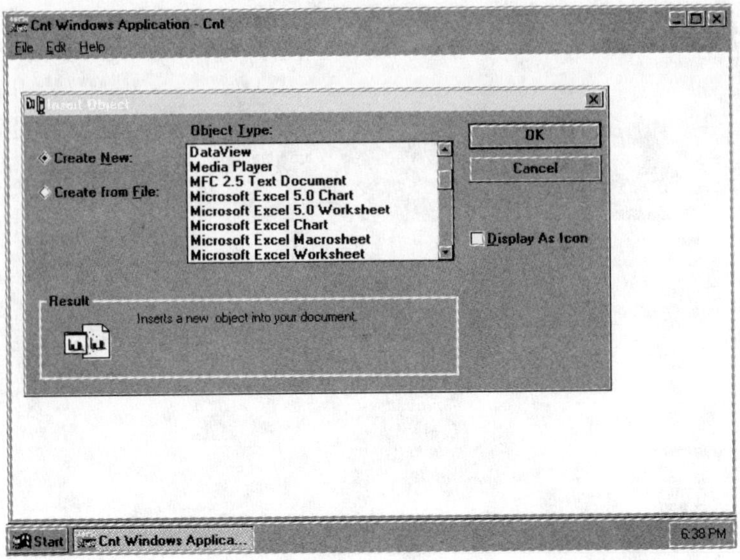

FIGURE 6-20. *The Insert Object dialog box lists the object sources*

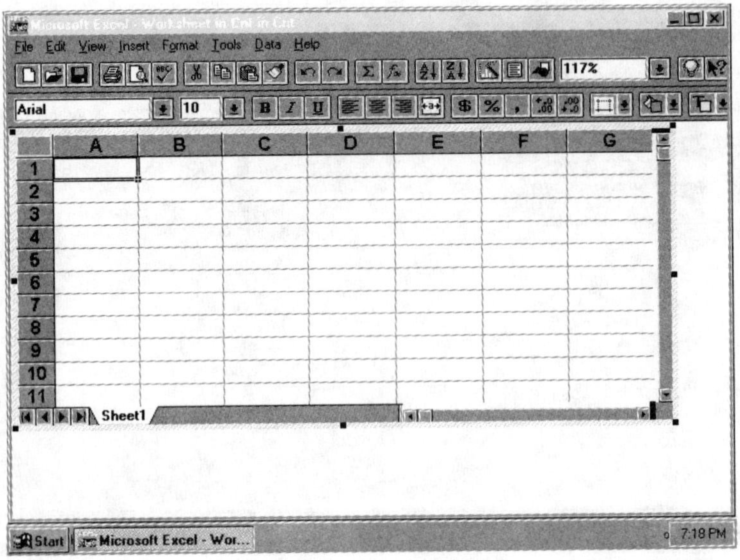

FIGURE 6-21. *The Excel server object is embedded into the container document*

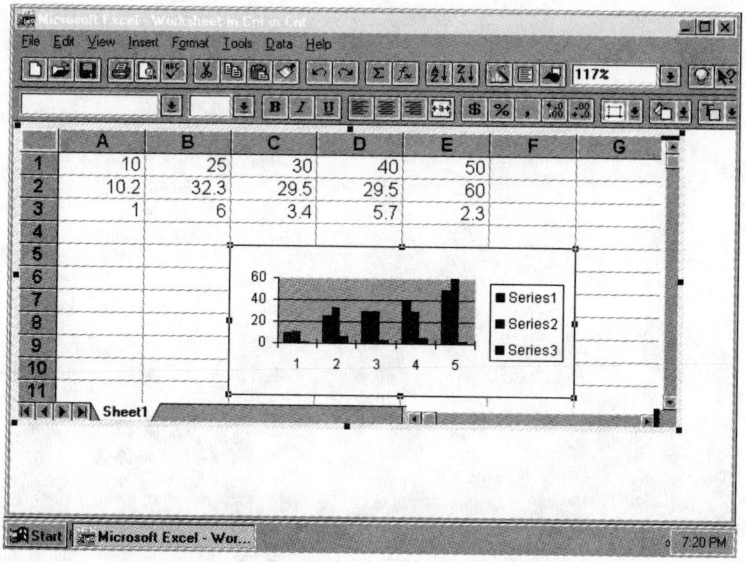

FIGURE 6-22. *Data can be entered in the server object that is embedded in the container*

CHAPTER 7

Developing OLE Server Applications

The server application for this chapter will be built in a manner similar to the container application of the previous chapter. This server will function as a mini-word processor. Acting as a server, this word processor can be inserted into applications with container abilities such as Microsoft Word, Microsoft Excel, or even the container application built in the previous chapter.

By using the AppWizard to generate your OLE application, your application will initialize OLE, register itself in the OLE registration database, support Visual Editing, support serialization of OLE storage streams, use an OLE class factory for creation of document objects, and obtain menu negotiation with the container.

Although servers tend to be more complicated than their container counterparts, the important thing to remember is that the template code is completely generated by the AppWizard. This server template code can be enhanced with your specific application features into a full-blown product. In this chapter we've added several enhancements to the template code.

Using the AppWizard

To generate the server application, named svr, proceed with the creation of a new project—just as you did in the container application from the previous chapter. Here are the six steps you will need to create while in the AppWizard:

1. Select a single document interface for the svr application.
2. No databases are used by the svr application.
3. Set the OLE options to Full Server for the svr application.
4. Choose the default features for the svr application.
5. Select additional file options for the svr application.
6. View the six new classes that will be generated by the AppWizard, but change **CSvrView**'s base class to **CEditView**.

In summary, these options reflect the six-step design process of the AppWizard. They include a single document interface, no database options, a full server option, default application features, detailed file comments, and so on.

When all the AppWizard selections are completed, click on the Finish push button to start the file-creation process. Finally, select the Ok button to build the files for the server application.

Once the svr files are generated, an executable file can be obtained by selecting the Build All option from the C/C++ compiler's Project menu. When the compile-and-link process is completed, you'll have an executable file named SVR.EXE with editing capabilities.

AppWizard Files

The files generated by the AppWizard produce a fully working server application named svr with editing capabilities. When the files are generated by the AppWizard, your subdirectory will contain the following C++ files: SVR.CPP, MAINFRM.CPP, SVRDOC.CPP, SVRVIEW.CPP, SRVRITEM.CPP, and IPFRAME.CPP. You will also be supplied with the necessary header and resource files.

The Server SVR.CPP File

Here is the wizard code for the SVR.CPP server file. As you examine this listing, you'll notice that dialog box colors have been altered. On a VGA screen, the background is now yellow and the text blue.

```
// svr.cpp : Defines the class behaviors for the application.
//

#include "stdafx.h"
#include "svr.h"

#include "mainfrm.h"
#include "ipframe.h"
#include "svrdoc.h"
#include "svrview.h"

#ifdef _DEBUG
#undef THIS_FILE
static char BASED_CODE THIS_FILE[] = __FILE__;
#endif

/////////////////////////////////////////////////////////////////////////////
// CSvrApp

BEGIN_MESSAGE_MAP(CSvrApp, CWinApp)
        //{{AFX_MSG_MAP(CSvrApp)
        ON_COMMAND(ID_APP_ABOUT, OnAppAbout)
                // NOTE - the ClassWizard will add and remove
                // mapping macros here.
                // DO NOT EDIT what you see in these blocks of
                // generated code!
        //}}AFX_MSG_MAP
        // Standard file based document commands
        ON_COMMAND(ID_FILE_NEW, CWinApp::OnFileNew)
        ON_COMMAND(ID_FILE_OPEN, CWinApp::OnFileOpen)
        // Standard print setup command
        ON_COMMAND(ID_FILE_PRINT_SETUP,CWinApp::OnFilePrintSetup)
END_MESSAGE_MAP()

/////////////////////////////////////////////////////////////////////////////
// CSvrApp construction

CSvrApp::CSvrApp()
```

```
{
        // TODO: add construction code here,
        // Place all significant initialization in InitInstance
}

/////////////////////////////////////////////////////////////////////////////
// The one and only CSvrApp object

CSvrApp theApp;

static const CLSID BASED_CODE clsid =
{ 0x27800, 0x0, 0x0, {0xc0, 0x0, 0x0, 0x0, 0x0, 0x0, 0x0, 0x46}};

/////////////////////////////////////////////////////////////////////////////
// CSvrApp initialization

BOOL CSvrApp::InitInstance()
{
        // Initialize OLE libraries
        if (!AfxOleInit())
        {
                AfxMessageBox(IDP_OLE_INIT_FAILED);
                return FALSE;
        }

        // Standard initialization
        // If you are not using these features and wish to
        // reduce the size of your final executable, you
        // should remove from the following the specific
        // initialization routines you do not need.

        COLORREF clrCtlBk, clrCtlText;

        // Set dialog box background to yellow and text to blue
        SetDialogBkColor(clrCtlBk=RGB(255,255,0),
                         clrCtlText=RGB(0,0,255));

        Enable3dControls();

        LoadStdProfileSettings(); //Load standard INI file options

        // Register the application's document templates.
```

```
// Document templates serve as the connection between
// documents, frame windows and views.

CSingleDocTemplate* pDocTemplate;
pDocTemplate = new CSingleDocTemplate(
        IDR_MAINFRAME,
        RUNTIME_CLASS(CSvrDoc),
        RUNTIME_CLASS(CMainFrame), //SDI frame window
        RUNTIME_CLASS(CSvrView));
pDocTemplate->SetServerInfo(
        IDR_SRVR_EMBEDDED, IDR_SRVR_INPLACE,
        RUNTIME_CLASS(CInPlaceFrame));
AddDocTemplate(pDocTemplate);

// Connect the COleTemplateServer to the document
// template.  The COleTemplateServer creates new
// documents on behalf of requesting OLE containers
// by using information specified in the document
// template.

m_server.ConnectTemplate(clsid, pDocTemplate, TRUE);
        // Note: SDI applications register server
        // objects only if /Embedding or /Automation
        // is present on the command line.

// Parse the command line to see if OLE server
if (RunEmbedded() || RunAutomated())
{
        // Register all OLE server (factories) as
        // running.  This enables the OLE libraries
        // to create objects from other applications.

        COleTemplateServer::RegisterAll();

        // Application was run with /Embedding or
        // /Automation.  Don't show the
        // main window in this case.

        return TRUE;
}
```

```
        // When a server application is launched stand-alone,
        // it is a good idea to update the system registry in
        // case it has been damaged.

        m_server.UpdateRegistry(OAT_INPLACE_SERVER);

        // create a new (empty) document
        OnFileNew();

        if (m_lpCmdLine[0] != '\0')
        {
                // TODO: add command line processing here
        }

        return TRUE;
}

/////////////////////////////////////////////////////////////////////
// CAboutDlg dialog used for App About

class CAboutDlg : public CDialog
{
public:
        CAboutDlg();

// Dialog Data
        //{{AFX_DATA(CAboutDlg)
        enum { IDD = IDD_ABOUTBOX };
        //}}AFX_DATA

// Implementation
protected:
        virtual void DoDataExchange(CDataExchange* pDX);
        // DDX/DDV support
        //{{AFX_MSG(CAboutDlg)
                // No message handlers
        //}}AFX_MSG
        DECLARE_MESSAGE_MAP()
};

CAboutDlg::CAboutDlg() : CDialog(CAboutDlg::IDD)
{
```

```
        //{{AFX_DATA_INIT(CAboutDlg)
        //}}AFX_DATA_INIT
}

void CAboutDlg::DoDataExchange(CDataExchange* pDX)
{
        CDialog::DoDataExchange(pDX);
        //{{AFX_DATA_MAP(CAboutDlg)
        //}}AFX_DATA_MAP
}

BEGIN_MESSAGE_MAP(CAboutDlg, CDialog)
        //{{AFX_MSG_MAP(CAboutDlg)
                // No message handlers
        //}}AFX_MSG_MAP
END_MESSAGE_MAP()

// App command to run the dialog
void CSvrApp::OnAppAbout()
{
        CAboutDlg aboutDlg;
        aboutDlg.DoModal();
}

///////////////////////////////////////////////////////////////
// CSvrApp commands
```

This server file, SVR.CPP, contains interesting code in **CSvrApp::InitInstance**. Examine the following portion of code edited from the previous listing.

```
BOOL CSvrApp::InitInstance()
{
    .
    .
    .

    CSingleDocTemplate* pDocTemplate;
    pDocTemplate = new CSingleDocTemplate(
        IDR_MAINFRAME,
        RUNTIME_CLASS(CSvrDoc),
        RUNTIME_CLASS(CMainFrame), // main SDI frame window
        RUNTIME_CLASS(CSvrView));
    pDocTemplate->SetServerInfo(
```

```
        IDR_SRVR_EMBEDDED, IDR_SRVR_INPLACE,
        RUNTIME_CLASS(CInPlaceFrame));
    .
    .
    .
```

In this portion of code, you will notice the normal implementation of a document template, but immediately following this piece of code is a call to the **SetServerInfo()** function. Document templates associate a document class with view and frame classes. This function associates additional information with the template: menus (IDR_SRVR_EMBEDDED and IDR_SRVR_INPLACE) and an in-place frame class (**CInPlaceFrame**). This is how the framework knows which menus and IP frame to create when the server is activated in place.

```
    .
    .
    .
if (RunEmbedded() || RunAutomated())
        {
                // Register all OLE server (factories) as
                // running.  This enables the OLE libraries
                // to create objects from other applications.

                COleTemplateServer::RegisterAll();

                // Application was run with /Embedding or
                // /Automation.  Don't show the
                // main window in this case.

                return TRUE;
        }

        // When a server application is launched stand-alone,
        // it is a good idea to update the system registry in
        // case it has been damaged.

        m_server.UpdateRegistry(OAT_INPLACE_SERVER);

        // create a new (empty) document
        OnFileNew();

        if (m_lpCmdLine[0] != '\0')
        {
```

```
                // TODO: add command line processing here
        }
    .
    .
    .
```

The class factory, **m_server**, is an instance of **COleTemplateServer**. This class is derived in the following manner:

```
CObject—
       CCmdTarget—
                 COleObjectFactory—
                                  COleTemplateServer
```

The factory(ies) is registered with a call to **COleTemplateServer::RegisterAll()**. With this in place, OLE libraries are able to create objects from other applications. Finally, **m_server.UpdateRegistry** registers the document and updates the registration database. This means that containers can now find your server in the registration database. In this case, OAT_INPLACE_SERVER is used to provide a full server interface. OAT_SERVER supports only embedding, OAT_CONTAINER supports links to embeddings, and OAT_DISPATCH_OBJECT makes the object IDispatch capable.

The Server MAINFRM.CPP File

Again this server file, MAINFRM.CPP, is essentially the same file as shown for the container application in the previous chapter. As you examine this listing, note the inclusion of the ID values for the server's menu selections.

```
// mainfrm.cpp : implementation of the CMainFrame class
//

#include "stdafx.h"
#include "svr.h"

#include "mainfrm.h"

#ifdef _DEBUG
#undef THIS_FILE
static char BASED_CODE THIS_FILE[] = __FILE__;
#endif

/////////////////////////////////////////////////////////////////////////////
// CMainFrame
```

```
IMPLEMENT_DYNCREATE(CMainFrame, CFrameWnd)

BEGIN_MESSAGE_MAP(CMainFrame, CFrameWnd)
        //{{AFX_MSG_MAP(CMainFrame)
        ON_WM_CREATE()
        //}}AFX_MSG_MAP
END_MESSAGE_MAP()

/////////////////////////////////////////////////////////////////
// arrays of IDs used to initialize control bars

// toolbar buttons - IDs are command buttons
static UINT BASED_CODE buttons[] =
{
        // same order as in the bitmap 'toolbar.bmp'
        ID_FILE_NEW,
        ID_FILE_OPEN,
        ID_FILE_SAVE,
                ID_SEPARATOR,
        ID_EDIT_CUT,
        ID_EDIT_COPY,
        ID_EDIT_PASTE,
                ID_SEPARATOR,
        ID_FILE_PRINT,
        ID_APP_ABOUT,
};

static UINT BASED_CODE indicators[] =
{
        ID_SEPARATOR,           // status line indicator
        ID_INDICATOR_CAPS,
        ID_INDICATOR_NUM,
        ID_INDICATOR_SCRL,
};

/////////////////////////////////////////////////////////////////
// CMainFrame construction/destruction

CMainFrame::CMainFrame()
{
```

```
        // TODO: add member initialization code here

}

CMainFrame::~CMainFrame()
{
}

int CMainFrame::OnCreate(LPCREATESTRUCT lpCreateStruct)
{
        if (CFrameWnd::OnCreate(lpCreateStruct) == -1)
                return -1;

        if (!m_wndToolBar.Create(this,
                  WS_CHILD | WS_VISIBLE | CBRS_TOP |
                  CBRS_TOOLTIPS | CBRS_FLYBY) ||
                !m_wndToolBar.LoadBitmap(IDR_MAINFRAME) ||
                !m_wndToolBar.SetButtons(buttons,
                  sizeof(buttons)/sizeof(UINT)))
        {
                TRACE0("Failed to create toolbar\n");
                return -1;      // fail to create
        }

        if (!m_wndStatusBar.Create(this) ||
                !m_wndStatusBar.SetIndicators(indicators,
                  sizeof(indicators)/sizeof(UINT)))
        {
                TRACE0("Failed to create status bar\n");
                return -1;      // fail to create
        }

        // TODO: Delete these three lines if you don't want the
        // toolbar to be dockable
        m_wndToolBar.EnableDocking(CBRS_ALIGN_ANY);
        EnableDocking(CBRS_ALIGN_ANY);
        DockControlBar(&m_wndToolBar);

        return 0;
}

/////////////////////////////////////////////////////////////////////////////
```

```
// CMainFrame diagnostics

#ifdef _DEBUG
void CMainFrame::AssertValid() const
{
        CFrameWnd::AssertValid();
}

void CMainFrame::Dump(CDumpContext& dc) const
{
        CFrameWnd::Dump(dc);
}

#endif //_DEBUG

/////////////////////////////////////////////////////////////////////////////
// CMainFrame message handlers
```

The constructor and destructor are empty in this file. Your specific code can be entered at this point. If you examine this listing, you'll notice that **CMainFrame::OnCreate** contains the tool and status bar code.

The Server SVRDOC.CPP File

The server file, SVRDOC.CPP, is responsible for implementing our **CSvrDoc** class. This class is derived from Microsoft's **COleServerDoc** class. The **COleServerDoc** class is derived in the following manner:

```
CObject—
       CCmdTarget—
                 CDocument—
                          COleDocument—
                                       COleLinkingDoc—
                                                     COleServerDoc
```

```
// svrdoc.cpp : implementation of the CSvrDoc class
//

#include "stdafx.h"
#include "svr.h"

#include "svrdoc.h"
#include "srvritem.h"
```

```
#include "svrview.h"

#ifdef _DEBUG
#undef THIS_FILE
static char BASED_CODE THIS_FILE[] = __FILE__;
#endif

/////////////////////////////////////////////////////////////////////
// CSvrDoc

IMPLEMENT_DYNCREATE(CSvrDoc, COleServerDoc)

BEGIN_MESSAGE_MAP(CSvrDoc, COleServerDoc)
        //{{AFX_MSG_MAP(CSvrDoc)
                // NOTE - the ClassWizard will add and remove
                // mapping macros here.
                // DO NOT EDIT what you see in these blocks of
                // generated code!
        //}}AFX_MSG_MAP
END_MESSAGE_MAP()

/////////////////////////////////////////////////////////////////////
// CSvrDoc construction/destruction

CSvrDoc::CSvrDoc()
{
        // TODO: add one-time construction code here

}

CSvrDoc::~CSvrDoc()
{
}

BOOL CSvrDoc::OnNewDocument()
{
        if (!COleServerDoc::OnNewDocument())
                return FALSE;

        // TODO: add reinitialization code here
        // (SDI documents will reuse this document)
```

```
        return TRUE;
}

//////////////////////////////////////////////////////////////////
// CSvrDoc server implementation

COleServerItem* CSvrDoc::OnGetEmbeddedItem()
{
        // OnGetEmbeddedItem is called by the framework to get
        // the COleServerItem that is associated with the
        // document.  It is only called when necessary.

        CSvrSrvrItem* pItem = new CSvrSrvrItem(this);
        ASSERT_VALID(pItem);
        return pItem;
}

//////////////////////////////////////////////////////////////////
// CSvrDoc serialization

void CSvrDoc::Serialize(CArchive& ar)
{
        if (ar.IsStoring())
        {
                // TODO: add storing code here
        }
        else
        {
                // TODO: add loading code here
        }

        ((CSvrView*)m_viewList.GetHead())->SerializeRaw(ar);
}

//////////////////////////////////////////////////////////////////
// CSvrDoc diagnostics

#ifdef _DEBUG
void CSvrDoc::AssertValid() const
{
        COleServerDoc::AssertValid();
}
```

```
void CSvrDoc::Dump(CDumpContext& dc) const
{
        COleServerDoc::Dump(dc);
}
#endif //_DEBUG

/////////////////////////////////////////////////////////////////
// CSvrDoc commands
```

This file contains an important piece of code unique to server applications.

```
/////////////////////////////////////////////////////////////////
// CSvrDoc server implementation

COleServerItem* CSvrDoc::OnGetEmbeddedItem()
{
        // OnGetEmbeddedItem is called by the framework to get
        // the COleServerItem that is associated with the
        // document.  It is only called when necessary.

        CSvrSrvrItem* pItem = new CSvrSrvrItem(this);
        ASSERT_VALID(pItem);
        return pItem;
}

/////////////////////////////////////////////////////////////////
```

This small portion of code implements the server for the selected item. Typically, there is one **COleServerItem** that represents the whole document during editing. When links are supported, additional items are used to represent portions of the document, rather than the whole document.

Another simple addition will allow the **CEditView** object to be saved to disk as raw text.

```
void CSvrDoc::Serialize(CArchive& ar)
{
        .
        .
        .
        ((CSvrView*)m_viewList.GetHead())->SerializeRaw(ar);
}
```

The Server SVRVIEW.CPP File

The server file, SVRVIEW.CPP, implements our **CSvrView** class. In this instance, the **CSvrView** class is derived from Microsoft's **CEditView** class.

```
// svrview.cpp : implementation of the CSvrView class
//

#include "stdafx.h"
#include "svr.h"

#include "svrdoc.h"
#include "svrview.h"

#ifdef _DEBUG
#undef THIS_FILE
static char BASED_CODE THIS_FILE[] = __FILE__;
#endif

/////////////////////////////////////////////////////////////////
// CSvrView

IMPLEMENT_DYNCREATE(CSvrView, CEditView)

BEGIN_MESSAGE_MAP(CSvrView, CEditView)
        //{{AFX_MSG_MAP(CSvrView)
                // NOTE - the ClassWizard will add and remove
                // mapping macros here.
                // DO NOT EDIT what you see in these blocks
                // of generated code!
        ON_COMMAND(ID_CANCEL_EDIT_SRVR, OnCancelEditSrvr)
        //}}AFX_MSG_MAP
        // Standard printing commands
        ON_COMMAND(ID_FILE_PRINT, CEditView::OnFilePrint)
        ON_COMMAND(ID_FILE_PRINT_PREVIEW,
                   CEditView::OnFilePrintPreview)
END_MESSAGE_MAP()

/////////////////////////////////////////////////////////////////
// CSvrView construction/destruction

CSvrView::CSvrView()
{
        // TODO: add construction code here
```

```
}

CSvrView::~CSvrView()
{
}

/////////////////////////////////////////////////////////////////
// CSvrView drawing

void CSvrView::OnDraw(CDC* pDC)
{
    CSvrDoc* pDoc = GetDocument();
        ASSERT_VALID(pDoc);


        // TODO: add draw code for native data here
}

/////////////////////////////////////////////////////////////////
// CSvrView printing

BOOL CSvrView::OnPreparePrinting(CPrintInfo* pInfo)
{
        // default CEditView preparation
        return CEditView::OnPreparePrinting(pInfo);
}

void CSvrView::OnBeginPrinting(CDC* pDC, CPrintInfo* pInfo)
{
        // Default CEditView begin printing.
        CEditView::OnBeginPrinting(pDC, pInfo);
}

void CSvrView::OnEndPrinting(CDC* pDC, CPrintInfo* pInfo)
{
        // Default CEditView end printing
        CEditView::OnEndPrinting(pDC, pInfo);
}

/////////////////////////////////////////////////////////////////
// OLE Server support
```

```
// The following command handler provides the standard keyboard
// user interface to cancel an in-place editing session.  Here,
// the server (not the container) causes the deactivation.
void CSvrView::OnCancelEditSrvr()
{
        GetDocument()->OnDeactivateUI(FALSE);
}

//////////////////////////////////////////////////////////////////////
// CSvrView diagnostics

#ifdef _DEBUG
void CSvrView::AssertValid() const
{
        CEditView::AssertValid();
}

void CSvrView::Dump(CDumpContext& dc) const
{
        CEditView::Dump(dc);
}

CSvrDoc* CSvrView::GetDocument() // non-debug version is inline
{
        ASSERT(m_pDocument->IsKindOf(RUNTIME_CLASS(CSvrDoc)));
        return (CSvrDoc*)m_pDocument;
}
#endif //_DEBUG

//////////////////////////////////////////////////////////////////////
// CSvrView message handlers
```

There is only a small portion of code in the previous listing that aids in OLE support.

```
//////////////////////////////////////////////////////////////////////
// OLE Server support

// The following command handler provides the standard keyboard
// user interface to cancel an in-place editing session.  Here,
// the server (not the container) causes the deactivation.
void CSvrView::OnCancelEditSrvr()
```

```
{
        GetDocument()->OnDeactivateUI(FALSE);
}

/////////////////////////////////////////////////////////////////////////////
```

Remember from the previous chapter that **OnDeactivateUI()** is used to cancel an in-place editing session. In the previous chapter, it was the container that dictated the deactivation. In this case, the server obtains the same ability.

The Server SRVRITEM.CPP File

This server file, SRVRITEM.CPP, is responsible for implementing our **CSvrSrvrItem** class. This class is derived from Microsoft's **COleServerItem** class in the following manner:

```
CObject—
       CCmdTarget—
                 CDocItem—
                         COleServerItem
```

```
// srvritem.cpp : implementation of the CSvrSrvrItem class
//

#include "stdafx.h"
#include "svr.h"

#include "svrdoc.h"
#include "srvritem.h"

#ifdef _DEBUG
#undef THIS_FILE
static char BASED_CODE THIS_FILE[] = __FILE__;
#endif

/////////////////////////////////////////////////////////////////////////////
// CSvrSrvrItem implementation

IMPLEMENT_DYNAMIC(CSvrSrvrItem, COleServerItem)

CSvrSrvrItem::CSvrSrvrItem(CSvrDoc* pContainerDoc)
        : COleServerItem(pContainerDoc, TRUE)
{
```

```
        // TODO: add one-time construction code here
        // (eg, adding additional clipboard formats to the
        // item's data source)
}

CSvrSrvrItem::~CSvrSrvrItem()
{
        // TODO: add cleanup code here
}

void CSvrSrvrItem::Serialize(CArchive& ar)
{
        // CSvrSrvrItem::Serialize will be called by the
        // framework if the item is copied to the clipboard.
        // This can happen automatically through the OLE
        // callback OnGetClipboardData.  A good default for
        // the embedded item is simply to delegate to the
        // document's Serialize function.  If you support
        // links, then you will want to serialize
        // just a portion of the document.

        if (!IsLinkedItem())
        {
                CSvrDoc* pDoc = GetDocument();
                ASSERT_VALID(pDoc);
                pDoc->Serialize(ar);
        }
}

BOOL CSvrSrvrItem::OnGetExtent(DVASPECT dwDrawAspect,
                               CSize& rSize)
{
        // Most applications, like this one, only handle drawing
        // the content aspect of the item.  If you wish to
        // support other aspects, such as DVASPECT_THUMBNAIL
        // (by overriding OnDrawEx), then this implementation of
        // OnGetExtent should be modified to handle the
        // additional aspect(s).
```

```
        if (dwDrawAspect != DVASPECT_CONTENT)
              return COleServerItem::OnGetExtent(dwDrawAspect,
                                                      rSize);

        // CSvrSrvrItem::OnGetExtent is called to get the extent
        // in HIMETRIC units of the entire item.  The default
        // implementation here simply returns a hard-coded
        // number of units.

        CSvrDoc* pDoc = GetDocument();
        ASSERT_VALID(pDoc);

        // TODO: replace this arbitrary size

        rSize = CSize(3000, 3000);  //3000x3000 HIMETRIC units

        return TRUE;
}

BOOL CSvrSrvrItem::OnDraw(CDC* pDC, CSize& rSize)
{
        CSvrDoc* pDoc = GetDocument();
        ASSERT_VALID(pDoc);

        // TODO: set mapping mode and extent
        // (The extent is usually the same as the size returned
        // from OnGetExtent)
        pDC->SetMapMode(MM_ANISOTROPIC);
        pDC->SetWindowOrg(100,100);
        pDC->SetWindowExt(3100, 3100);

        // TODO: add drawing code here.  Optionally, fill in the
        // HIMETRIC extent.
        // All drawing takes place in the metafile device
        // context (pDC).

        return TRUE;
}
```

```
/////////////////////////////////////////////////////////////////
// CSvrSrvrItem diagnostics

#ifdef _DEBUG
void CSvrSrvrItem::AssertValid() const
{
        COleServerItem::AssertValid();
}

void CSvrSrvrItem::Dump(CDumpContext& dc) const
{
        COleServerItem::Dump(dc);
}
#endif

/////////////////////////////////////////////////////////////////
```

Document information is saved to the storage stream transparently; just include **pDoc->Serialize(ar)** as shown in the previous listing. Now serialization is redirected to the OLE container's storage stream.

For the server to draw correctly, two additional items are needed: **CSvrSrvrItem::OnGetExtent()** and **CSvrSrvrItem::OnDraw()**.

```
BOOL CSvrSrvrItem::OnGetExtent(DVASPECT dwDrawAspect,
                                CSize& rSize)
{
        // Most applications, like this one, only handle drawing
        // the content aspect of the item.  If you wish to
        // support other aspects, such as DVASPECT_THUMBNAIL
        // (by overriding OnDrawEx), then this implementation of
        // OnGetExtent should be modified to handle the
        // additional aspect(s).

        if (dwDrawAspect != DVASPECT_CONTENT)
                return COleServerItem::OnGetExtent(dwDrawAspect,
                                                   rSize);

        // CSvrSrvrItem::OnGetExtent is called to get the extent
        // in HIMETRIC units of the entire item.  The default
        // implementation here simply returns a hard-coded
        // number of units.

        CSvrDoc* pDoc = GetDocument();
```

```
        ASSERT_VALID(pDoc);

        // TODO: replace this arbitrary size

        rSize = CSize(3000, 3000);  //3000x3000 HIMETRIC units

        return TRUE;
}
```

This portion of code is called to retrieve the size of the OLE item. The drawing units are, by default, MM_HIMETRIC, the drawing mode required by OLE. In this example, the AppWizard hardwired **Csize()** to 3000 by 3000 units. These values can be changed if necessary.

Now here's a rub—we'll have to switch drawing modes, as you'll see in the following piece of code.

```
BOOL CSvrSrvrItem::OnDraw(CDC* pDC, CSize& rSize)
{
        CSvrDoc* pDoc = GetDocument();
        ASSERT_VALID(pDoc);

        // TODO: set mapping mode and extent
        // (The extent is usually the same as the size returned
        // from OnGetExtent)
        pDC->SetMapMode(MM_ANISOTROPIC);
        pDC->SetWindowOrg(100,100);
        pDC->SetWindowExt(3100, 3100);

        // TODO: add drawing code here.  Optionally, fill in the
        // HIMETRIC extent.
        // All drawing takes place in the metafile device
        // context (pDC).

        return TRUE;
}
```

This member function is used to draw the item. Since CDC is a metafile, the mapping mode must be set to MM_ANISOTROPIC. It is at this point that you can optionally set the window's origin and extent. The AppWizard sets the origin at 100, 100 and the extent to 3100, 3100.

The Server IPFRAME.CPP File

This server file, IPFRAME.CPP, implements our **CInPlaceFrame** class. This class is derived from Microsoft's **COleIPFrameWnd** class in the following manner:

```
CObject—
      CCmdTarget—
              CWnd—
                  CFrameWnd—
                          COleIPFrameWnd
```

This class allows Visual Editing when a server document is being edited in place.

```
// ipframe.cpp : implementation of the CInPlaceFrame class
//

#include "stdafx.h"
#include "svr.h"

#include "ipframe.h"

#ifdef _DEBUG
#undef THIS_FILE
static char BASED_CODE THIS_FILE[] = __FILE__;
#endif

/////////////////////////////////////////////////////////////////
// CInPlaceFrame

IMPLEMENT_DYNCREATE(CInPlaceFrame, COleIPFrameWnd)

BEGIN_MESSAGE_MAP(CInPlaceFrame, COleIPFrameWnd)
        //{{AFX_MSG_MAP(CInPlaceFrame)
        ON_WM_CREATE()
        //}}AFX_MSG_MAP
END_MESSAGE_MAP()

/////////////////////////////////////////////////////////////////
// arrays of IDs used to initialize control bars

// toolbar buttons - IDs are command buttons
static UINT BASED_CODE buttons[] =
{
        // same order as in the bitmap 'itoolbar.bmp'
        ID_EDIT_CUT,
        ID_EDIT_COPY,
        ID_EDIT_PASTE,
```

```
                ID_SEPARATOR,
        ID_APP_ABOUT,
};

/////////////////////////////////////////////////////////////////
// CInPlaceFrame construction/destruction

CInPlaceFrame::CInPlaceFrame()
{
}

CInPlaceFrame::~CInPlaceFrame()
{
}

int CInPlaceFrame::OnCreate(LPCREATESTRUCT lpCreateStruct)
{
        if (COleIPFrameWnd::OnCreate(lpCreateStruct) == -1)
                return -1;

        // CResizeBar implements in-place resizing.
        if (!m_wndResizeBar.Create(this))
        {
                TRACE0("Failed to create resize bar\n");
                return -1;      // fail to create
        }

        // By default, it is a good idea to register a
        // drop-target that does nothing with your frame window.
        // This prevents drops from "falling through" to a
        // container that supports drag-drop.
        m_dropTarget.Register(this);

        return 0;
}

// OnCreateControlBars is called by the framework to create
// control bars on the container application's windows.
// pWndFrame is the top level frame window of the container
// and is always non-NULL.  pWndDoc is the doc level frame
// window and will be NULL when the container is an SDI
// application.  A server application can place MFC control
```

```
// bars on either window.
BOOL CInPlaceFrame::OnCreateControlBars(CWnd* pWndFrame,
                                         CWnd* pWndDoc)
{
        // Create toolbar on client's frame window
        if (!m_wndToolBar.Create(pWndFrame) ||
                !m_wndToolBar.LoadBitmap(IDR_SRVR_INPLACE) ||
                !m_wndToolBar.SetButtons(buttons,
                        sizeof(buttons)/sizeof(UINT)))
        {
                TRACE0("Failed to create toolbar\n");
                return FALSE;
        }
        // Set owner to this window, so messages are delivered
        // to correct app
        m_wndToolBar.SetOwner(this);

        return TRUE;
}

/////////////////////////////////////////////////////////////////
// CInPlaceFrame diagnostics

#ifdef _DEBUG
void CInPlaceFrame::AssertValid() const
{
        COleIPFrameWnd::AssertValid();
}

void CInPlaceFrame::Dump(CDumpContext& dc) const
{
        COleIPFrameWnd::Dump(dc);
}
#endif //_DEBUG

/////////////////////////////////////////////////////////////////
// CInPlaceFrame commands
```

This class is also responsible for creating and placing control bars within the container application's document window, as you can see in the following portion of the previous listing.

```
BOOL CInPlaceFrame::OnCreateControlBars(CWnd* pWndFrame,
                                         CWnd* pWndDoc)
{
        // Create toolbar on client's frame window
        if (!m_wndToolBar.Create(pWndFrame) ||
                !m_wndToolBar.LoadBitmap(IDR_SRVR_INPLACE) ||
                !m_wndToolBar.SetButtons(buttons,
                         sizeof(buttons)/sizeof(UINT)))
        {
                TRACE0("Failed to create toolbar\n");
                return FALSE;
        }
        // Set owner to this window, so messages are delivered
        // to correct app
        m_wndToolBar.SetOwner(this);

        return TRUE;
}
```

A call to **SetOwner()** ensures that messages are sent to the correct application.

Working with the Server Application

The server application can now be tested. Remember that this application was created under Windows 95; however, it can be run under Windows NT, too.

As an example, we'll let Microsoft's Excel serve as a container. Open Excel in the normal manner and choose the Object... item from the Insert menu, as shown in Figure 7-1.

From the Object dialog box, choose the Svr Document as the object to embed in this container.

Figure 7-2 shows the initial insertion of the object into the container document.

Notice that the window caption now reads "Svr - Svr in Book1." This indicates that the server object has been properly embedded.

Figure 7-3 shows that text can be entered in the embedded object that is now part of the Excel container.

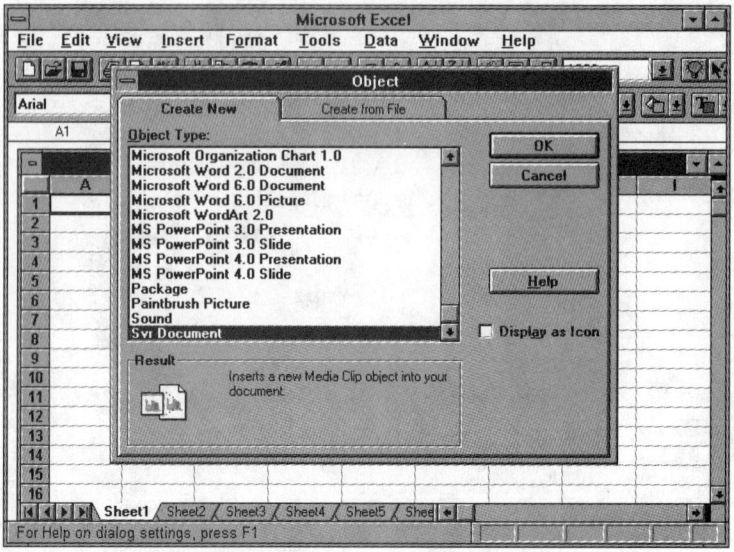

FIGURE 7-1. *The Object dialog box lists the object sources for this container*

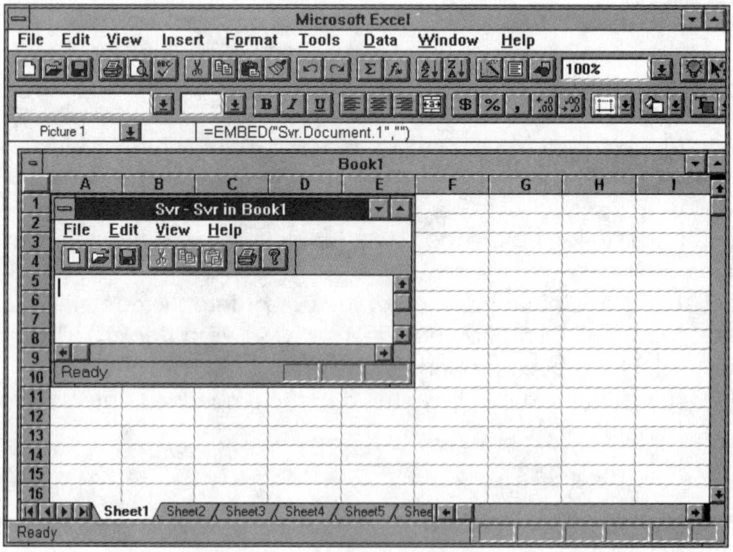

FIGURE 7-2. *The server object is embedded into the Excel container document*

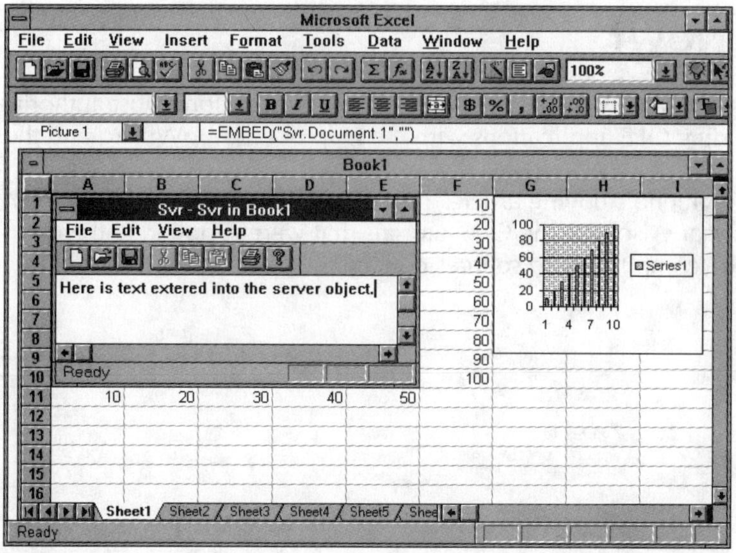

FIGURE 7-3. *Text can be entered in the server object that is embedded in the Excel container*

A Word on OLE Automation

When building both containers and servers, you might have noticed an option for automation. What is automation? Automation is a programming interface that allows an API to be visible to OLE applications. For example, a Visual Basic application may make a call to your application. Some mechanism must be present that will inform the Visual Basic application that your application has a valid automation class and exposed functions and arguments. If you select the automation option when building your container or server, the protocol IDispatch will be used to achieve this visibility. A dispatch map will be added to your document class in order to map virtual member functions to unique IDispatch IDs. This eliminates the need for writing the code that details which functions and arguments are to be exposed.

Experiment with the automation option, and discover the added benefits to your server applications.

What Now?

OLE is a complicated subject, but it is worth your attention. Most authorities now suggest building OLE applications with the help of the AppWizard and the MFC libraries.

We recommend studying articles on OLE, which can be found in the *Microsoft Systems Journal*. Also, use the OLE tutorials that were supplied with your Microsoft Visual C/C++ compiler. Both sources contain a wealth of information.

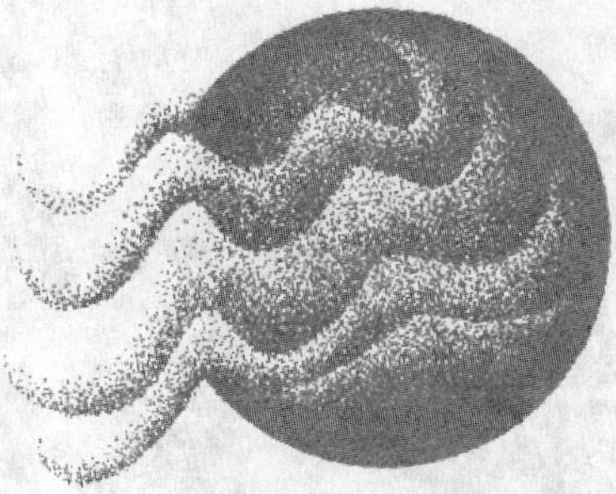

CHAPTER 8

Custom Controls: Concepts and Definitions

As Windows has evolved, so has one of Windows' most visible components: controls. Everyone who has used Windows is familiar with standard controls such as push buttons, radio buttons, scroll bars, and so on. However, what do you do when you need the functionality of a control that is not part of the standard package? Starting with earlier versions of Visual Basic, another type of control began to emerge—the custom control. These custom controls, also known as *VBXs* (after their file extension, .VBX), are specialty items. They are actually small *dynamic link libraries* (DLLs) with .VBX file extensions. A good example of a custom control is a slide bar that might be used to control the volume in a CD-ROM player application. However, custom controls can also be much more complicated.

While many programmers have incorporated Visual Basic's VBXs into their applications, C and C++ have needed their own mechanism for handling custom controls. At the same time the solution to this problem was being pondered, Microsoft began the migration from (16-bit) Windows 3.1 to (32-bit) Windows NT and Windows 95. It turns out that the hardware-specific 16-bit VBX controls will not serve the new 32-bit multiple platform environments as well as desired. Thus, Microsoft decided that rather than expand the VBX specifications, it would redesign the custom control architecture to include both 16-bit and 32-bit platforms. Under Windows 95 and Windows NT, OLE controls will be the natural replacement for the older VBX custom controls of Visual Basic. These new custom controls will serve container applications such as Microsoft Access, Excel, Word, PowerPoint, and so on. As a result, OLE controls have a very large potential market and should attract third-party vendors capable of designing eye-appealing as well as functional custom controls.

The good news about OLE controls, for the C++ developer, is that custom controls have a Microsoft C++ Wizard, the ControlWizard, to aid in their design, too. Like earlier OLE applications, the code developed for OLE custom controls is generated in object-oriented C++ with full use of the Microsoft Foundation Class (MFC) library.

To develop good custom controls, you will need to install the Microsoft OLE Custom Control Developer's Kit (CDK), in addition to your Microsoft Visual C++ Compiler.

Once developed, your controls can be tested with Microsoft's Test Container application provided with the developer's kit or with a container application such as Microsoft Access.

Microsoft has declared support for VBX and OLE controls in 16-bit environments. So, developers using the 16-bit version of Visual C++ will be able to continue using both types of controls. However, controls developed for 32-bit environments, using the 32-bit version of Visual C++ (version 2.0 or later), will only support OLE custom controls.

A Standard Control

Standard controls usually show up as dialog box items in most Windows programs. Here radio buttons, push buttons, and check boxes aid in data entry and user interaction with the application. These controls are typically entered with the use of the dialog box editor. The dialog editor is integrated into the Visual C++ compiler and is listed, as an option, when the Resource menu is selected and the

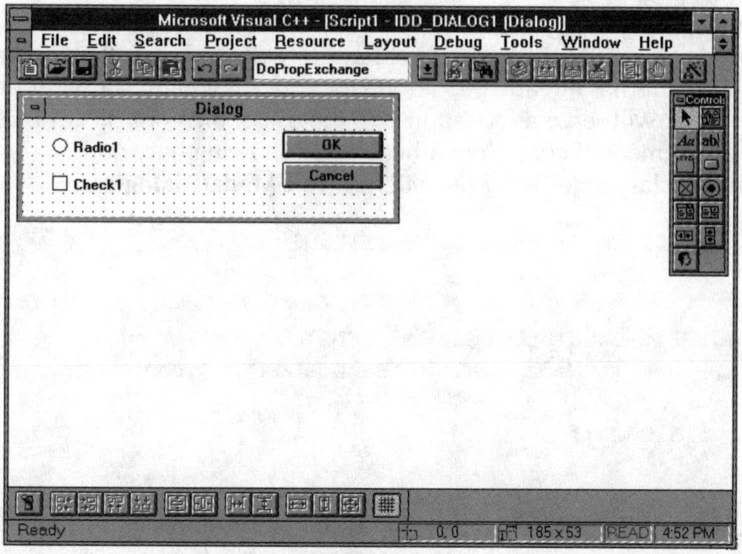

FIGURE 8-1. *A dialog box being constructed with two push buttons, a radio button, and a check box*

New menu item is chosen from the Visual C++ menu bar. Figure 8-1 shows a dialog box under construction in the resource editor. Notice that two push buttons, a radio button, and a check box have been added to the dialog box.

That dialog box information, if saved to a resource script file, will contain information used by the resource compiler when drawing and placing the controls within the dialog box. Here is a portion of a resource script file showing the four previously created standard controls.

```
IDD_DIALOG1 DIALOG DISCARDABLE  0, 0, 185, 42
STYLE DS_MODALFRAME|WS_POPUP|WS_VISIBLE|WS_CAPTION|WS_SYSMENU
CAPTION "Dialog"
FONT 8, "MS Sans Serif"
BEGIN
  DEFPUSHBUTTON "OK",IDOK,129,6,50,14
  PUSHBUTTON "Cancel",IDCANCEL,129,23,50,14
  CONTROL "Radio Button Control",IDC_RADIO1,"Button",
          BS_AUTORADIOBUTTON,4,7,104,10
  CONTROL "Check Box Control",IDC_CHECK1,"Button",
          BS_AUTOCHECKBOX|WS_TABSTOP,5,28,89,10
END
```

The beauty of standards control is in the implementation of the control—Windows handles it! You do not have to write the code that creates and places a control, this has already been done for you. All you must do is write the code segment that will serve as a response to the use of the control. For example, here is a small segment of code from a header file showing how our **CBarDataDialog** class is derived from Microsoft's **CModalDialog** class.

```
class CBarDataDialog : public CModalDialog
{
public:
  CBarDataDialog(CWnd* pParentWnd=NULL)
               : CModalDialog("BarDiaBox",pParentWnd)
               {  }
  virtual void OnOK();
};
```

The next listing shows an example of how an application's code might respond to the push of a standard OK push button located in a dialog box.

```
void CBarDataDialog::OnOK()
{
  GetDlgItemText(DM_TITLE,szTString,20);
  iBarSize[0]=GetDlgItemInt(DM_P1,NULL,0);
  iBarSize[1]=GetDlgItemInt(DM_P2,NULL,0);
  iBarSize[2]=GetDlgItemInt(DM_P3,NULL,0);
  iBarSize[3]=GetDlgItemInt(DM_P4,NULL,0);
  iBarSize[4]=GetDlgItemInt(DM_P5,NULL,0);
  iBarSize[5]=GetDlgItemInt(DM_P6,NULL,0);
  CModalDialog::OnOK();
}
```

Standard controls do not have to worry about a coupling between themselves and the application because the coupling, or communications link, is handled internally by Windows. The code for a standard control can even reside in a static link library. We are not as lucky, as you might suspect, when dealing with custom controls.

OLE Custom Controls

Standard controls can also show up as dialog box items in Windows programs. They can be placed beside standard controls such as radio buttons, push buttons, check boxes, and so on. They are, however, inherently more difficult to implement.

Unless a custom control has been supplied by a commercial vendor, you, the programmer, will be responsible for the design and implementation of a custom control. The problem is now twofold. First, during the design phase, you must create, write, and compile the code that draws the control and implements all of the control's methods, and so on. This code eventually becomes a dynamic link library with either a .DLL or .OCX file extension. Second, the application that is to use the custom control must now interface with the control's methods, data, and so on. You, too, must properly design this interface.

A properly designed OLE custom control must be independent from the application in which it is used. In other words, it must be completely reentrant. Remember that a custom control is really a dynamic linked library that is not linked to any particular application. A separate instance for data for each use of the control is required for reentrance in a DLL. The only communication allowed between an application and a custom control is via messages. Hence, a custom control must be defined in a dynamic link library.

OLE Custom Control Design Criterion

When entering the design phase for a custom control, several decisions must be made to make the custom control as appealing and functional as possible.

First, you must decide how the custom control will be drawn and displayed. Here some talent will be required to produce both attractive and functional custom controls. Custom controls are, perhaps, Microsoft's first flirt with relaxing its "common-look-and-feel standard" for all Windows applications. As a result, a tremendously profitable commercial market should open for predesigned custom controls.

Next, the custom control should be designed to take advantage of changes in control properties resulting from the automation interface of the control. Note that for custom controls so designed, property pages will allow the user to change properties at run time.

Arguments should be assigned custom controls in order to control events, set their names, and determine when they should be fired.

A control's methods should be defined in terms of arguments and return types.

Finally, the persistence of a control's various property states must be determined and implemented.

The COleControl Class

OLE custom controls are derived from Microsoft's **COleControl** class.

The next listing contains an edited portion of the AFXCTL.H header file from Microsoft's CDK, mentioned earlier. If you are interested in examining the full header file, you should be able to locate it in the CDK's **include** subdirectory.

```
///////////////////////////////////////////////////////////////
// COleControl - base class for a control implemented in C++
//               with MFC

class COleControl : public CWnd
{
  DECLARE_DYNAMIC(COleControl)

// Constructors
public:
  COleControl();

// Operations

   // Initialization
   void SetInitialSize(int cx, int cy);
   void InitializeIIDs(const IID* piidPrimary,
                       const IID* piidEvents);

   // Invalidating
   void InvalidateControl(LPCRECT lpRect = NULL);

   // Modified flag
   BOOL IsModified();
   void SetModifiedFlag(BOOL bModified = TRUE);

   // Drawing operations
   void DoSuperclassPaint(CDC* pDC, const CRect& rcBounds);

   // Property exchange
   BOOL ExchangeExtent(CPropExchange* pPX);
   void ExchangeStockProps(CPropExchange* pPX);
   BOOL ExchangeVersion(CPropExchange* pPX,
                        DWORD dwVersionDefault,
                        BOOL bConvert = TRUE);
   BOOL IsConvertingVBX();

   // Stock methods
   void Refresh();
```

```
void DoClick();

// Stock properties
OLE_COLOR GetBackColor();
void SetBackColor(OLE_COLOR);
short GetBorderStyle();
void SetBorderStyle(short);
BOOL GetEnabled();
void SetEnabled(BOOL);
CFontHolder& InternalGetFont();
LPFONTDISP GetFont();
void SetFont(LPFONTDISP);
OLE_COLOR GetForeColor();
void SetForeColor(OLE_COLOR);
OLE_HANDLE GetHwnd();
const CString& InternalGetText();
BSTR GetText();
void SetText(LPCTSTR);

// Using colors
COLORREF TranslateColor(OLE_COLOR clrColor,
                        HPALETTE hpal = NULL);

// Using fonts
CFont* SelectStockFont(CDC* pDC);
CFont* SelectFontObject(CDC* pDC, CFontHolder& fontHolder);

// Client site access
LPOLECLIENTSITE GetClientSite();

// Generic ambient property access
BOOL GetAmbientProperty(DISPID dispid, VARTYPE vtProp,
                        void* pvProp);
BOOL GetAmbientProperty(LPCTSTR pszPropName, VARTYPE vtProp,
                        void* pvProp);
BOOL WillAmbientsBeValidDuringLoad();

// Specific ambient properties
OLE_COLOR AmbientBackColor();
CString AmbientDisplayName();
LPFONTDISP AmbientFont();
OLE_COLOR AmbientForeColor();
```

```
LCID AmbientLocaleID();
CString AmbientScaleUnits();
short AmbientTextAlign();
BOOL AmbientUserMode();
BOOL AmbientUIDead();
BOOL AmbientShowGrabHandles();
BOOL AmbientShowHatching();

// Firing events
void FireEvent(DISPID dispid, BYTE FAR* pbParams, ...);

// Firing functions for stock events
void FireKeyDown(USHORT* pnChar, short nShiftState);
void FireKeyUp(USHORT* pnChar, short nShiftState);
void FireKeyPress(USHORT* pnChar);
void FireMouseDown(short nButton, short nShiftState,
  OLE_XPOS_PIXELS x, OLE_YPOS_PIXELS y);
void FireMouseUp(short nButton, short nShiftState,
  OLE_XPOS_PIXELS x, OLE_YPOS_PIXELS y);
void FireMouseMove(short nButton, short nShiftState,
  OLE_XPOS_PIXELS x, OLE_YPOS_PIXELS y);
void FireClick();
void FireDblClick();
void FireError(SCODE scode, LPCTSTR lpszDescription,
               UINT nHelpID = 0);

// Changing size and/or rectangle
BOOL GetRectInContainer(LPRECT lpRect);
BOOL SetRectInContainer(LPCRECT lpRect);
void GetControlSize(int* pcx, int* pcy);
BOOL SetControlSize(int cx, int cy);

// Window management
void RecreateControlWindow();

// Modal dialog operations
void PreModalDialog(HWND hWndParent = NULL);
void PostModalDialog(HWND hWndParent = NULL);

// Data binding operations
void BoundPropertyChanged(DISPID dispid);
BOOL BoundPropertyRequestEdit(DISPID dispid);
```

```
    BOOL BoundPropertyShowEditView(DISPID dispid);
    BOOL BoundPropertyValidateAndSave(DISPID dispid);
    BOOL BoundPropertyCancelEdit(DISPID dispid);
      .
      .
      .
      .

// Implementation
public:
    ~COleControl();

#ifdef _DEBUG
    void AssertValid() const;
    void Dump(CDumpContext& dc) const;
#endif // _DEBUG

protected:
    // Interface IDs
    const IID* m_piidPrimary;
    const IID* m_piidEvents;
    LPUNKNOWN GetInterfaceHook(const void* piid);

    // Type lib implementation
    CTypeLibCache* m_pTypeLibCache;

    // Shutdown
    virtual void OnFinalRelease();
    BOOL m_bFinalReleaseCalled;

    // Window management
    BOOL CreateControlWindow(HWND hWndParent, const CRect& rcPos);

    // Serialization
    HRESULT SaveState(IStream* pStm);
    HRESULT LoadState(IStream* pStm);
    virtual void Serialize(CArchive& ar);

    // Drawing
    void DrawContent(CDC* pDC, CRect& rc);
    void DrawMetafile(CDC* pDC, CRect& rc);
    BOOL GetMetafileData(LPFORMATETC lpFormatEtc,
```

```
                                LPSTGMEDIUM lpStgMedium);

    AFX_MODULE_STATE* m_pModuleState;
        .
        .
        .
        .
    // Stock events
    void KeyDown(UINT nChar);
    void KeyUp(UINT nChar);
    void ButtonDown(USHORT iButton, UINT nFlags, CPoint point);
    void ButtonUp(USHORT iButton, UINT nFlags, CPoint point);
    void ButtonDblClk(USHORT iButton, UINT nFlags, CPoint point);
    USHORT m_iButtonState : 3;
    USHORT m_iDblClkState : 3;

    // Masks identify which stock events and properties are used
    void InitStockEventMask();
    DWORD m_dwStockEventMask;

    void InitStockPropMask();
    DWORD m_dwStockPropMask;
        .
        .
        .
        .
// Message maps
protected:
    //{{AFX_MSG(COleControl)
    afx_msg void OnKeyDown(UINT nChar, UINT nRepCnt, UINT nFlags);
    afx_msg void OnKeyUp(UINT nChar, UINT nRepCnt, UINT nFlags);
    afx_msg void OnChar(UINT nChar, UINT nRepCnt, UINT nFlags);
    afx_msg void OnMouseMove(UINT nFlags, CPoint point);
    afx_msg void OnLButtonDown(UINT nFlags, CPoint point);
    afx_msg void OnLButtonUp(UINT nFlags, CPoint point);
    afx_msg void OnLButtonDblClk(UINT nFlags, CPoint point);
    afx_msg void OnMButtonDown(UINT nFlags, CPoint point);
    afx_msg void OnMButtonUp(UINT nFlags, CPoint point);
    afx_msg void OnMButtonDblClk(UINT nFlags, CPoint point);
    afx_msg void OnRButtonDown(UINT nFlags, CPoint point);
    afx_msg void OnRButtonUp(UINT nFlags, CPoint point);
    afx_msg void OnRButtonDblClk(UINT nFlags, CPoint point);
```

```
    afx_msg void OnInitMenuPopup(CMenu*, UINT, BOOL);
    afx_msg void OnMenuSelect(UINT nItemID, UINT nFlags,
                              HMENU hSysMenu);
    afx_msg LRESULT OnSetMessageString(WPARAM wParam,
                                       LPARAM lParam);
    afx_msg void OnEnterIdle(UINT nWhy, CWnd* pWho);
    afx_msg void OnCancelMode();
    afx_msg void OnPaint(CDC* pDC);
    afx_msg void OnSysKeyDown(UINT nChar, UINT nRepCnt,
                              UINT nFlags);
    afx_msg void OnSysKeyUp(UINT nChar, UINT nRepCnt,
                            UINT nFlags);
    afx_msg int  OnMouseActivate(CWnd *pDesktopWnd,
                                 UINT nHitTest, UINT message);
    afx_msg LRESULT OnSetText(WPARAM wParam, LPARAM lParam);
    afx_msg BOOL OnNcCreate(LPCREATESTRUCT lpCreateStruct);
    afx_msg void OnDestroy();
    afx_msg void OnKillFocus(CWnd* pNewWnd);
    afx_msg void OnSetFocus(CWnd* pOldWnd);
    //}}AFX_MSG
    DECLARE_MESSAGE_MAP()

// Interface maps
protected:
    // IPersistStorage
    BEGIN_INTERFACE_PART(PersistStorage, IPersistStorage)
      INIT_INTERFACE_PART(COleControl, PersistStorage)
        STDMETHOD(GetClassID)(LPCLSID);
        STDMETHOD(IsDirty)();
        STDMETHOD(InitNew)(LPSTORAGE);
        STDMETHOD(Load)(LPSTORAGE);
        STDMETHOD(Save)(LPSTORAGE, BOOL);
        STDMETHOD(SaveCompleted)(LPSTORAGE);
        STDMETHOD(HandsOffStorage)();
    END_INTERFACE_PART(PersistStorage)

      // IPersistStreamInit
    BEGIN_INTERFACE_PART(PersistStreamInit, IPersistStreamInit)
      INIT_INTERFACE_PART(COleControl, PersistStreamInit)
        STDMETHOD(GetClassID)(LPCLSID);
        STDMETHOD(IsDirty)();
        STDMETHOD(Load)(LPSTREAM);
```

```
    STDMETHOD(Save)(LPSTREAM, BOOL);
    STDMETHOD(GetSizeMax)(ULARGE_INTEGER FAR *);
    STDMETHOD(InitNew)();
END_INTERFACE_PART(PersistStreamInit)
    .
    .
    .
    .
// IDispatch
BEGIN_INTERFACE_PART(Dispatch, IDispatch)
  INIT_INTERFACE_PART(COleControl, Dispatch)
  STDMETHOD(GetTypeInfoCount)(unsigned int FAR* pctinfo);
  STDMETHOD(GetTypeInfo)(unsigned int itinfo, LCID lcid,
    ITypeInfo FAR* FAR* pptinfo);
  STDMETHOD(GetIDsOfNames)(REFIID riid, LPTSTR FAR* rgszNames,
    unsigned int cNames, LCID lcid, DISPID FAR* rgdispid);
  STDMETHOD(Invoke)(DISPID dispidMember, REFIID riid,
                    LCID lcid,
    unsigned short wFlags, DISPPARAMS FAR* pdispparams,
    VARIANT FAR* pvarResult, EXCEPINFO FAR* pexcepinfo,
    unsigned int FAR* puArgErr);
END_INTERFACE_PART(Dispatch)
    .
    .
    .
    .
// IProvideClassInfo
BEGIN_INTERFACE_PART(ProvideClassInfo, IProvideClassInfo)
  INIT_INTERFACE_PART(COleControl, ProvideClassInfo)
  STDMETHOD(GetClassInfo)(LPTYPEINFO FAR* ppTypeInfo);
END_INTERFACE_PART(ProvideClassInfo)

// ISpecifyPropertyPages
BEGIN_INTERFACE_PART(SpecifyPropertyPages,
                     ISpecifyPropertyPages)
  INIT_INTERFACE_PART(COleControl, SpecifyPropertyPages)
    STDMETHOD(GetPages)(CAUUID FAR*);
END_INTERFACE_PART(SpecifyPropertyPages)

// IPerPropertyBrowsing
BEGIN_INTERFACE_PART(PerPropertyBrowsing, IPerPropertyBrowsing)
  INIT_INTERFACE_PART(COleControl, PerPropertyBrowsing)
```

```
      STDMETHOD(GetDisplayString)(DISPID dispid,
                                  BSTR FAR* lpbstr);
      STDMETHOD(MapPropertyToPage)(DISPID dispid,
                                   LPCLSID lpclsid);
    STDMETHOD(GetPredefinedStrings)(DISPID dispid,
      CALPOLESTR FAR* lpcaStringsOut,
      CADWORD FAR* lpcaCookiesOut);
    STDMETHOD(GetPredefinedValue)(DISPID dispid, DWORD dwCookie,
                                  VARIANT FAR* lpvarOut);
  END_INTERFACE_PART(PerPropertyBrowsing)

  // IConnectionPointContainer
  BEGIN_INTERFACE_PART(ConnPtContainer,
                       IConnectionPointContainer)
    INIT_INTERFACE_PART(COleControl, ConnPtContainer)
    STDMETHOD(EnumConnectionPoints)(LPENUMCONNECTIONPOINTS
                                    FAR* ppEnum);
    STDMETHOD(FindConnectionPoint)(REFIID iid,
                                   LPCONNECTIONPOINT
                                   FAR* ppCP);
  END_INTERFACE_PART(ConnPtContainer)
    .
    .
    .
    .
```

Our intention in showing this partial listing was not to explain each section of the listing in detail, but to provide you with a reference as we introduce some new terms. You'll find those sections with **boldface** headers in the previous listing.

Events

Events are actions or responses that are triggered by the control in reaction to an action on the control—for example, a keypress or mouse button click.

Since your class will be derived from Microsoft's **COleControl** class, it will be able to use a new map that enables messages. These messages or events are sent to the application using the OLE control. This application is called the *control container*. The application or container will receive information about an event when something happens to the control. This event could be as simple as clicking the mouse within the control. Additional information can be provided by using event parameters. Examine the message map area of the previous listing.

A control communicates with its application (container) by firing events. OLE now provides stock and custom events to be used by your control. See the section marked **Stock events** in the previous listing. Stock events are handled by the

COleControl as a default. Custom events might be used to signal the application (container) when a control event occurs, such as receiving a message.

Methods and Properties

To make a custom control interactive, the control must expose a set of *methods* (functions) and *properties* (interface) to the application using the control. Methods are control functions that permit external code to alter characteristics of the control. Typical characteristics include appearance, properties, or behavior. Control properties, on the other hand, include the color, text, font, and so on, used in the control. Methods and properties form the basic mechanism whereby the application (container) communicates with the control. This communication allows the appearance and values of the control to be changed. Methods and properties are defined by the developer while using Microsoft's ClassWizard. Find the section defining stock methods in the previous listing. Stock methods are implemented automatically by the **COleControl** class. Custom methods can be added by the programmer if additional custom features are needed by the control.

A primary interface to the control allows early bound access to the control's methods and properties. Here object methods are exposed as methods and properties as get/set method pairs. **IDispatch** is used for late bound access. The application using the control (container) decides which type of binding is provided the user. Examine the **IDispatch** section in the previous header file.

Next find two sections in the previous listing: **Type lib implementation** and **IProvideClassInfo**. **IProvideClassInfo** returns a **CoClass TypeInfo** that describes the control.

OLE controls also provide extended properties, methods, and events. Usually this information is control-specific information needed only by the application (container).

Persistence Controls support persistence to streams through **IPersistStream** and persistence to storage through **IPersistStorage**. Both implementations can be found in the **Interface maps** section of the previous listing. **IPersistStorage** is necessary for continued support of compound document applications (containers). **IPersistStream** allows embedded controls to be saved to streams, where feasible.

Persistence permits the OLE control to read or write property values to and from a file or stream. An application (container) can use persistence to store property values for the control. These property values can then be retrieved if a new instance of the control is created.

For example, the parameter PX_Blob is used to exchange a control property that stores Binary Large Object (BLOB) data, while PX_Bool is used to exchange a control property of type BOOL.

Control Containers The standard compound document interface required for an in-place embedding container has the attributes necessary for a control container. OLE container applications were discussed in Chapter 6. In addition to the container attributes inherent in this type of container, the container must also provide two additional items: *events* and *ambient properties*.

A control actually serves as a converter when dealing with events. As such, a control must convert events from the user into events that are meaningful to the container. For each event, so converted, the container must supply an entry point in order to respond to the event.

Ambient properties refers to container properties that typically apply to all controls in the container. Examples of ambient properties include default colors and fonts.

At the time of this writing, OLE custom controls could be designed in Microsoft Visual C++ (version 2.0 and later) and tested in the Microsoft Test Container application included with the CDK. Microsoft Access also serves as a container for OLE custom controls, as you'll see in Chapter 10.

CHAPTER 9

Developing Simple Custom Controls

Custom controls developed with the 32-bit Microsoft Visual C++ compiler are actually dynamic link libraries with .OCX file extensions. The older VBX custom controls, developed with Microsoft's Visual Basic, will continue to work with applications created with the 16-bit version of Microsoft Visual C++. However, starting with the 32-bit version of Microsoft Visual C++ (version 2.0), only OLE custom controls (OCX) are allowed.

As with the OLE containers and servers created in Chapters 6 and 7, Microsoft Wizards will help make the creation of custom controls a breeze.

The custom control Wizard is named ControlWizard. This Wizard can be found by dropping down the Tools menu from the Visual C++ menu bar.

The ControlWizard will automatically create a default custom control, with only a minimal amount of additional information from the developer. The control can then be customized to suit the needs of the project. A special container application, called the Microsoft Test Container, can then be used to test the features of the custom control.

In this chapter, you will first learn the step-by-step process of creating a default custom control, named bull1. That application will be expanded and refined later in the chapter into a functional bull's-eye control, named bull2.

Creating Our First Custom Control with the ControlWizard

In this section, you will learn the step-by-step approach to creating a default custom control. Then, each of the control's C++ files will be examined and studied to better understand their function.

You'll find that building this default custom control is even easier than building OLE containers and servers. Remember that Microsoft's Wizards generate Microsoft Foundation Class (MFC) library code. If you need to review object-oriented coding techniques using the MFC library, study the material in Chapters 3 and 4.

Using ControlWizard Defaults

From the Microsoft Visual C++ menu bar, select the Tools menu. Next, choose the ControlWizard from the list of menu items, as shown in Figure 9-1.

The ControlWizard's main dialog box will then request the name of the project. Our default custom control will be named bull1. Note, in Figure 9-2, that we set our directory for the control's files off of the C drive's root directory.

At this time, no other options need to be set in the ControlWizard's main dialog box for a default custom control. Accept these values by clicking the OK push button in this dialog box.

The ControlWizard will immediately display the New Control Information dialog box, as shown in Figure 9-3.

For this example, simply click on the Create push button to accept these values.

The ControlWizard will generate two project files (files with a .MAK extension). The first project file, BULL1.MAK, can be used by the 16-bit Visual C++ compiler to generate a 16-bit version of the control. The second project file, BULL132.MAK,

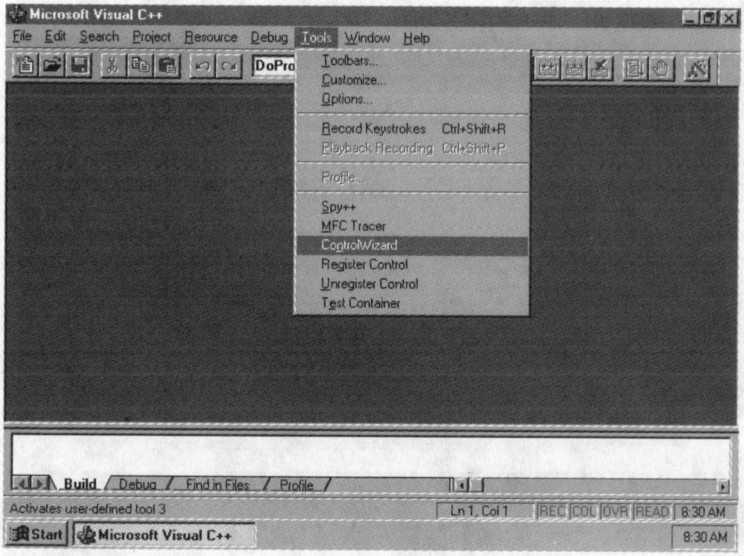

FIGURE 9-1. *Custom controls are created with the ControlWizard, located in the Tools menu*

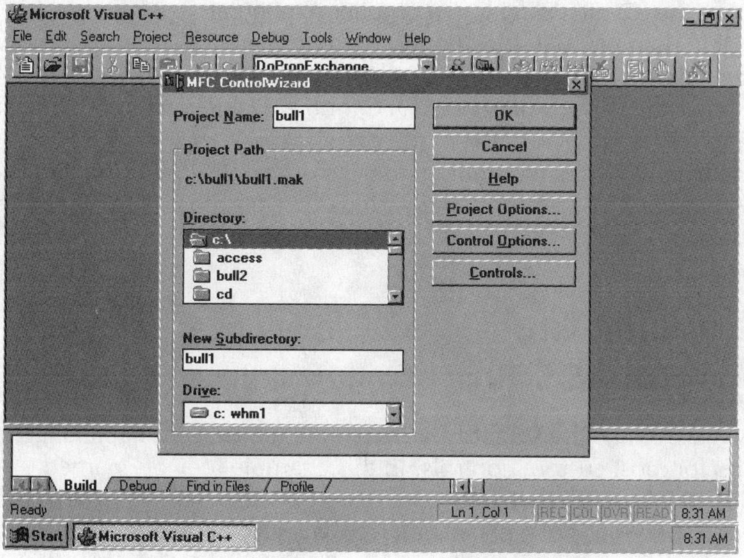

FIGURE 9-2. *The ControlWizard's main dialog box allows you to name the project and the location of the directory for the project's files*

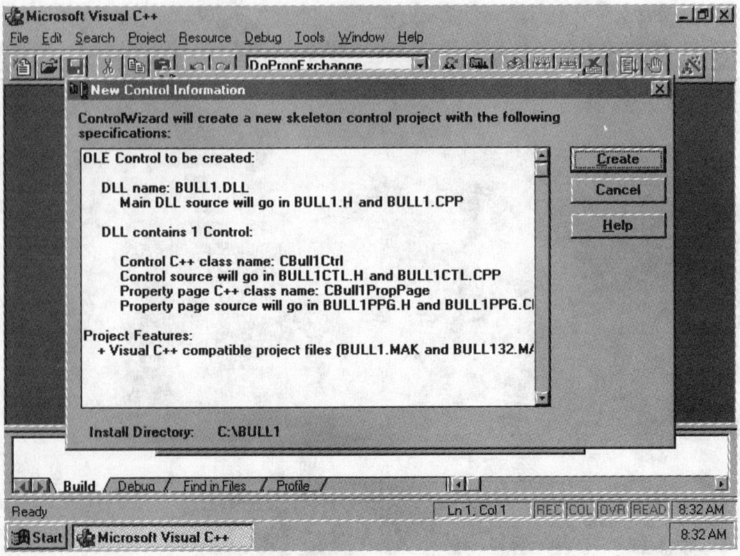

FIGURE 9-3. *The New Control Information dialog box shows a list of files that will contain information regarding the default custom control*

can be used by the 32-bit Visual C++ compiler to generate a 32-bit version of the control. For this example, we selected the 32-bit project file in order to build a 32-bit custom control for either Win95 or Windows NT.

Figure 9-4 shows the various files generated for the 32-bit version of this default custom control.

Before actually building (compiling) the custom control by using the Microsoft Visual C++ compiler, let's examine the various C++ files that were generated with the ControlWizard.

Understanding the ControlWizard's Code

The ControlWizard, like the Wizards we've studied in earlier chapters, generates four C++ files for most custom controls. In this example they are named STDAFX.CPP, BULL1.CPP, BULL1PPG.CPP, and BULL1CTL.CPP. These files, like the examples in previous chapters, also have their support header files, and so on.

This section will examine the role each of these C++ files plays in the development of the custom control, rather than discussing each OLE function in detail. You'll discover that as you add or delete features from the default custom control, some of these files will be used more than others.

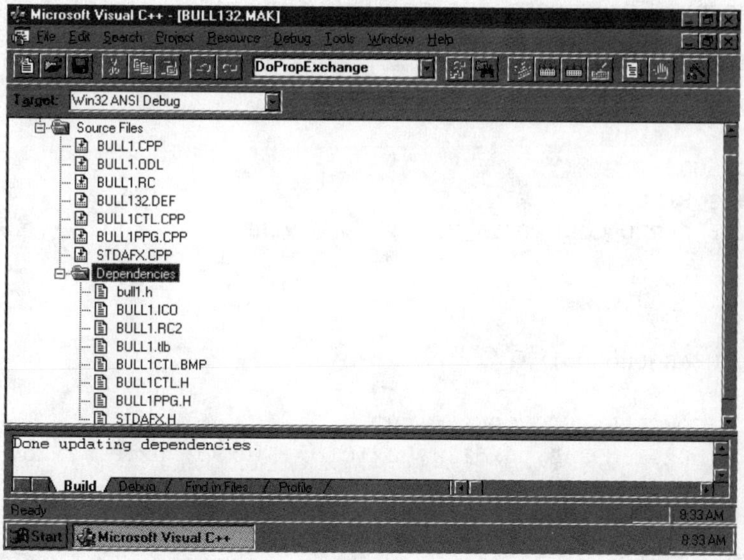

FIGURE 9-4. *The files generated by the ControlWizard for the 32-bit version of this custom control*

The STDAFX.CPP File

This is a simple source file that will use the STDAFX.H header file.

```
// stdafx.cpp : source file that includes just the standard
// includes
// stdafx.pch will be the pre-compiled header
// stdafx.obj will contain the pre-compiled type information


#include "stdafx.h"
```

This file is used to include all the standard header files that your custom control will need. Recall that for each project that uses the MFC library, the compiler creates a header file STDAFX.H that serves as a container for system and project headers. These are frequently used files whose contents do not change frequently.

The BULL1.CPP File

This file is responsible for the implementation of the **CBull1App** class and the registration of the subsequent DLL.

```
// bull1.cpp : Implementation of CBull1App and DLL registration.

#include "stdafx.h"
#include "bull1.h"

#ifdef _DEBUG
#undef THIS_FILE
static char BASED_CODE THIS_FILE[] = __FILE__;
#endif


CBull1App NEAR theApp;

const GUID CDECL BASED_CODE _tlid =
          { 0xea3d9342, 0xd13a, 0x101b, { 0x9d, 0xf9, 0x2a,
            0xa, 0x20, 0xf1, 0x29, 0x9 } };
const WORD _wVerMajor = 1;
const WORD _wVerMinor = 0;


////////////////////////////////////////////////////////////////
// CBull1App::InitInstance - DLL initialization

BOOL CBull1App::InitInstance()
{
     BOOL bInit = COleControlModule::InitInstance();

     if (bInit)
     {
          // TODO: Add your own module initialization code
          // here.
     }

     return bInit;
}


////////////////////////////////////////////////////////////////
// CBull1App::ExitInstance - DLL termination

int CBull1App::ExitInstance()
{
     // TODO: Add your own module termination code here.
```

```
    return COleControlModule::ExitInstance();
}


/////////////////////////////////////////////////////////////////
// DllRegisterServer - Adds entries to the system registry

STDAPI DllRegisterServer(void)
{
    AFX_MANAGE_STATE(_afxModuleAddrThis);

    if (!AfxOleRegisterTypeLib(AfxGetInstanceHandle(),_tlid))
        return ResultFromScode(SELFREG_E_TYPELIB);

    if (!COleObjectFactoryEx::UpdateRegistryAll(TRUE))
        return ResultFromScode(SELFREG_E_CLASS);

    return NOERROR;
}


/////////////////////////////////////////////////////////////////
// DllUnregisterServer - Removes entries from the
//                       system registry

STDAPI DllUnregisterServer(void)
{
    AFX_MANAGE_STATE(_afxModuleAddrThis);

    if (!AfxOleUnregisterTypeLib(_tlid))
        return ResultFromScode(SELFREG_E_TYPELIB);

    if (!COleObjectFactoryEx::UpdateRegistryAll(FALSE))
        return ResultFromScode(SELFREG_E_CLASS);

    return NOERROR;
}
```

As you examine the listing, notice that we've boldfaced four comments that precede four sections of code. These sections of code are responsible for DLL initialization and termination as well as for registration and deregistration of entries in the system registry.

Initialization The **InitInstance()** function is used to initialize the initial and subsequent instances for this control. Room is also provided so that programmers can add initialization code for any modules that they've written.

Termination The **ExitInstance()** function is called whenever an instance of the control is terminated. Specific module termination code can also be added to this section by programmers.

Registration Here **AfxOleRegisterTypeLib()** works in conjunction with the **UpdateRegistryAllEx()** function, with a **TRUE** parameter, to ensure that all of the application's object factories are registered with the OLE system registry. This is usually done when the application is first launched.

Deregistration Here **AfxOleUnregisterTypeLib()** works in conjunction with the **UpdateRegistryAllEx()** function, with a **FALSE** parameter, to ensure that the application's object factories are deregistered with the OLE system registry.

The BULL1PPG.CPP File

This file derives the **CBull1PropPage** class from Microsoft's **COlePropertyPage** class. Examine the following listing.

```
// bull1ppg.cpp : Implementation of the CBull1PropPage
//                property page class.

#include "stdafx.h"
#include "bull1.h"
#include "bull1ppg.h"

#ifdef _DEBUG
#undef THIS_FILE
static char BASED_CODE THIS_FILE[] = __FILE__;
#endif


IMPLEMENT_DYNCREATE(CBull1PropPage, COlePropertyPage)


/////////////////////////////////////////////////////////////////
// Message map

BEGIN_MESSAGE_MAP(CBull1PropPage, COlePropertyPage)
     //{{AFX_MSG_MAP(CBull1PropPage)
```

```
    // NOTE - ClassWizard will add and remove message map
    //        entries
    //    DO NOT EDIT what you see in these blocks of
    //    generated code !

    //}}AFX_MSG_MAP
END_MESSAGE_MAP()


/////////////////////////////////////////////////////////////
// Initialize class factory and guid

IMPLEMENT_OLECREATE_EX(CBull1PropPage, "BULL1.Bull1PropPage.1",
    0xea3d9343, 0xd13a, 0x101b, 0x9d, 0xf9, 0x2a, 0xa, 0x20,
    0xf1, 0x29, 0x9)


/////////////////////////////////////////////////////////////
// CBull1PropPage::CBull1PropPageFactory::UpdateRegistry -
// Adds or removes system registry entries for CBull1PropPage

BOOL CBull1PropPage::CBull1PropPageFactory::UpdateRegistry(BOOL
                                                   bRegister)
{
    if (bRegister)
        return AfxOleRegisterPropertyPageClass(
            AfxGetInstanceHandle(),
            m_clsid, IDS_BULL1_PPG);
    else
        return AfxOleUnregisterClass(m_clsid, NULL);
}


/////////////////////////////////////////////////////////////
// CBull1PropPage::CBull1PropPage - Constructor

CBull1PropPage::CBull1PropPage() :
    COlePropertyPage(IDD, IDS_BULL1_PPG_CAPTION)
{
    //{{AFX_DATA_INIT(CBull1PropPage)
    // NOTE: ClassWizard will add member initialization here
    //    DO NOT EDIT what you see in these blocks of
```

```
    //    generated code !

    //}}AFX_DATA_INIT
}


/////////////////////////////////////////////////////////////////////////////
// CBull1PropPage::DoDataExchange - Moves data between page
//                                  and properties

void CBull1PropPage::DoDataExchange(CDataExchange* pDX)
{
    //{{AFX_DATA_MAP(CBull1PropPage)
    // NOTE: ClassWizard will add DDP, DDX, and DDV calls here
    //    DO NOT EDIT what you see in these blocks of
    //    generated code !

    //}}AFX_DATA_MAP
    DDP_PostProcessing(pDX);
}


/////////////////////////////////////////////////////////////////////////////
// CBull1PropPage message handlers
```

The **AfxOleRegisterPropertyPageClass()** function is used to register the property page class with the registration database. This permits the property page to be used by other OLE containers that are made aware of OLE custom controls. The registry, with the property page name and its location on the system, will be updated after this function is called.

In this file also notice that **COlePropertyPage**, from which our **CBull1PropPage** class is derived, can use the constructor to identify the dialog-template resource on which the property page is based and also the string resource containing the caption.

The **DoDataExchange()** function is generally used by the framework to exchange and validate dialog data. Here its specific job is to move data between the page and properties of the control.

The BULL1CTL.CPP File

This file is used for the actual implementation of the custom control's OLE class. In this example, that class is **CBull1Ctrl**. This is the file you will most likely spend most of your time editing. In this file, you will be able to create unique implementations of your custom control from the default custom control provided by the ControlWizard. These specific pieces of code will be examined, as they are added, in this and the following chapter.

Let's examine the specific code allotted to the default custom control. Study the following listing.

```
// bull1ctl.cpp : Implementation of the CBull1Ctrl OLE control
//              class.

#include "stdafx.h"
#include "bull1.h"
#include "bull1ctl.h"
#include "bull1ppg.h"


#ifdef _DEBUG
#undef THIS_FILE
static char BASED_CODE THIS_FILE[] = __FILE__;
#endif


IMPLEMENT_DYNCREATE(CBull1Ctrl, COleControl)


/////////////////////////////////////////////////////////////
// Message map

BEGIN_MESSAGE_MAP(CBull1Ctrl, COleControl)
     //{{AFX_MSG_MAP(CBull1Ctrl)
     // NOTE - ClassWizard will add and remove message map
     //         entries
     //    DO NOT EDIT what you see in these blocks of
     //    generated code !

     //}}AFX_MSG_MAP
     ON_OLEVERB(AFX_IDS_VERB_PROPERTIES, OnProperties)
END_MESSAGE_MAP()


/////////////////////////////////////////////////////////////
// Dispatch map

BEGIN_DISPATCH_MAP(CBull1Ctrl, COleControl)
     //{{AFX_DISPATCH_MAP(CBull1Ctrl)
```

```
    // NOTE - ClassWizard will add and remove dispatch map
    //        entries
    //    DO NOT EDIT what you see in these blocks of
    //    generated code !

    //}}AFX_DISPATCH_MAP
    DISP_FUNCTION_ID(CBull1Ctrl, "AboutBox", DISPID_ABOUTBOX,
                     AboutBox, VT_EMPTY, VTS_NONE)
END_DISPATCH_MAP()


/////////////////////////////////////////////////////////////
// Event map

BEGIN_EVENT_MAP(CBull1Ctrl, COleControl)
    //{{AFX_EVENT_MAP(CBull1Ctrl)
    // NOTE - ClassWizard will add and remove event map
    //        entries
    //    DO NOT EDIT what you see in these blocks of
    //    generated code !

    //}}AFX_EVENT_MAP
END_EVENT_MAP()


/////////////////////////////////////////////////////////////
// Property pages

// TODO: Add more property pages as needed. Remember to
//       increase the count!
BEGIN_PROPPAGEIDS(CBull1Ctrl, 1)
    PROPPAGEID(CBull1PropPage::guid)
END_PROPPAGEIDS(CBull1Ctrl)


/////////////////////////////////////////////////////////////
// Initialize class factory and guid

IMPLEMENT_OLECREATE_EX(CBull1Ctrl, "BULL1.Bull1Ctrl.1",
    0x3f926480, 0xcbb7, 0x101b, 0x9d, 0xf9, 0x2a, 0xa,
    0x20, 0xf1, 0x29, 0x9)
```

```
/////////////////////////////////////////////////////////////
// Type library ID and version

IMPLEMENT_OLETYPELIB(CBull1Ctrl, _tlid, _wVerMajor,
                    _wVerMinor)


/////////////////////////////////////////////////////////////
// Interface IDs

const IID BASED_CODE IID_DBull1 =
          { 0xea3d9340, 0xd13a, 0x101b, { 0x9d, 0xf9, 0x2a,
            0xa, 0x20, 0xf1, 0x29, 0x9 } };
const IID BASED_CODE IID_DBull1Events =
          { 0xea3d9341, 0xd13a, 0x101b, { 0x9d, 0xf9, 0x2a,
            0xa, 0x20, 0xf1, 0x29, 0x9 } };


/////////////////////////////////////////////////////////////
// Control type information

static const DWORD BASED_CODE _dwBull1OleMisc =
     OLEMISC_ACTIVATEWHENVISIBLE ¦
     OLEMISC_SETCLIENTSITEFIRST ¦
     OLEMISC_INSIDEOUT ¦
     OLEMISC_CANTLINKINSIDE ¦
     OLEMISC_RECOMPOSEONRESIZE;

IMPLEMENT_OLECTLTYPE(CBull1Ctrl, IDS_BULL1, _dwBull1OleMisc)


/////////////////////////////////////////////////////////////
// CBull1Ctrl::CBull1CtrlFactory::UpdateRegistry -
// Adds or removes system registry entries for CBull1Ctrl

BOOL CBull1Ctrl::CBull1CtrlFactory::UpdateRegistry(BOOL
                                    bRegister)
{
     if (bRegister)
          return AfxOleRegisterControlClass(
```

```
                AfxGetInstanceHandle(),
                m_clsid,
                m_lpszProgID,
                IDS_BULL1,
                IDB_BULL1,
                FALSE,                //  Not insertable
                _dwBull1OleMisc,
                _tlid,
                _wVerMajor,
                _wVerMinor);
    else
        return AfxOleUnregisterClass(m_clsid, m_lpszProgID);
}


/////////////////////////////////////////////////////////////////////////////
// CBull1Ctrl::CBull1Ctrl - Constructor

CBull1Ctrl::CBull1Ctrl()
{
    InitializeIIDs(&IID_DBull1, &IID_DBull1Events);

    // TODO: Initialize your control's instance data here.
}


/////////////////////////////////////////////////////////////////////////////
// CBull1Ctrl::~CBull1Ctrl - Destructor

CBull1Ctrl::~CBull1Ctrl()
{
    // TODO: Cleanup your control's instance data here.

}


/////////////////////////////////////////////////////////////////////////////
// CBull1Ctrl::OnDraw - Drawing function

void CBull1Ctrl::OnDraw(
                CDC* pdc, const CRect& rcBounds,
                const CRect& rcInvalid)
```

```
{
    // TODO: Replace the following code with your own
    //       drawing code.
    pdc->FillRect(rcBounds,
CBrush::FromHandle((HBRUSH)GetStockObject(WHITE_BRUSH)));
    pdc->Ellipse(rcBounds);
}


/////////////////////////////////////////////////////////////
// CBull1Ctrl::DoPropExchange - Persistence support

void CBull1Ctrl::DoPropExchange(CPropExchange* pPX)
{
    ExchangeVersion(pPX, MAKELONG(_wVerMinor, _wVerMajor));
    COleControl::DoPropExchange(pPX);

    // TODO: Call PX_ functions for each persistent custom
    //       property.

}


/////////////////////////////////////////////////////////////
// CBull1Ctrl::OnResetState - Reset control to default state

void CBull1Ctrl::OnResetState()
{
    COleControl::OnResetState();

    // TODO: Reset any other control state here.
}


/////////////////////////////////////////////////////////////
// CBull1Ctrl::AboutBox - Display an "About" box to the user


void CBull1Ctrl::AboutBox()
{
    CDialog dlgAbout(IDD_ABOUTBOX_BULL1);
    dlgAbout.DoModal();
```

```
}


///////////////////////////////////////////////////////////////////////
// CBull1Ctrl message handlers
```

Notice that the message map, dispatch map, and event map are automatically created and edited by Microsoft's Wizards. Under most circumstances, you will not edit these maps.

Recall that message maps are important because they provide an alternative to the switch statement used in procedure-oriented programs to handle messages. OLE Automation includes techniques to call methods and access properties across several applications. These requests are dispatched via the dispatch map. The event map helps process custom control events.

Examine the listing and notice the boldfaced section of code used to implement the OLE type library. In general, OLE custom controls need to exchange information concerning various properties and methods. The best way to provide this information is through a type library.

As you continue reading down the listing, you will see code for updating the system registry as well as constructor code for initializing instances of the control. Three important sections of code make up the remainder of the listing.

Drawing Function This section of code is responsible for drawing the default control shape in the bounding rectangle.

```
// CBull1Ctrl::OnDraw - Drawing function

void CBull1Ctrl::OnDraw(
            CDC* pdc, const CRect& rcBounds,
            const CRect& rcInvalid)
{
    // TODO: Replace the following code with your own
    //       drawing code.
    pdc->FillRect(rcBounds,
CBrush::FromHandle((HBRUSH)GetStockObject(WHITE_BRUSH)));
    pdc->Ellipse(rcBounds);
}
```

The default shape is determined by the **Ellipse()** function. The control is bound by the bounding rectangle specified with *rcBounds* values. The rectangle is filled with the stock WHITE_BRUSH.

Persistence Support Recall that persistence permits an OLE control to read or write property values to and from a file or stream. An application (container) can use persistence to store property values for the control. These property values can then be retrieved if a new instance of the control is created. For example, the parameter *PX_Blob* is used to exchange a control property that stores binary large object (BLOB) data while *PX_Bool* is used to exchange a control property of type BOOL.

Here is the section of code that permits persistence support.

```
/////////////////////////////////////////////////////////////////////////////
// CBull1Ctrl::DoPropExchange - Persistence support

void CBull1Ctrl::DoPropExchange(CPropExchange* pPX)
{
     ExchangeVersion(pPX, MAKELONG(_wVerMinor, _wVerMajor));
     COleControl::DoPropExchange(pPX);

     // TODO: Call PX_ functions for each persistent custom
     //       property.

}
```

Notice that PX functions can be added by the programmer for each persistent property that is included.

The About Box The ControlWizard designs a default about box. The contents of this simple dialog box can be edited to suit your project's needs or used as is.

```
// CBull1Ctrl::AboutBox - Display an "About" box to the user

void CBull1Ctrl::AboutBox()
{
     CDialog dlgAbout(IDD_ABOUTBOX_BULL1);
     dlgAbout.DoModal();
}
```

As you examine the listing, note that this about box is a standard modal dialog box.

Building and Testing the Control The bull1 custom control can be built as a 16- or 32-bit control. To build this control as a 32-bit control, select the BULL132.MAK project file while running in the 32-bit version of Visual C++ (version 2.0 or later). To build this control as a 16-bit control, select the BULL1.MAK file while running in the 16-bit version of Visual C++ (version 1.5 or later).

One additional step is required if you choose to build the 16-bit version of this control. After selecting BULL1.MAK as the make file, create a type library by dropping down the Tools menu and selecting the Make TypeLib menu item. This menu item will not be present on the 32-bit Visual C++ compiler, since this process is automatic.

Compiling

From this point on, the build process is identical for both versions of the control. From the Project menu, select the Build bull1 menu item, as shown in Figure 9-5.

The 16-bit Visual C++ compiler will generate a BULL1.DLL custom control file, while the 32-bit Visual C++ compiler will generate a BULL1.OCX custom control file.

Registering the Control

Before testing a new control, the control must be registered. New custom controls can be registered and unregistered from the Visual C++ compiler's Tools menu, as shown in Figure 9-6.

For this example, select the Register Control menu item, as shown in the previous figure.

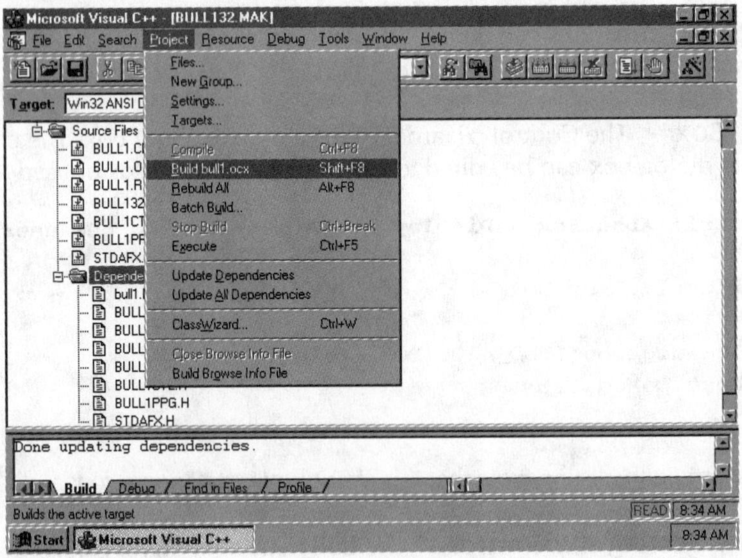

FIGURE 9-5. *Starting the build process for the bull1 custom control*

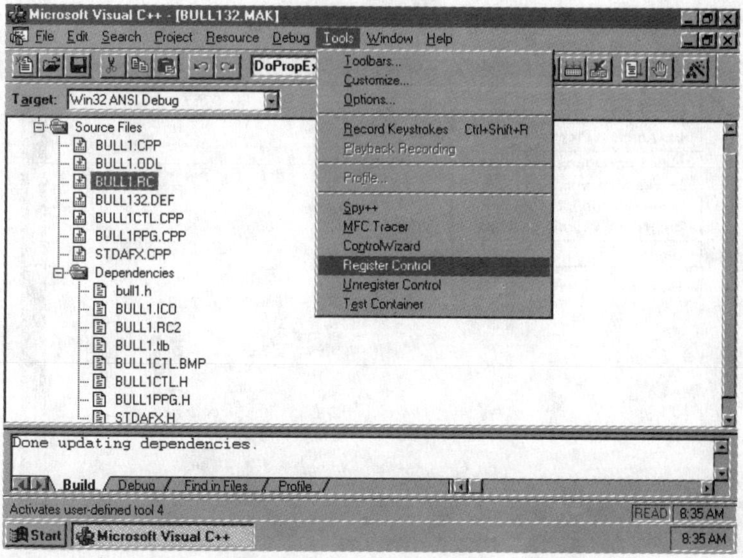

FIGURE 9-6. *Custom Controls can be registered or unregistered from within the Visual C++ compiler*

The Test Container

The Test Container is a Microsoft CDK application designed to test new custom controls. After you have properly installed your CDK tools, the option to start the Test Container application will be added to your Visual C++ Tools menu. The Test Container can be started by selecting the Test Container menu item.

To test a new control, use the Edit menu from the Test Container's menu bar to select the Insert OLE Control... menu item, as shown in Figure 9-7.

When this selection is made, the Insert OLE Control dialog box will appear, as shown in Figure 9-8.

In this case, only one control has been registered. Select the Bull1 Control item to insert your new custom control in the Test Container. Figure 9-9 shows the new control in the Test Container.

The Test Container allows the developer to put a custom control through its paces, before inserting it into a new container. For example, the Test Container will allow you to view an event log, invoke methods, set ambient properties, draw

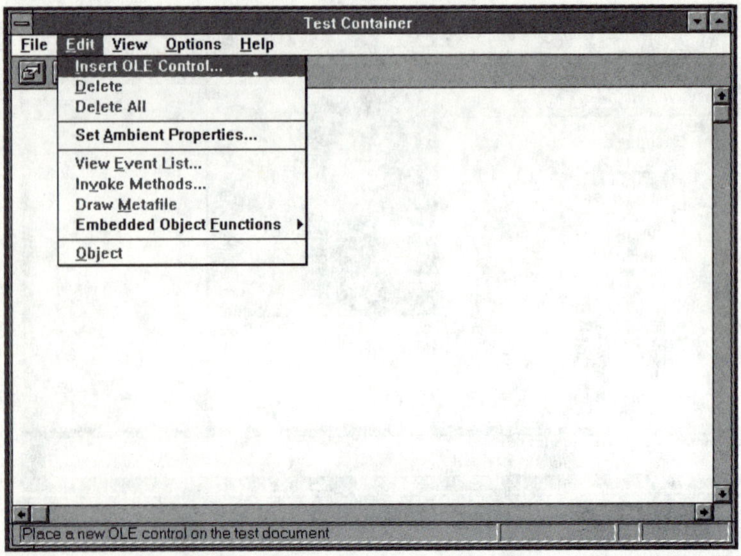

FIGURE 9-7. *The Test Container's Edit menu allows you to select your new control for testing*

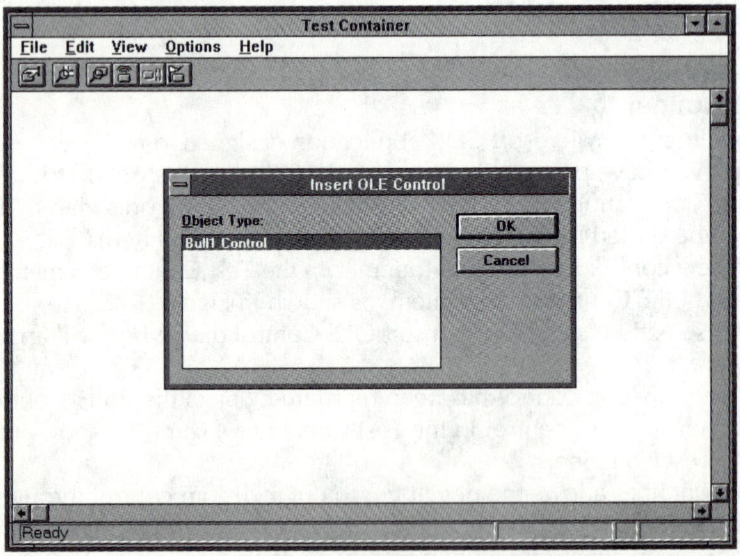

FIGURE 9-8. *The Insert OLE Control dialog box lists all registered OLE controls*

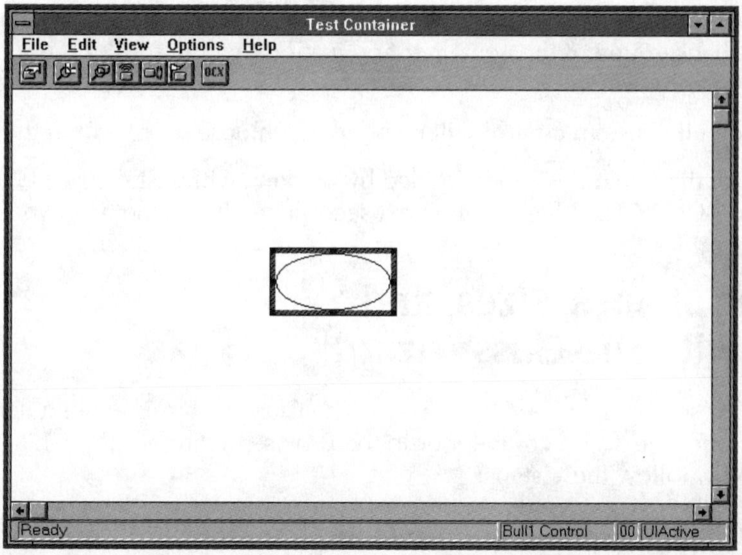

FIGURE 9-9. *A new custom control inserted in the Test Container application*

metafiles, load or save property sets, and so on. You'll learn how to use these options in later sections.

In the next section, we'll take the default custom control, which we named bull1, and create a unique custom control to meet our specific needs—a true bull's-eye control.

Creating a Bull's-eye Control

A unique custom control can be built from the default custom control produced by the ControlWizard, with the help of the ClassWizard.

To build the unique custom control for this section, repeat all of the steps in the previous section dealing with the ControlWizard, but name this default custom control bull2.

The bull2 custom control will include a number of unique features not present in the default control produced by the ControlWizard. Here is what we're going to add:

- Instead of drawing a default ellipse, the bull2 custom control will draw four different colored circles in the form of a target with a bull's-eye.

- The background of the bull2 custom control will be changed to match the background of the container application that houses the bull2 custom control.
- The bull2 custom control will respond to a mouse event within the control.
- All of these features can be added by working with just the BULL2CTL.CPP and BULL2CTL.H files. In the next section, we'll add the first two features.

Altering Shapes, Sizes, and Colors with the ClassWizard

Start the Microsoft Visual C++ ClassWizard. The ClassWizard is a menu item in the Project menu for the 32-bit compiler or in the Browse menu for the 16-bit compiler. Now follow these steps:

1. Select the OLE Automation tab.
2. Select **CBull2Ctrl** from the Class Name list box.
3. Select the Add Property button and display the Add Property dialog box.
4. In the edit control of the External Name combo box, type **BullShape**.
5. For an Implementation, select Member Variable.
6. Select BOOL from the Type list box, and observe that the Notification Function edit control contains OnBullShapeChanged.
7. Close the Add Property dialog box by selecting the OK button, and return to the OLE Automation tab.
8. Select the Add Property button, once again, and display the Add Property dialog box.
9. In the edit control of the External Name combo box, select BackColor from the list of items available.
10. For an Implementation, select Stock.
11. Close the Add Property dialog box by selecting the OK button, and return to the OLE Automation tab.
12. Select the OK push button to accept the choices and close the ClassWizard.

The ClassWizard will automatically create the code to add the BullShape and BackColor properties to the **CBull2Ctrl** class. The **CBull2Ctrl** class's dispatch map will be altered to accommodate the BullShape property, and the BackColor property is added to the BULL2.ODL library file. A declaration for **OnBullShapedChanged()** is added to the BULL2CTL.H header file.

These changes are added automatically by the ClassWizard. Now the code that reacts to these changes must be added. As we mentioned at the start of this section, these features can be added by working just the BULL2CTL.CPP and BULL2CTL.H files.

The BULL2CTL.H Header File

One small insertion must be made in the header file to accommodate a function that will be used for correctly sizing the bull's-eye target. Insert **GetDrawRect( )** immediately under the destructor shown in the following partial listing of the BULL2CTL.H header file.

```
// Implementation
 protected:
      ~CBull2Ctrl();
           .
           .
           .
      void GetDrawRect(CRect* rc);      // Draw a perfect circle
           .
           .
           .
      DECLARE_OLECREATE_EX(CBull2Ctrl) //Class factory and guid
```

Now the unique drawing code can be added to the BULL2CTL.CPP file.

The BULL2CTL.CPP File

The following code listing shows the important parts of the BULL2CTL.CPP file. This file is identical to the default file returned by the ControlWizard, except for the boldfaced code, which implements several new features.

```
// bull2ctl.cpp : Implementation of the CBull2Ctrl OLE
// control class.
      .
      .
      .
```

```
/////////////////////////////////////////////////////////////////
// CBull2Ctrl::OnDraw - Drawing function

void CBull2Ctrl::OnDraw(CDC* pdc, const CRect& rcBounds,
                        const CRect& rcInvalid)
{
    CBrush* pOldBrush;
    CBrush  NewBrush(TranslateColor(GetBackColor()));
    CPen* pOldPen;
    CRect rc1 = rcBounds;
    CRect rc2;

    // Use BackColor property to paint background
    pdc->FillRect(rcBounds, &NewBrush);

    // Prepare to draw bull's-eye target

    GetDrawRect(&rc1);
    pOldPen=(CPen*)pdc->SelectStockObject(BLACK_PEN);

    // Calculate incremental changes for circle sizes
    int deltax = (rc1.right - rc1.left)/8;
    int deltay = (rc1.bottom - rc1.top)/8;

    // Draw the largest (red) circle
    rc2.left=rc1.left;
    rc2.right=rc1.right;
    rc2.top=rc1.top;
    rc2.bottom=rc1.bottom;
    NewBrush.CreateSolidBrush(RGB(255,0,0));
    pOldBrush=(CBrush*)pdc->SelectObject(&NewBrush);
    pdc->Ellipse(rc2);

    // Draw the next size (blue) circle
    rc2.left+=deltax;
    rc2.right-=deltax;
    rc2.top+=deltay;
    rc2.bottom-=deltay;
    NewBrush.CreateSolidBrush(RGB(0,0,255));
    pOldBrush=(CBrush*)pdc->SelectObject(&NewBrush);
    pdc->Ellipse(rc2);
```

```
    // Draw the next size (yellow) circle
    rc2.left+=deltax;
    rc2.right-=deltax;
    rc2.top+=deltay;
    rc2.bottom-=deltay;
    NewBrush.CreateSolidBrush(RGB(255,255,0));
    pOldBrush=(CBrush*)pdc->SelectObject(&NewBrush);
    pdc->Ellipse(rc2);

    // Draw the (black) bull's-eye

    rc2.left+=deltax;
    rc2.right-=deltax;
    rc2.top+=deltay;
    rc2.bottom-=deltay;
    NewBrush.CreateSolidBrush(RGB(0,0,0));
    pOldBrush=(CBrush*)pdc->SelectObject(&NewBrush);
    pdc->Ellipse(rc2);

    pdc->SelectObject(pOldPen);
    pdc->SelectObject(pOldBrush);
}
    .
    .
    .
/////////////////////////////////////////////////////////////////////////////
//
// CBull2Ctrl message handlers

void CBull2Ctrl::OnBullShapeChanged()
{
    // TODO: Add notification handler code

    SetModifiedFlag();
}

void CBull2Ctrl::GetDrawRect(CRect* rc)
{
  int dx = rc->right - rc->left;
  int dy = rc->bottom - rc->top;
```

```
  if (dx > dy)
  {
    rc->left += (dx - dy) / 2;
    rc->right = rc->left + dy;
  }
  else
  {
    rc->top += (dy - dx) / 2;
    rc->bottom = rc->top + dx;
  }
}
```

The Control's Background Color The control's background color can be set to match the container's background color with just a few lines of code.

```
CBrush  NewBrush(TranslateColor(GetBackColor()));
   .
   .
   .
 // Use BackColor property to paint background
    pdc->FillRect(rcBounds, &NewBrush);
```

The **FillRect()** function will fill the bounding rectangle of the custom control with a color described by the brush returned by **TranslateColor**(**GetBackColor**()) function calls.

Selecting a background color to match the container's background eliminates a boxed-in appearance that would otherwise accompany the new control.

The Control's Shape and Size The bull's-eye target is made by drawing four concentric circles. The largest circle is drawn and filled first. In the portion of code shown next, a black pen is used to draw the shape of the circle, while the **CreateSolidBrush()** function specifies the circle's fill brush.

```
CBrush* pOldBrush;
          .
          .
          .
    CPen* pOldPen;
    CRect rc1 = rcBounds;
    CRect rc2;
          .
          .
          .
```

```
    // Prepare to draw bull's-eye target

    GetDrawRect(&rc1);
    pOldPen=(CPen*)pdc->SelectStockObject(BLACK_PEN);

    // Calculate incremental changes for circle sizes
    int deltax = (rc1.right - rc1.left)/8;
    int deltay = (rc1.bottom - rc1.top)/8;

    // Draw the largest (red) circle

    rc2.left=rc1.left;
    rc2.right=rc1.right;
    rc2.top=rc1.top;
    rc2.bottom=rc1.bottom;
    NewBrush.CreateSolidBrush(RGB(255,0,0));
    pOldBrush=(CBrush*)pdc->SelectObject(&NewBrush);
    pdc->Ellipse(rc2);
         .
         .
         .
    pdc->SelectObject(pOldPen);
    pdc->SelectObject(pOldBrush);
}
```

The three remaining circles that make up the target are drawn in a similar manner.

In order not to end up with an elliptical bull's-eye target, the smaller of the x or y extent of the bounding rectangle is used to specify the maximum diameter of the largest circle. This information is returned by a call to the **GetDrawRect()** function that we added to this listing.

So, while *rcBounds* continues to describe the bounding rectangle for the control, *rc1* (and hence *rc2*) will describe a square whose size is described by the smaller of the x or y extents of *rcBounds*.

Responding to Mouse Events

In this section, you'll learn how to make your control respond to a mouse event. Specifically, if the left mouse button is pressed while the cursor is on the bull's-eye, the bull's-eye will change color. This color change notifies the user that a "hit" has occurred.

Start the Microsoft Visual C++ ClassWizard. Again, the ClassWizard is a menu item in the Project menu for the 32-bit compiler, or in the Browse menu for the 16-bit compiler. Here are the steps needed to implement these features:

1. Select the OLE Automation tab.
2. Select **CBull2Ctrl** from the Class Name list box.
3. Select the Add Property button and display the Add Property dialog box.
4. In the edit control of the External Name combo box, type **HitColor**.
5. For an Implementation, check to make sure Member Variable is selected.
6. Select OLE_COLOR from the Type list box, and clear the Notification Function edit control.
7. Close the Add Property dialog box by selecting the OK button, and return to the OLE Automation tab.
8. Select the Message Maps tab.
9. Select **CBull2Ctrl** from the Class Name list box.
10. From the Object IDs list box, select **CBull2Ctrl**, and then view a list of messages in the Messages list box.
11. Select WM_LBUTTONDOWN from the Messages list box.
12. Choose the Add Function button.
13. Repeat this process by selecting WM_LBUTTONUP.
14. Select the OK push button to accept the choices and close the ClassWizard.

The ClassWizard will automatically create the code to add the HitColor property and the outlines for the above function implementations for the **CBull2Ctrl** class.

These changes are added automatically by the ClassWizard. Now the code that reacts to these changes must be added. Again, these features can be added by working just the BULL2CTL.CPP and BULL2CTL.H files.

The BULL2CTL.H Header File

Two additional insertions must be made in the header file to accommodate both a function that will determine if the mouse was clicked within the bull's-eye, and a function that will change the bull's-eye color when a hit occurs. Insert **InCircle()** and **HitColor()** just under the destructor shown in the following partial listing of the BULL2CTL.H header file.

```
// Implementation
protected:
    ~CBull2Ctrl();
        .
        .
        .
    BOOL InCircle(CPoint& point);      // Hit the bull's-eye?
    void HitColor(CDC* pdc)            // Blink the color if hit
    void GetDrawRect(CRect* rc);       // Draw a perfect circle
        .
        .
        .
    DECLARE_OLECREATE_EX(CBull2Ctrl) //Class factory and guid
```

Now the code can be added to detect mouse clicks within the control.

The BULL2CTL.CPP File

The first insertion in this listing is needed to specify the color that the bull's-eye must change to when a hit occurs. This is handled by the **DoPropExchange()** function. Here is the **DoPropExchange()** function in this program. The new line is in boldface.

```
void CBull2Ctrl::DoPropExchange(CPropExchange* pPX)
{
    ExchangeVersion(pPX, MAKELONG(_wVerMinor, _wVerMajor));
    COleControl::DoPropExchange(pPX);

    PX_Long(pPX, _T("HitColor"), (long &)m_hitColor,
            RGB(127,127,127));
}
```

This function is responsible for initializing the *m_hitColor* member variable to gray. The variable *m_hitColor* must be cast to a long, since it is an unsigned long value.

Next, the action for the mouse left button down and up must be specified. The ClassWizard added the **OnLButtonDown()** and **OnLButtonUp()** function outlines. The boldfaced code in the following listing, is our unique code for this application.

```
void CBull2Ctrl::OnLButtonDown(UINT nFlags, CPoint point)
{
    CDC* pdc;

    // Blink the color if within the bull's-eye
```

```
    if (InCircle(point))
    {
        pdc = GetDC();
        HitColor(pdc);
        ReleaseDC(pdc);
    }
    COleControl::OnLButtonDown(nFlags, point);
}

void CBull2Ctrl::OnLButtonUp(UINT nFlags, CPoint point)
{
    if (InCircle(point))
        InvalidateControl();

    COleControl::OnLButtonUp(nFlags, point);
}
```

This code checks to make sure the left mouse button was clicked within the bull's-eye. If so, the **HitColor()** function will be called to change the color of the whole bull's-eye target control.

When the left mouse button is released, the **OnLButtonUp()** function merely invalidates the control, forcing a repaint in the normal colors.

The **InCircle()** function is used to determine if the left mouse button was depressed within the bull's-eye. All of the following code must be added to the end of the BULL2CTL.CPP listing.

```
BOOL CBull2Ctrl::InCircle(CPoint& point)
{
  CRect rc;
    GetClientRect(rc);
    GetDrawRect(&rc);

    // Determine center point
    double h = (rc.right - rc.left) / 2;
    double k = (rc.bottom - rc.top) / 2;

    // Determine x, y values
    double x = point.x - (rc.right + rc.left) / 2;
    double y = point.y - (rc.bottom + rc.top) / 2;

    // Use ellipse equation for point within bull's-eye
```

```
    return ((x * x) / (h * h) + (y * y) / (k * k)) <= .125;
}
```

This function locates the center of the bull's-eye target control, then determines if the hit occurred within the actual bull's-eye—hence the .125 value in the equation for an ellipse.

If the point is within the bull's-eye, the **HitColor()** function is called. All of the code in the following function must be added to the end of the BULL2CTL.CPP listing.

```
void CBull2Ctrl::HitColor(CDC* pdc)
{
    CBrush* pOldBrush;
        CBrush hitBrush(TranslateColor(m_hitColor));
        CPen* pOldPen;
        CRect rc;

        // If mouse point is within bull's-eye only, change color
        // of whole target
        GetClientRect(rc);
        GetDrawRect(&rc);
        pOldBrush=pdc->SelectObject(&hitBrush);
        pOldPen=(CPen*)pdc->SelectStockObject(BLACK_PEN);
        pdc->Ellipse(rc);
        pdc->SelectObject(pOldPen);
        pdc->SelectObject(pOldBrush);
}
```

This function merely selects the gray brush, described earlier, and repaints the entire target area. Recall that the **OnDraw()** function painted four different colored circles.

Build the control, in the normal manner, with your Visual C++ compiler. Remember that one additional step is required if you choose to build the 16-bit version of this control. After selecting the 16-bit BULL2.MAK project file, create a type library by dropping down the Tools menu and selecting the Make TypeLib menu item. This menu item will not be present on the 32-bit Visual C++ compiler, since this process is automatic.

Remember also to register the control while in the Visual C++ compiler.

The Test Container

Now the Test Container can be used to test our unique bull's-eye control.

To test the bull's-eye control, use the Edit menu from the Test Container's menu bar to select the Insert OLE Control... menu item, as shown earlier in this chapter.

When this selection is made, the new control will be available from the Insert OLE Control dialog box. Select the Bull2 Control item to insert your new custom control in the test container. Figure 9-10 shows the bull's-eye control inserted in the Microsoft Test Container.

The Test Container can be used to test several features of a new control. For example, Figure 9-11 shows how the control responds to a mouse hit at the center of the control.

The Test Container can be used to view control properties. From the View menu select the Properties... menu item, as shown in Figure 9-12.

The Properties dialog box, shown in Figure 9-13, will allow you to select the property you wish to change. In this example, we'll alter the BackColor property.

Once the property is selected, click on the Value box and display the group of colors that can be substituted for the current background color, as shown in Figure 9-14.

It is also possible to alter the BackColor value by entering a new color value in the Value box. Try testing some of the control's other properties.

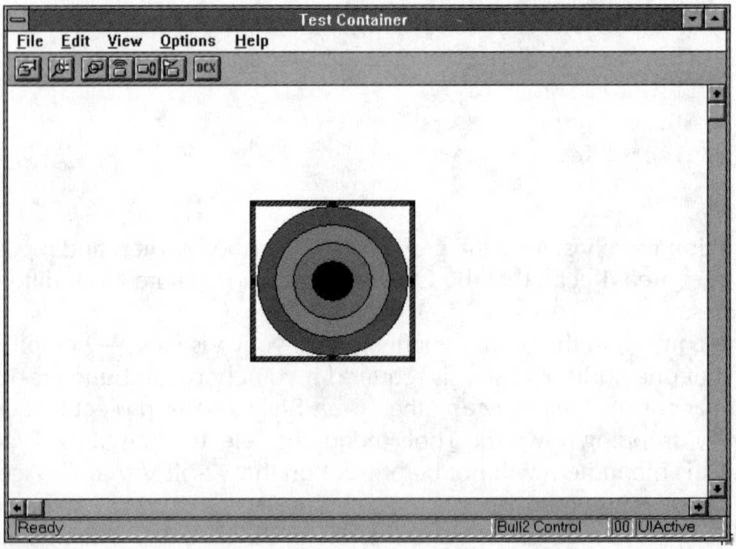

FIGURE 9-10. *The new bull's-eye target control*

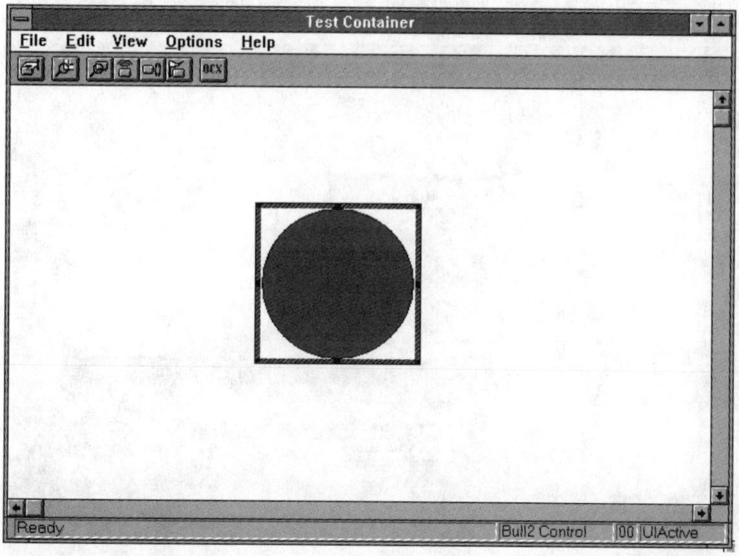

FIGURE 9-11. *The bull's-eye target control will turn gray when a mouse hit occurs in the bull's-eye*

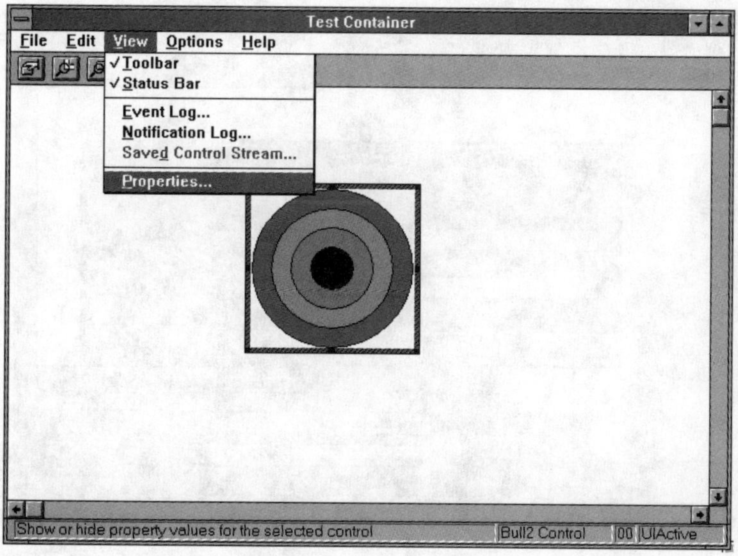

FIGURE 9-12. *Control properties can be viewed and changed from within the Test Container*

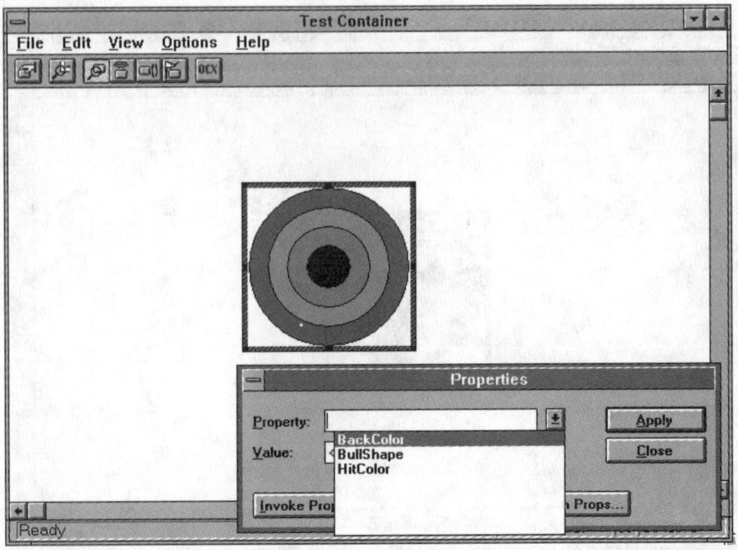

FIGURE 9-13. *The Properties dialog box allows you to select the property you wish to alter*

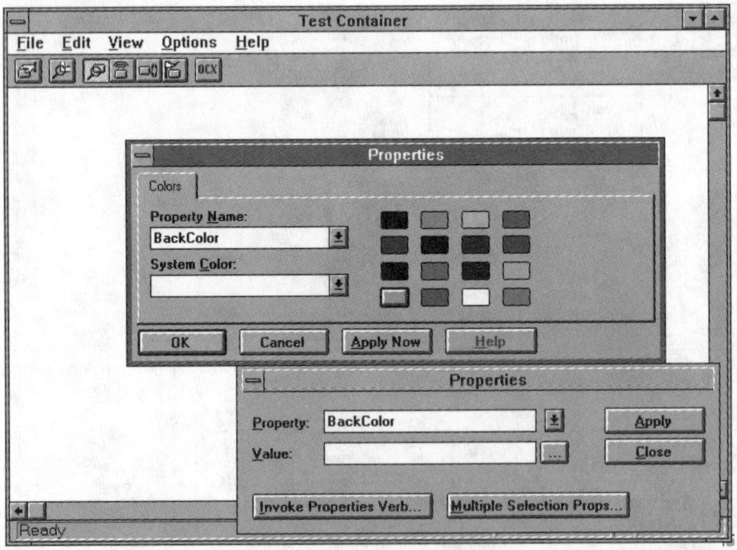

FIGURE 9-14. *The BackColor value will be changed by selecting a new color from the palette*

What's Next?

In the next chapter, you will learn how to incorporate more advanced features into a custom control. These features include adding custom notification properties, custom get/set properties, custom events, text and fonts, and so on.

CHAPTER 10

Developing More Complex Custom Controls

The custom control developed in this chapter will include many of the features of the previous bull's-eye custom control and yet add new features such as captions, labels, property page modifications, and data binding.

We'll start building our new custom control with the help of the ControlWizard, which automatically creates a default custom control. The control will then be customized to suit this project. Near the end of this chapter, the completed control will be tested in the Microsoft Test Container application. Here you'll see a demonstration of many of the new custom control features.

Creating a Temperature Control

The custom control developed in this chapter is a temperature custom control. This custom control can be built from the default custom control produced by the ControlWizard, with the help of the ClassWizard.

To build the temperature custom control for this chapter, repeat all of the steps from the previous chapter to build a default custom control. However, for this control, name the control htcd. This stands for "hot-cold," which will be an important feature of this control.

The temperature custom control will include a number of features. See if you can identify the features in this control that were not present in the previous chapter. To the default custom control, we'll add the following:

- Instead of drawing a default ellipse, the control will draw a rounded rectangle that will serve as the shape for the control.
- The background of the control will be changed to match the background of the container application that houses the custom control.
- The control will respond to both left and right mouse button events when depressed within the control.

The control will change foreground colors to reflect a hit. Three colors are used to indicate different temperature settings.

- The control will allow us to place a caption in the control in a specified font.
- The control will indicate the date and time the hot or cold temperatures were set.
- The control will allow us to enter a string of details relating to the control.

Most of these features can be added by working with just the HTCDCTL.CPP and HTCDCTL.H files. In the next section, we'll add the first two features to the default control.

Altering Shapes, Sizes, and Colors with the ClassWizard

To start this section, you must have successfully built a default custom control, with the ControlWizard, named htcdctl. If you have not completed the default custom control, follow the steps in the previous chapter for using the ControlWizard.

Use either the 16-bit or 32-bit project files (HTCD.MAK or NTCD32.MAK) and start the ClassWizard from within Microsoft Visual C++. Remember that the ClassWizard is a menu item in the Project menu for the 32-bit compiler, or in the Browse menu for the 16-bit compiler. Now follow these steps:

1. Select the OLE Automation tab.
2. Select **CHtcdCtrl** from the Class Name list box.
3. Select the Add Property button and display the Add Property dialog box.
4. In the edit control of the External Name combo box, select BackColor from the list of items available.
5. For an Implementation, select Stock.
6. Close the Add Property dialog box by selecting the OK button, and return to the OLE Automation tab.
7. Select the OK push button to accept the choices and close the ClassWizard.

The ClassWizard will automatically create the code to add the BackColor properties to the **CHtcdCtrl** class. The **CHtcdCtrl** class's dispatch map will be altered to accommodate the property, and BackColor is added to the HTCDCTL.ODL library file.

This background color change feature is added automatically by the ClassWizard. Now the code that reacts to this change as well as the code for drawing the basic control must be added.

The HTCDCTL.CPP File

The following code shows the changes that were made in the HTCDCTL.CPP file. This file is identical to the default file returned by the ControlWizard, except for the new code added to the **OnDraw()** function.

```
/////////////////////////////////////////////////////////////////////
// CHtcdCtrl::OnDraw - Drawing function

void CHtcdCtrl::OnDraw(
        CDC* pdc, const CRect& rcBounds, const CRect& rcInvalid)
{
  CBrush* pOldBrush;
  CBrush NewBrush(TranslateColor(GetBackColor()));
  CPen* pOldPen;
  CRect rc = rcBounds;
  POINT pt;

  // Fill background with brush color returned by BackColor()
  pdc->FillRect(rcBounds, &NewBrush);

  // Draw control using defined pen
  pOldPen = (CPen*)pdc->SelectStockObject(BLACK_PEN);

  pt.x = 40; // rounding values for RoundRect() function
  pt.y = 40;
  NewBrush.CreateSolidBrush(RGB(0, 255, 0));  // green brush
  pOldBrush = (CBrush*)pdc->SelectObject(&NewBrush);
  pdc->RoundRect(rcBounds, pt);

  pdc->SelectObject(pOldPen);
  pdc->SelectObject(pOldBrush);
}
```

The Background Color The control's background color can be set to match the container's background color with just a few lines of code.

```
CBrush  NewBrush(TranslateColor(GetBackColor()));
      .
      .
      .
// Fill background with brush color returned by BackColor()
pdc->FillRect(rcBounds, &NewBrush);
```

The **FillRect()** function will fill the bounding rectangle, which holds the custom control, with a color described by the brush returned by **TranslateColor(GetBackColor())** function calls.

It is best to set the background color to match the container's background. This prevents a boxed-in appearance that would otherwise accompany the new control.

The Control's Shape The new control is drawn with a black pen and filled with green, as can be seen in the following partial listing of **OnDraw()**.

```
CBrush* pOldBrush;
  CBrush NewBrush(TranslateColor(GetBackColor()));
  CPen* pOldPen;
     .
     .
     .
  POINT pt;
     .
     .
     .
  // Draw control using defined pen
  pOldPen = (CPen*)pdc->SelectStockObject(BLACK_PEN);

  pt.x = 40; // rounding values for RoundRect() function
  pt.y = 40;
  NewBrush.CreateSolidBrush(RGB(0, 255, 0));  // green brush
  pOldBrush = (CBrush*)pdc->SelectObject(&NewBrush);
  pdc->RoundRect(rcBounds, pt);
```

As you study this listing, notice the rounding values that are used for the **RoundRect**() function. You might want to experiment with different values. Depending on the values selected, the rounded rectangle can be changed from a rectangle, with little rounding, to an ellipse with a lot of rounding.

Responding to Mouse Events

In this section, the control will be made to respond to two specific mouse events: a depressed left or a depressed right mouse button. Specifically, if the left mouse button is pressed while the cursor is in the control, the control will turn red to indicate a hot temperature. If the right mouse button is pressed while the cursor is in the control, the control will turn blue to indicate a cold temperature. Either color change notifies the user that a hit has occurred.

To add these features, start the Microsoft Visual C++ ClassWizard. Recall that the ClassWizard is a menu item in the Project menu for the 32-bit compiler, or in the Browse menu for the 16-bit compiler. Here are the steps needed to implement these features:

1. Select the OLE Automation tab.
2. Select **CHtcdCtrl** from the Class Name list box.

3. Select the Add Property button and display the Add Property dialog box.
4. In the edit control of the External Name combo box, type **HotColor**.
5. For an Implementation, check to make sure Member Variable is selected.
6. Select OLE_COLOR from the Type list box, and clear the Notification Function edit control.
7. Again, select the Add Property button and display the Add Property dialog box.
8. In the edit control of the External Name combo box, type **ColdColor**.
9. For an Implementation, check to make sure Member Variable is selected.
10. Select OLE_COLOR from the Type list box, and clear the Notification Function edit control.
11. Close the Add Property dialog box by selecting the OK button, and return to the OLE Automation tab.
12. Select the Message Maps tab.
13. Select **CHtcdCtrl** from the Class Name list box.
14. From the Object IDs list box, select **CHtcdCtrl**, and then view a list of messages in the Messages list box.
15. Select WM_LBUTTONDOWN from the Messages list box.
16. Choose the Add Function button.
17. Now repeat this process and select WM_RBUTTONDOWN.
18. Choose the Add Function button.
19. Select the OK push button to accept the choices and close the ClassWizard.

The ClassWizard will automatically create the code to add the HotColor property and the ColdColor property code outlines to the **CHtcdCtrl** class.

These changes are added automatically by the ClassWizard. Once these steps are completed, the code that reacts to these changes must be added.

The HTCDCTL.H Header File

Two additional insertions must be made in the header file to accommodate the functions that will determine whether a left or right mouse button was clicked within the control. Insert **HotColor()** and **ColdColor()**, shown in boldface, just under the destructor in the following partial listing of the HTCDCTL.H header file.

```
// Implementation
protected:
  ~CHtcdCtrl();
  void HotColor(CDC* pdc);          // Hot color function
  void ColdColor(CDC* pdc);         // Cold color function
  DECLARE_OLECREATE_EX(CHtcdCtrl) // Class factory and guid
      .
      .
      .
```

Now the code for both functions can be added to the HTCDCTL.CPP file.

The HTCDCTL.CPP File

Several insertions are made in this file by the ClassWizard. Other changes must be made by the developer. Let's examine them one by one.

DoPropExchange() Function The first piece of code is needed to specify the color that the control must change to when a left or right mouse hit occurs. This is handled by the **DoPropExchange()** function. Here is the **DoPropExchange()** function for this program, showing the new lines of code in boldface.

```
////////////////////////////////////////////////////////////////////
// CHtcdCtrl::DoPropExchange - Persistence support

void CHtcdCtrl::DoPropExchange(CPropExchange* pPX)
{
  ExchangeVersion(pPX, MAKELONG(_wVerMinor, _wVerMajor));
  COleControl::DoPropExchange(pPX);

  PX_Long(pPX, _T("HotColor"), (long &)m_hotColor,
          RGB(255,0,0));  // red
  PX_Long(pPX, _T("ColdColor"), (long &)m_coldColor,
          RGB(0,0,255));  // blue
}
```

This function is responsible for initializing the *m_hotColor* member variable to red and *m_coldColor* to blue. These variables must be cast to a long, since they return an unsigned long value.

The OnLButtonDown() and OnRButtonDown() Functions

Next, the action for the left or right mouse button down must be added. Recall that the ClassWizard added the **OnLButtonDown()** and **OnRButtonDown()** function outlines. The boldface code in the following listing is our unique code for this application.

```
/////////////////////////////////////////////////////////////////////
// CHtcdCtrl message handlers

void CHtcdCtrl::OnLButtonDown(UINT nFlags, CPoint point)
{
  CDC* pdc;

  // change to hot color (red)
  pdc = GetDC();
  HotColor(pdc);
  ReleaseDC(pdc);

  COleControl::OnLButtonDown(nFlags, point);
}

void CHtcdCtrl::OnRButtonDown(UINT nFlags, CPoint point)
{
  CDC* pdc;

  // change to cold color (blue)
  pdc = GetDC();
  ColdColor(pdc);
  ReleaseDC(pdc);

  COleControl::OnRButtonDown(nFlags, point);
}
```

This code checks to make sure the left or right mouse button was clicked within the control. If so, the **HotColor()** or **ColdColor()** function will be called to change the color of the whole control.

When the appropriate mouse button is released, the control color will remain as changed.

The HotColor() and ColdColor() Functions If the left mouse button is clicked, the **HotColor()** function will be called. If the right button is clicked, the **ColdColor()** function will be called.

All of the code in the listing must be added to the end of the HTCDCTL.CPP listing.

```
void CHtcdCtrl::HotColor(CDC* pdc)
{
```

```
  CBrush* pOldBrush;
  CBrush NewBrush(TranslateColor(m_hotColor));
  CPen* pOldPen;
  CRect rc;
  POINT pt;
  struct tm *date_time;
  time_t timer;

  GetClientRect(rc);
  pOldBrush = pdc->SelectObject(&NewBrush);
  pOldPen = (CPen*)pdc->SelectStockObject(BLACK_PEN);

  pt.x=40;  // rounding values for RoundRect() function
  pt.y=40;
  pdc->RoundRect(rc, pt);

  // get date and time information
  time(&timer);
  date_time=localtime(&timer);
  const CString& strtime = asctime(date_time);

  pdc->SetTextAlign(TA_CENTER | TA_TOP);
  pdc->ExtTextOut((rc.left + rc.right) / 2,
               rc.top + rc.bottom - tm.tmHeight,
               ETO_CLIPPED, rc, strtime,
               strtime.GetLength()-1, NULL);

  pdc->SelectObject(pOldPen);
  pdc->SelectObject(pOldBrush);
}

void CHtcdCtrl::ColdColor(CDC* pdc)
{
  CBrush* pOldBrush;
  CBrush NewBrush(TranslateColor(m_coldColor));
  CPen* pOldPen;
  CRect rc;
  POINT pt;
  struct tm *date_time;
  time_t timer;

  GetClientRect(rc);
```

```
    pOldBrush = pdc->SelectObject(&NewBrush);
    pOldPen = (CPen*)pdc->SelectStockObject(BLACK_PEN);

    pt.x=40;  // rounding values for RoundRect() function
    pt.y=40;
    pdc->RoundRect(rc, pt);

    // get date and time information
    time(&timer);
    date_time=localtime(&timer);
    const CString& strtime = asctime(date_time);

    pdc->SetTextAlign(TA_CENTER | TA_TOP);
    pdc->ExtTextOut((rc.left + rc.right) / 2,
                    rc.top + rc.bottom - tm.tmHeight,
                    ETO_CLIPPED, rc, strtime,
                    strtime.GetLength()-1, NULL);

    pdc->SelectObject(pOldPen);
    pdc->SelectObject(pOldBrush);
}
```

If you study the listing, you will note that both functions are similar. When either function is called, the control will be redrawn with a black pen and filled with the appropriate brush (red or blue). Additionally, the date and time the control was set to hot or cold will be recorded and printed in the control. Standard C/C++ function calls are used for this purpose.

You could rebuild and test the control at this point, but there are several other features that we want to add first.

Stock Fonts and Captions

Many developers and users find the ability to add labels and captions to controls a useful feature. In this section we'll show you how to select a stock font, set its drawing color, and then how to create a caption within the control.

To add these features, start the Microsoft Visual C++ ClassWizard. Here are the steps needed to implement these three features:

1. Select the OLE Automation tab.
2. Select **CHtcdCtrl** from the Class Name list box.
3. Select the Add Property button and display the Add Property dialog box.

4. In the edit control of the External Name combo box, select Caption.
5. For an Implementation, choose Stock.
6. Choose OK to close the Add Property dialog box.
7. Again, select the Add Property button and display the Add Property dialog box.
8. In the edit control of the External Name combo box, select Font.
9. For an Implementation, choose Stock.
10. Choose OK to close the Add Property dialog box.
11. Again, select the Add Property button and display the Add Property dialog box.
12. In the edit control of the External Name combo box, select ForeColor.
13. For an Implementation, choose Stock.
14. Choose OK to close the Add Property dialog box.
15. Select the OK push button to accept the choices and close the ClassWizard.

The ClassWizard will automatically add the Caption, ForeColor, and Font properties to the **CHtcdCtrl** class and make them available for our use.

The HTCDCTL.CPP File

Again, the changes needed to implement these features are added either by the ClassWizard or by the developer. For example, the Dispatch map is modified automatically by the ClassWizard, while the feature-specific code must be added in the **OnDraw()**, **HotColor()**, and **ColdColor()** functions.

The Dispatch Map The ClassWizard has modified the class dispatch map, in the HTCDCTL.CPP file, to add these properties. Examine the following partial listing for all three features.

```
/////////////////////////////////////////////////////////////////////
// Dispatch map

BEGIN_DISPATCH_MAP(CHtcdCtrl, COleControl)
  //{{AFX_DISPATCH_MAP(CHtcdCtrl)
  DISP_PROPERTY(CHtcdCtrl, "HotColor", m_hotColor, VT_COLOR)
  DISP_PROPERTY(CHtcdCtrl, "ColdColor", m_coldColor, VT_COLOR)
  DISP_PROPERTY_EX(CHtcdCtrl, "Details", GetDetails,
```

```
                    SetDetails, VT_BSTR)
  DISP_STOCKPROP_BACKCOLOR()
  DISP_STOCKPROP_CAPTION()
  DISP_STOCKPROP_FONT()
  DISP_STOCKPROP_FORECOLOR()
  //}}AFX_DISPATCH_MAP
  DISP_FUNCTION_ID(CHtcdCtrl, "AboutBox", DISPID_ABOUTBOX,
                    AboutBox, VT_EMPTY, VTS_NONE)
END_DISPATCH_MAP()
```

The Property Page ID Table Three property pages will be needed for the addition of the color and font features. Make the changes, shown in boldface, to your Property page section.

```
/////////////////////////////////////////////////////////////////////////////
// Property pages

// TODO: Add more property pages as needed.
// Remember to increase the count!
BEGIN_PROPPAGEIDS(CHtcdCtrl, 3)
  PROPPAGEID(CHtcdPropPage::guid)
  PROPPAGEID(CLSID_CColorPropPage)
  PROPPAGEID(CLSID_CFontPropPage)
END_PROPPAGEIDS(CHtcdCtrl)
```

Now it is just a matter of modifying the **OnDraw()**, **HotColor()**, and **ColdColor()** functions to take advantage of these features.

The OnDraw(), HotColor(), and ColdColor() Functions

Since all three of these functions are similar, we'll show you the changes that were made to the **OnDraw()** function. You should also add this code to the **HotColor()** and **ColdColor()** functions. The additions are shown in boldface.

```
/////////////////////////////////////////////////////////////////////////////
// CHtcdCtrl::OnDraw - Drawing function

void CHtcdCtrl::OnDraw(
      CDC* pdc, const CRect& rcBounds, const CRect& rcInvalid)
{
  CBrush* pOldBrush;
  CBrush NewBrush(TranslateColor(GetBackColor()));
  CPen* pOldPen;
```

```
   CRect rc = rcBounds;
   CFont* pOldFont;
   TEXTMETRIC tm;
   const CString& strCaption = InternalGetText();
   POINT pt;

   // Fill background with brush color returned by BackColor()
   pdc->FillRect(rcBounds, &NewBrush);

   // Background mode to transparent
   pdc->SetBkMode(TRANSPARENT);

   // Set foreground color for text
   pdc->SetTextColor(TranslateColor(GetForeColor()));

   // Draw control using defined pen
   pOldPen = (CPen*)pdc->SelectStockObject(BLACK_PEN);

   pt.x=40;  // rounding values for RoundRect() function
   pt.y=40;
   NewBrush.CreateSolidBrush(RGB(0, 255, 0));   // green brush
   pOldBrush=(CBrush*)pdc->SelectObject(&NewBrush);
   pdc->RoundRect(rcBounds, pt);

   // Draw the control's caption
   pOldFont = SelectStockFont(pdc);
   pdc->GetTextMetrics(&tm);
   pdc->SetTextAlign(TA_CENTER | TA_TOP);
   pdc->ExtTextOut((rc.left + rc.right) / 2,
               rc.top,
               ETO_CLIPPED, rc, strCaption,
               strCaption.GetLength(), NULL);

   pdc->SelectObject(pOldPen);
   pdc->SelectObject(pOldBrush);
   pdc->SelectObject(pOldFont);
}
```

Note a couple of things about this rather straightforward implementation. The TRANSPARENT background mode is used so that the color surrounding each character of the caption will match the background of the control. The **SetTextAlign()** and **ExtTextOut()** functions set the alignment and placement of the caption within the control. The caption will be clipped to fit the control's bounding rectangle, then centered horizontally at the top of the control.

Again, these new features could be tested at this point, but there are two features that need to be added before our control is complete.

Altering the Default Property Page

In the previous section, we altered the number of property page IDs to accommodate the addition of fonts and colors. The ControlWizard supplied a default property page to this project. The default property page is a dialog box that can be edited in the Resource Editor like any other dialog box.

Open the HTCD.RC resource file for editing in either the 16-bit or 32-bit version Visual C++ compiler. While the actual steps vary between the two compiler versions, the process is essentially the same. You will need to open and edit the IDD_PROPPAGE_HTCD dialog box. When that dialog box is opened, you will find it initially empty. Alter this dialog box by adding the controls shown in Figure 10-1.

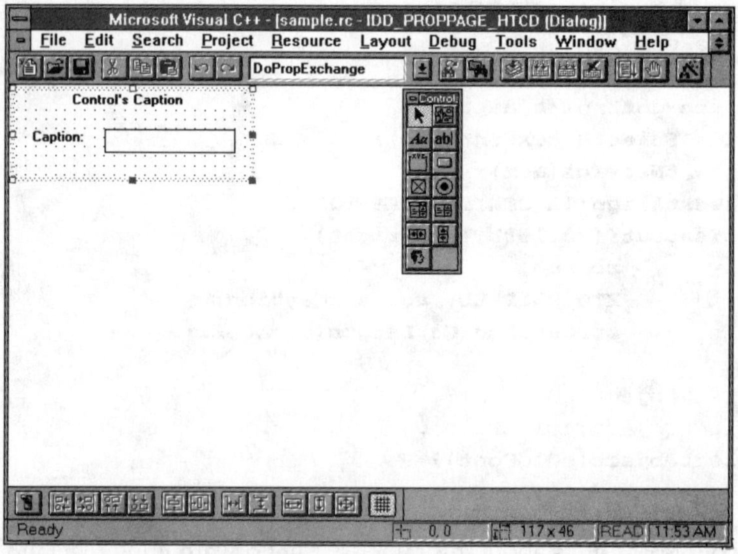

FIGURE 10-1. *The IDD_PROPPAGE_HTCD dialog box is changed to accommodate controls that will allow the control's caption to be altered*

Remember to change the edit control's ID to IDC_CAPTION, and then simply save the new contents of the file.

Now the default property page controls must be linked to the control's properties. Here are the steps that are needed from within the ClassWizard:

1. Select the Member Variables tab.
2. Select **CHtcdPropPage** from the Class Name list box.
3. Select the IDC_CAPTION in the Control IDs list box.
4. Select the Add Variable button and display the Add Variable dialog box.
5. Alter the Member Variable Name edit control so that it reads **m_caption**.
6. Select Value in the Category drop-down box, and CString in the Variable Type drop-down box.
7. Select Caption in the Optional OLE Property Name combo box.
8. Choose OK to close the Add Member Variable box.
9. Select the OK push button to accept the choices and close the ClassWizard.

The ClassWizard will alter the HTCDPPG.H header file as well as the HTCDPPG.CPP source file.

In the HTCDPPG.H header file, notice the addition of **CString m_caption** under **CPropertyPageDialog**.

Likewise, in the HTCDPPG.CPP source file, locate the following two changes. In the **CPropertyPageDialog()** function, there will be the addition of

```
m_caption = _T("");
```

Under the **DoDataExchange()** function, there will be the addition of

```
DDP_Text(pDX, IDC_CAPTION, m_caption, _T("Caption"));
```

DDP_ macros are only used in OLE custom controls, unlike their cousin DDX_ macros used in MFC dialog boxes.

You'll see how property page member variables can be manipulated when the control is tested in the final section of this chapter.

Data Binding

Data binding enables control properties to be linked through the container to a data source. This important OLE custom control feature is used whenever a bound property is changed. The control notifies the container via the **BoundPropertyChanged()** function. This is called *optimistic* data binding, because the control optimistically assumes that the changes can be made to the bound property. This is the type of data binding illustrated in this section. It is also possible to use *pessimistic* data binding, which requires that the control get permission from the container via the **BoundPropertyRequestEdit()** function.

In the previous section, we added a caption capability to the default property page. To illustrate the concept of data binding, the default property page will be further modified. Recall that the default property page is a dialog box that can be edited in the Resource Editor like any other dialog box.

Adding a Details Property

The following is added to the default property page dialog, IDD_PROPPAGE_HTCD.

Open the HTCD.RC resource file for editing in either the 16-bit or 32-bit version Visual C++ compiler. Remember that while the actual steps vary between the two compiler versions, the process is essentially the same. You will need to open and edit the IDD_PROPPAGE_HTCD dialog. When that dialog box is opened, you will find that it looks like the altered dialog box of Figure 10-1, shown earlier. Alter the dialog box by adding the controls shown in Figure 10-2.

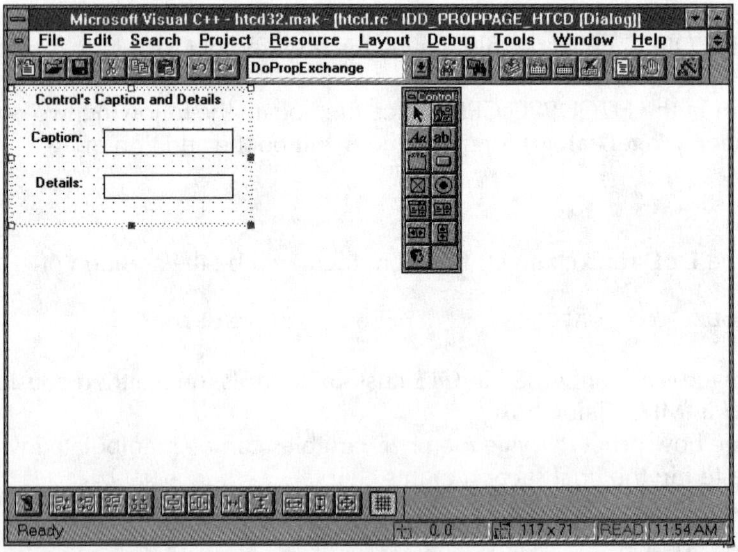

FIGURE 10-2. *The IDD_PROPPAGE_HTCD dialog box is again altered to accommodate new controls that will allow simple data binding*

Remember to change the new edit control's ID to IDC_DETAILS, and then simply save the new contents of the file.

Defining the Details Property

The Details property is a Get/Set property of type BSTR. The following steps will add this property and create the **GetDetails()** and **SetDetails()** function outlines. Here are the steps that are needed from within the ClassWizard:

1. Select the OLE Automation tab.
2. Select **CHtcdCtrl** from the Class Name list box.
3. Select the Add Property button and display the Add Property dialog box.
4. Alter the External Name edit control to read **Details**.
5. For an Implementation, select Get/Set Methods.
6. Select BSTR from the Type drop-down list box.
7. Choose OK to close the Add Property dialog box.
8. Now select the Member Variables tab.
9. Select **CHtcdPropPage** from the Class Name list box.
10. Select IDC_DETAILS in the Control IDs list box.
11. Select the Add Variable button and display the Add Variable dialog box.
12. Alter the variable name to read **m_details**.
13. Select Value in the Category drop-down list box, and CString in the Variable Type drop-down list box.
14. Enter **Details** into the Optional OLE Property Name drop-down combo box.
15. Choose OK to close the Add Member Variable box.
16. Select the OK push button to accept the choices and close the ClassWizard.

The ClassWizard will alter the HTCD.ODL, HTCDCTL.CPP, and HTCDCTL.H files to accommodate the Details property. It is now up to us to alter detail-specific code. Additionally, the edit control will be linked with the Details property.

The HTCDCTL.H Header File A small addition needs to be made to the HTCDCTL.H header file. The change is shown in boldface. This is a partial listing of this header file.

```
// Implementation
protected:
  ~CHtcdCtrl();
  CString m_details;
  void HotColor(CDC* pdc);          // Hot color function
  void ColdColor(CDC* pdc);         // Cold color function
    .
    .
    .
```

Now the details of the Get/Set properties will be added to the HTCDCTL.CPP source file.

The HTCDCTL.CPP Source File To ensure persistence support of the Details property, make the following change to the **DoPropExchange()** function. The change is shown in boldface in the following listing.

```
/////////////////////////////////////////////////////////////////////
// CHtcdCtrl::DoPropExchange - Persistence support

void CHtcdCtrl::DoPropExchange(CPropExchange* pPX)
{
  ExchangeVersion(pPX, MAKELONG(_wVerMinor, _wVerMajor));
  COleControl::DoPropExchange(pPX);

  PX_Long(pPX, _T("HotColor"), (long &)m_hotColor,
          RGB(255, 0, 0));
  PX_Long(pPX, _T("ColdColor"), (long &)m_coldColor,
          RGB(0, 0, 255));
  PX_String(pPX, _T("Details"), m_details, _T(""));
}
```

Alter the **OnDraw()**, **HotColor()**, and **ColdColor()** functions to reflect the boldfaced changes shown in the following listing. Note: This is a partial listing of the **OnDraw()** function.

```
    .
    .
    .
// Draw the control's caption and details
  pOldFont = SelectStockFont(pdc);
  pdc->GetTextMetrics(&tm);
```

```
  pdc->SetTextAlign(TA_CENTER | TA_TOP);
  pdc->ExtTextOut((rc.left + rc.right) / 2,
                  rc.top,
                  ETO_CLIPPED, rc, strCaption,
                  strCaption.GetLength(), NULL);

  pdc->ExtTextOut((rc.left + rc.right) / 2,
                  ((rc.top + rc.bottom - tm.tmHeight) / 2),
                  ETO_CLIPPED, rc, m_details,
                  m_details.GetLength(), NULL);

  pdc->SelectObject(pOldPen);
      .
      .
      .
```

The details string will be clipped, then centered horizontally and vertically within the control.

The ClassWizard automatically creates the outlines for the **GetDetails()** and **SetDetails()** functions in the HTCDCTL.CPP file. For this unique application, modify these functions to conform to the following listing.

```
BSTR CHtcdCtrl::GetDetails()
{
  CString s;

  return s.AllocSysString();
}

void CHtcdCtrl::SetDetails(LPCTSTR lpszNewValue)
{
  if(m_details != lpszNewValue)
  {
    m_details = lpszNewValue;
    SetModifiedFlag();
    InvalidateControl();
  }
}
```

The **InvalidateControl()** is called to force a repainting of the control when a new string exists.

Binding the Details Property

To make the Details property bindable, the following changes must be made. Here are the steps that are needed from within the ClassWizard:

1. Select the OLE Automation tab.
2. Select **CHtcdCtrl** from the Class Name list box.
3. In the Name list box, select Details.
4. Select the Data Binding button and view the Data Binding dialog box.
5. Select the Bindable Property check box. Leave other options unchecked at this time.
6. Choose OK to close the Data Binding dialog box.
7. Select the OK push button to accept the choices and close the ClassWizard.

This change is automatically added to the HTCD.ODL file by the ClassWizard.

The HTCDCTL.CPP Source File One change is needed in the **SetDetails()** function in order to bind this property. That change is shown in boldface in the following partial listing of the HTCDCTL.CPP source file.

```
void CHtcdCtrl::SetDetails(LPCTSTR lpszNewValue)
{
  if(m_details != lpszNewValue)
  {
    m_details = lpszNewValue;
    SetModifiedFlag();
    InvalidateControl();
    BoundPropertyChanged(dispidDetails);
  }
}
```

Notice that when a new string exists, the **BoundPropertyChanged()** function is used to implement an optimistic data binding. Optimistic and pessimistic data binding were discussed at the beginning of this section.

A Final Check We have worked with a large number of additions and changes to the default ControlWizard files. Most of those changes have occurred in the HTCDCTL.CPP source file. Here is a final look at the contents of this whole file, with all code additions in boldface.

```
// htcdctl.cpp : Implementation of the CHtcdCtrl OLE control
// class.

#include "stdafx.h"
#include "htcd.h"
#include "htcdctl.h"
#include "htcdppg.h"


#ifdef _DEBUG
#undef THIS_FILE
static char BASED_CODE THIS_FILE[] = __FILE__;
#endif


IMPLEMENT_DYNCREATE(CHtcdCtrl, COleControl)


/////////////////////////////////////////////////////////////
// Message map

BEGIN_MESSAGE_MAP(CHtcdCtrl, COleControl)
  //{{AFX_MSG_MAP(CHtcdCtrl)
  ON_WM_LBUTTONDOWN()
  ON_WM_RBUTTONDOWN()
  //}}AFX_MSG_MAP
  ON_OLEVERB(AFX_IDS_VERB_PROPERTIES, OnProperties)
END_MESSAGE_MAP()


/////////////////////////////////////////////////////////////
// Dispatch map

BEGIN_DISPATCH_MAP(CHtcdCtrl, COleControl)
  //{{AFX_DISPATCH_MAP(CHtcdCtrl)
  DISP_PROPERTY(CHtcdCtrl, "HotColor", m_hotColor, VT_COLOR)
  DISP_PROPERTY(CHtcdCtrl, "ColdColor", m_coldColor, VT_COLOR)
  DISP_PROPERTY_EX(CHtcdCtrl, "Details", GetDetails,
                   SetDetails, VT_BSTR)
  DISP_STOCKPROP_BACKCOLOR()
  DISP_STOCKPROP_CAPTION()
```

```
  DISP_STOCKPROP_FONT()
  DISP_STOCKPROP_FORECOLOR()
  //}}AFX_DISPATCH_MAP
  DISP_FUNCTION_ID(CHtcdCtrl, "AboutBox", DISPID_ABOUTBOX,
                AboutBox, VT_EMPTY, VTS_NONE)
END_DISPATCH_MAP()


/////////////////////////////////////////////////////////////
// Event map

BEGIN_EVENT_MAP(CHtcdCtrl, COleControl)
  //{{AFX_EVENT_MAP(CHtcdCtrl)

  // NOTE - ClassWizard will add and remove event map entries
  //    DO NOT EDIT what you see in these blocks of generated
  //    code !
  //}}AFX_EVENT_MAP
END_EVENT_MAP()


/////////////////////////////////////////////////////////////
// Property pages

// TODO: Add more property pages as needed.
// Remember to increase the count!
BEGIN_PROPPAGEIDS(CHtcdCtrl, 3)
  PROPPAGEID(CHtcdPropPage::guid)
  PROPPAGEID(CLSID_CColorPropPage)
  PROPPAGEID(CLSID_CFontPropPage)
END_PROPPAGEIDS(CHtcdCtrl)


/////////////////////////////////////////////////////////////
// Initialize class factory and guid

IMPLEMENT_OLECREATE_EX(CHtcdCtrl, "HTCD.HtcdCtrl.1",
  0x23def10f, 0xf847, 0x11cd, 0x8e, 0xea, 0x90, 0x1d, 0xca,
  0xea, 0x63, 0x2e)


/////////////////////////////////////////////////////////////
```

```
// Type library ID and version

IMPLEMENT_OLETYPELIB(CHtcdCtrl, _tlid, _wVerMajor, _wVerMinor)


/////////////////////////////////////////////////////////////
// Interface IDs

const IID BASED_CODE IID_DHtcd =
    { 0x23def111, 0xf847, 0x11cd, { 0x8e, 0xea, 0x90, 0x1d,
      0xca, 0xea, 0x63, 0x2e } };
const IID BASED_CODE IID_DHtcdEvents =
    { 0x23def113, 0xf847, 0x11cd, { 0x8e, 0xea, 0x90, 0x1d,
      0xca, 0xea, 0x63, 0x2e } };


/////////////////////////////////////////////////////////////
// Control type information

static const DWORD BASED_CODE _dwHtcdOleMisc =
  OLEMISC_ACTIVATEWHENVISIBLE ¦
  OLEMISC_SETCLIENTSITEFIRST ¦
  OLEMISC_INSIDEOUT ¦
  OLEMISC_CANTLINKINSIDE ¦
  OLEMISC_RECOMPOSEONRESIZE;

IMPLEMENT_OLECTLTYPE(CHtcdCtrl, IDS_HTCD, _dwHtcdOleMisc)


/////////////////////////////////////////////////////////////
// CHtcdCtrl::CHtcdCtrlFactory::UpdateRegistry -
// Adds or removes system registry entries for CHtcdCtrl

BOOL CHtcdCtrl::CHtcdCtrlFactory::UpdateRegistry(BOOL bRegister)
{
  if (bRegister)
    return AfxOleRegisterControlClass(
      AfxGetInstanceHandle(),
      m_clsid,
      m_lpszProgID,
      IDS_HTCD,
      IDB_HTCD,
```

```
      FALSE,                        //  Not insertable
      _dwHtcdOleMisc,
      _tlid,
      _wVerMajor,
      _wVerMinor);
  else
    return AfxOleUnregisterClass(m_clsid, m_lpszProgID);
}


/////////////////////////////////////////////////////////////////
// CHtcdCtrl::CHtcdCtrl - Constructor

CHtcdCtrl::CHtcdCtrl()
{
  InitializeIIDs(&IID_DHtcd, &IID_DHtcdEvents);

  // TODO: Initialize your control's instance data here.
}


/////////////////////////////////////////////////////////////////
// CHtcdCtrl::~CHtcdCtrl - Destructor

CHtcdCtrl::~CHtcdCtrl()
{
  // TODO: Cleanup your control's instance data here.

}


/////////////////////////////////////////////////////////////////
// CHtcdCtrl::OnDraw - Drawing function

void CHtcdCtrl::OnDraw(
      CDC* pdc, const CRect& rcBounds, const CRect& rcInvalid)
{
  CBrush* pOldBrush;
  CBrush NewBrush(TranslateColor(GetBackColor()));
  CPen* pOldPen;
  CRect rc = rcBounds;
```

```
    CFont* pOldFont;
    TEXTMETRIC tm;
    const CString& strCaption = InternalGetText();
    POINT pt;

    // Fill background with brush color returned by BackColor()
    pdc->FillRect(rcBounds, &NewBrush);

    // Background mode to transparent
    pdc->SetBkMode(TRANSPARENT);

    // Set foreground color for text
    pdc->SetTextColor(TranslateColor(GetForeColor()));

    // Draw control using defined pen
    pOldPen = (CPen*)pdc->SelectStockObject(BLACK_PEN);

    pt.x=40;  // rounding values for RoundRect() function
    pt.y=40;
    NewBrush.CreateSolidBrush(RGB(0, 255, 0));  // green brush
    pOldBrush=(CBrush*)pdc->SelectObject(&NewBrush);
    pdc->RoundRect(rcBounds, pt);

    // Draw the control's caption and details
    pOldFont = SelectStockFont(pdc);
    pdc->GetTextMetrics(&tm);
    pdc->SetTextAlign(TA_CENTER | TA_TOP);
    pdc->ExtTextOut((rc.left + rc.right) / 2,
                    rc.top,
                    ETO_CLIPPED, rc, strCaption,
                    strCaption.GetLength(), NULL);

    pdc->ExtTextOut((rc.left + rc.right) / 2,
                    ((rc.top + rc.bottom - tm.tmHeight) / 2),
                    ETO_CLIPPED, rc, m_details,
                    m_details.GetLength(), NULL);

    pdc->SelectObject(pOldPen);
    pdc->SelectObject(pOldBrush);
    pdc->SelectObject(pOldFont);
}
```

```
////////////////////////////////////////////////////////////////
// CHtcdCtrl::DoPropExchange - Persistence support

void CHtcdCtrl::DoPropExchange(CPropExchange* pPX)
{
  ExchangeVersion(pPX, MAKELONG(_wVerMinor, _wVerMajor));
  COleControl::DoPropExchange(pPX);

  PX_Long(pPX, _T("HotColor"), (long &)m_hotColor,
        RGB(255,0,0));
  PX_Long(pPX, _T("ColdColor"), (long &)m_coldColor,
        RGB(0,0,255));
  PX_String(pPX, _T("Details"), m_details, _T(""));
}


////////////////////////////////////////////////////////////////
// CHtcdCtrl::OnResetState - Reset control to default state

void CHtcdCtrl::OnResetState()
{
  COleControl::OnResetState(); //Resets DoPropExchange default

  // TODO: Reset any other control state here.
}


////////////////////////////////////////////////////////////////
// CHtcdCtrl::AboutBox - Display an "About" box to the user

void CHtcdCtrl::AboutBox()
{
  CDialog dlgAbout(IDD_ABOUTBOX_HTCD);
  dlgAbout.DoModal();
}


////////////////////////////////////////////////////////////////
// CHtcdCtrl message handlers

void CHtcdCtrl::OnLButtonDown(UINT nFlags, CPoint point)
```

```
{
  CDC* pdc;

  // change to hot color (red)
  pdc = GetDC();
  HotColor(pdc);
  ReleaseDC(pdc);

  COleControl::OnLButtonDown(nFlags, point);
}

void CHtcdCtrl::OnRButtonDown(UINT nFlags, CPoint point)
{
  CDC* pdc;

  // change to cold color (blue)
  pdc = GetDC();
  ColdColor(pdc);
  ReleaseDC(pdc);

  COleControl::OnRButtonDown(nFlags, point);
}

void CHtcdCtrl::HotColor(CDC* pdc)
{
  CBrush* pOldBrush;
  CBrush NewBrush(TranslateColor(m_hotColor));
  CPen* pOldPen;
  CRect rc;
  CFont* pOldFont;
  CFont NewFont;
  TEXTMETRIC tm;
  const CString& strCaption = InternalGetText();
  POINT pt;
  struct tm *date_time;
  time_t timer;

  // Background mode to transparent
  pdc->SetBkMode(TRANSPARENT);

  // Set foreground color for text
  pdc->SetTextColor(TranslateColor(GetForeColor()));
```

```
    GetClientRect(rc);
    pOldBrush = pdc->SelectObject(&NewBrush);
    pOldPen = (CPen*)pdc->SelectStockObject(BLACK_PEN);

    pt.x=40;  // rounding values for RoundRect() function
    pt.y=40;
    pdc->RoundRect(rc, pt);

    // Draw the control's caption
    pOldFont = SelectStockFont(pdc);
    pdc->GetTextMetrics(&tm);
    pdc->SetTextAlign(TA_CENTER | TA_TOP);
    pdc->ExtTextOut((rc.left + rc.right) / 2,
                  rc.top,
                  ETO_CLIPPED, rc, strCaption,
                  strCaption.GetLength(), NULL);

    pdc->ExtTextOut((rc.left + rc.right) / 2,
                  ((rc.top + rc.bottom - tm.tmHeight) / 2),
                  ETO_CLIPPED, rc, m_details,
                  m_details.GetLength(), NULL);

    // get date and time information
    time(&timer);
    date_time=localtime(&timer);
    const CString& strtime = asctime(date_time);

    pdc->SetTextAlign(TA_CENTER | TA_TOP);
    pdc->ExtTextOut((rc.left + rc.right) / 2,
                  rc.top + rc.bottom - tm.tmHeight,
                  ETO_CLIPPED, rc, strtime,
                  strtime.GetLength()-1, NULL);

    pdc->SelectObject(pOldPen);
    pdc->SelectObject(pOldBrush);
    pdc->SelectObject(pOldFont);
}

void CHtcdCtrl::ColdColor(CDC* pdc)
{
    CBrush* pOldBrush;
```

```
CBrush NewBrush(TranslateColor(m_coldColor));
CPen* pOldPen;
CRect rc;
CFont* pOldFont;
CFont NewFont;
TEXTMETRIC tm;
const CString& strCaption = InternalGetText();
POINT pt;
struct tm *date_time;
time_t timer;

// Background mode to transparent
pdc->SetBkMode(TRANSPARENT);

// Set foreground color for text
pdc->SetTextColor(TranslateColor(GetForeColor()));

GetClientRect(rc);
pOldBrush = pdc->SelectObject(&NewBrush);
pOldPen = (CPen*)pdc->SelectStockObject(BLACK_PEN);

pt.x=40;  // rounding values for RoundRect() function
pt.y=40;
pdc->RoundRect(rc, pt);

// Draw the control's caption
pOldFont = SelectStockFont(pdc);
pdc->GetTextMetrics(&tm);
pdc->SetTextAlign(TA_CENTER | TA_TOP);
pdc->ExtTextOut((rc.left + rc.right) / 2,
               rc.top,
               ETO_CLIPPED, rc, strCaption,
               strCaption.GetLength(), NULL);

pdc->ExtTextOut((rc.left + rc.right) / 2,
               ((rc.top + rc.bottom - tm.tmHeight) / 2),
               ETO_CLIPPED, rc, m_details,
               m_details.GetLength(), NULL);

// get date and time information
time(&timer);
date_time=localtime(&timer);
```

```
  const CString& strtime = asctime(date_time);

  pdc->SetTextAlign(TA_CENTER | TA_TOP);
  pdc->ExtTextOut((rc.left + rc.right) / 2,
                  rc.top + rc.bottom - tm.tmHeight,
                  ETO_CLIPPED, rc, strtime,
                  strtime.GetLength()-1, NULL);

  pdc->SelectObject(pOldPen);
  pdc->SelectObject(pOldBrush);
  pdc->SelectObject(pOldFont);
}

BSTR CHtcdCtrl::GetDetails()
{
  CString s;

  return s.AllocSysString();
}

void CHtcdCtrl::SetDetails(LPCTSTR lpszNewValue)
{
  if(m_details != lpszNewValue)
  {
    m_details = lpszNewValue;
    SetModifiedFlag();
    InvalidateControl();
    BoundPropertyChanged(dispidDetails);
  }
}
```

If your code matches this code and you have made the changes to the other files as you have worked your way through this chapter, you are now ready to compile your custom control!

From the Visual C++ compiler's Project menu, select the Rebuild All option. With a successful compilation, the new control is ready to be tested in the Microsoft Test Container application.

The Test Container

The Test Container can now be used to test our unique temperature custom control, named htcd.

To test the temperature custom control in the Test Container, use the Edit menu from the Test Container's menu bar to select the Insert OLE Control... menu item. This should be very familiar to you by now. When this selection is made, the new control will be available from the Insert OLE Control dialog box. Select the htcd item to insert your new custom control in the Test Container. Figure 10-3 shows the temperature control inserted in the Test Container.

As you view this figure, also notice the last icon on the toolbar. This icon is the icon for the temperature control. The Test Container can be used to test several features of our new control. For example, Figure 10-4 shows how the control responds to a left mouse button hit within the control.

Select the Test Containers Edit menu and choose the Htcd Control Object menu item. The Htcd Control Properties dialog box, shown in Figure 10-5, will allow you to alter the Caption and Details strings.

As you can see in the previous figure, the caption is changed to "Temperature" and the details are set to "Ice Cream Mixer." Figure 10-6 shows the resulting control, when the OK push button is clicked.

Captions are centered at the top of the control, while details are centered horizontally and vertically within the control.

Here is an interesting experiment. Open the Notification Log by selecting it from the Test Container's View menu. If it is not blank, simply clear it with the push

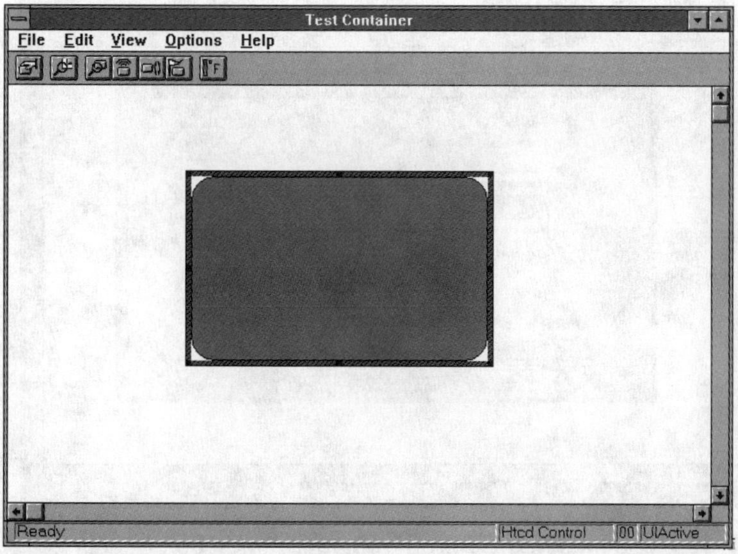

FIGURE 10-3. *The new temperature control*

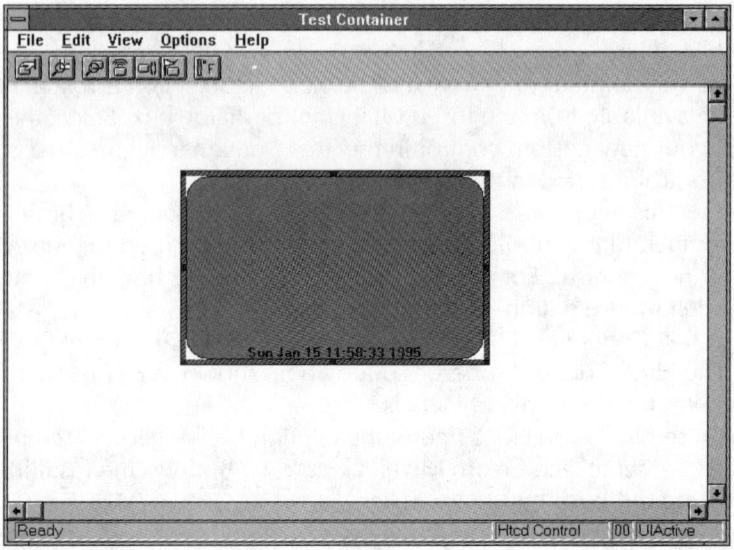

FIGURE 10-4. *The temperature control will turn red and display the date and time when the left mouse button is depressed while in the control*

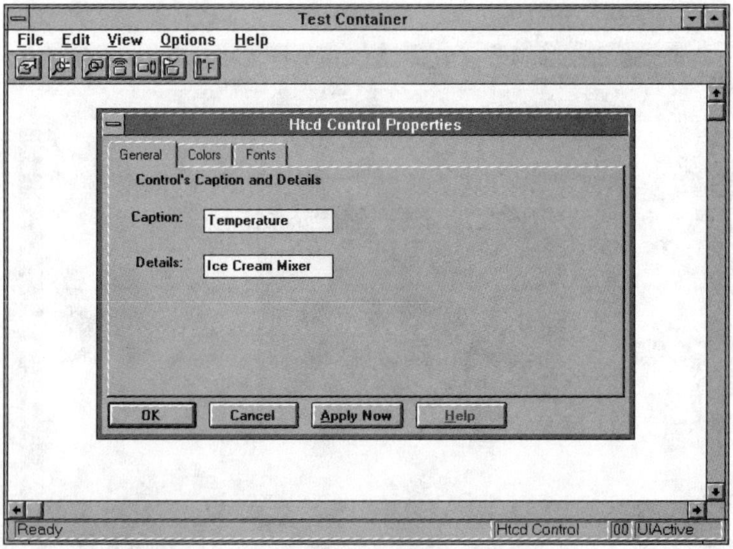

FIGURE 10-5. *Use the Htcd Control Properties dialog box to change properties such as strings, fonts, and colors*

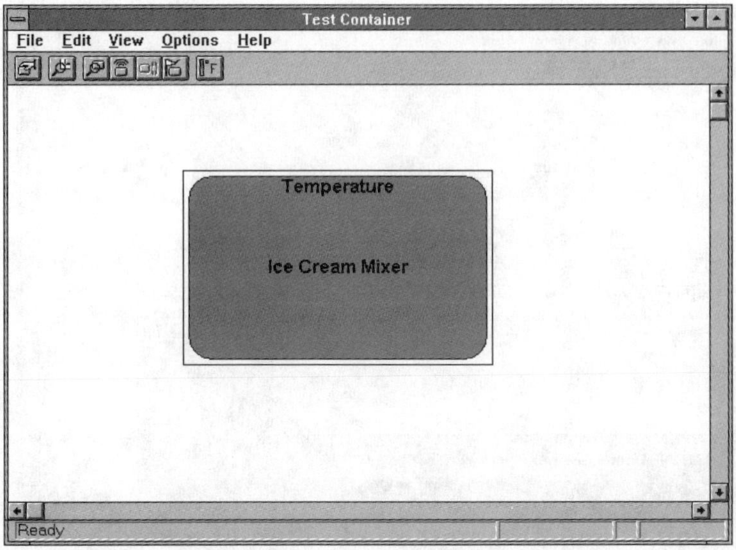

FIGURE 10-6. *The custom control now has a unique caption and details comment*

button provided. Now change the caption and details strings, as we did in the previous section. If you do this, your Notification Log might resemble Figure 10-7.

The Notification Log will notify you of changes to items that are bound. Here the notification tells you that the Details property (a bound item) has changed.

Ambient Properties for this control can be changed by selecting the Set Ambient Properties... menu item from the Test Container's Edit menu, as shown in Figure 10-8.

Figure 10-9 shows the Ambient Properties dialog box being used to change the ForeColor of the control. Basic and custom colors are available for testing.

It is possible to change other ambient properties with this dialog box. To see a list of properties, click on the down arrow of the Standard Property list box.

Using Microsoft Access as a Container

Microsoft Access was the first container application to take advantage of OLE 2 custom controls. Custom controls can be installed in a database form, under

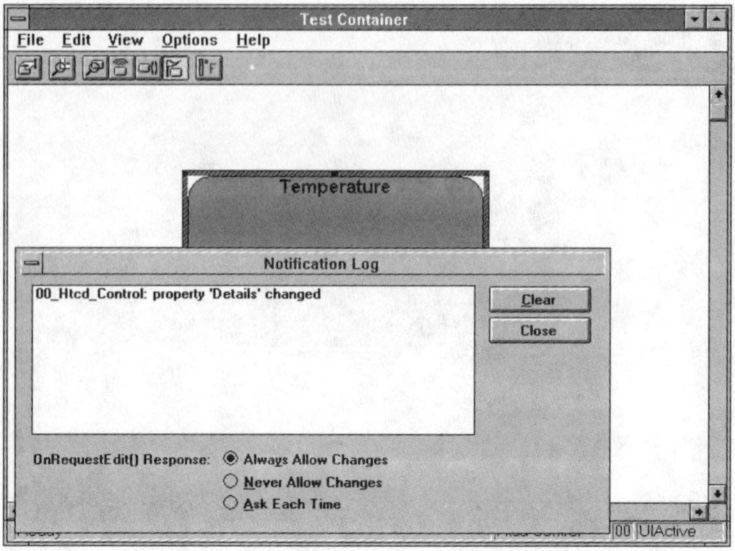

FIGURE 10-7. *The Notification Log will notify you of changes to bound items*

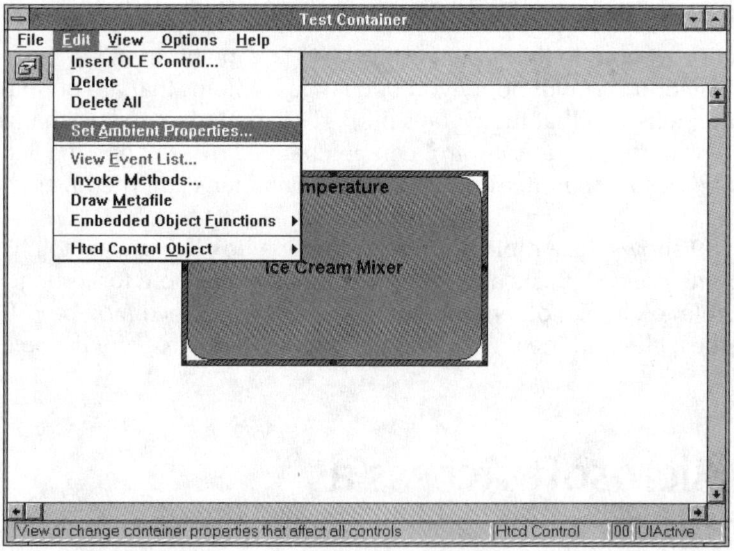

FIGURE 10-8. *Ambient Properties such as fonts and colors can be tested by selecting the Set Ambient Properties... menu item from the Edit menu*

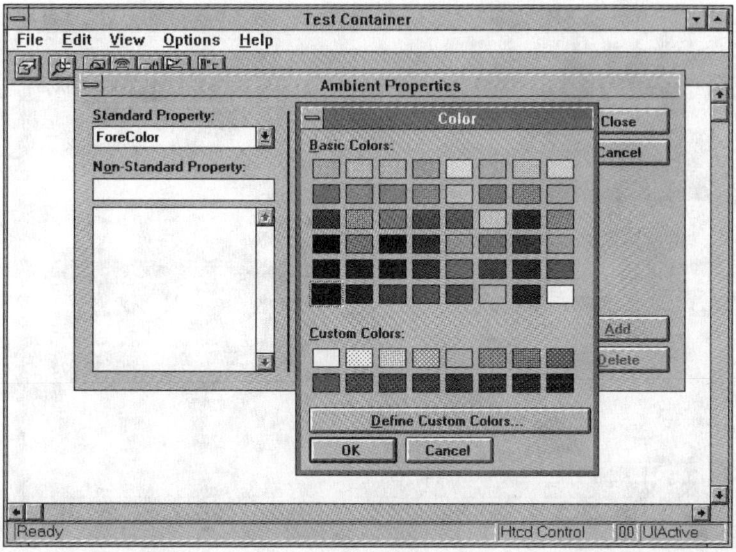

FIGURE 10-9. *The ForeColor property is about to be changed by using the Ambient Properties dialog box*

design, by selecting the Insert Object... menu item from the Edit menu. The Insert Object dialog box will then give you a choice of register controls. For this example, we've selected our Htcd custom control and installed it in a Microsoft Access sample form, as shown in Figure 10-10.

It is now a simple matter to move and resize the custom control to any location on the database form. Figure 10-11 shows the size and location of the edited form.

If the right mouse button is clicked while in the custom control, a dialog box will be displayed. Figure 10-12 shows that this dialog box will allow the control's properties to be viewed or changed.

If the Properties... item is selected from the dialog box, a complete list of the custom control's properties will be displayed.

If you want to set the Caption and Details strings, simply choose Htcd Control Object from this same list. The Htcd Control Properties dialog box will then be displayed, as shown in Figure 10-13.

Figure 10-14 shows the Htcd custom control with its new label and details string placed on the database form.

Notice that while the control was originally designed to reflect temperature settings of hot, mild, and cold, it is being used in a database form to reflect sales prospects for a company. Truly versatile custom controls can take on a number of faces!

Figure 10-15 shows the working version of the Access database form with a working Htcd custom control.

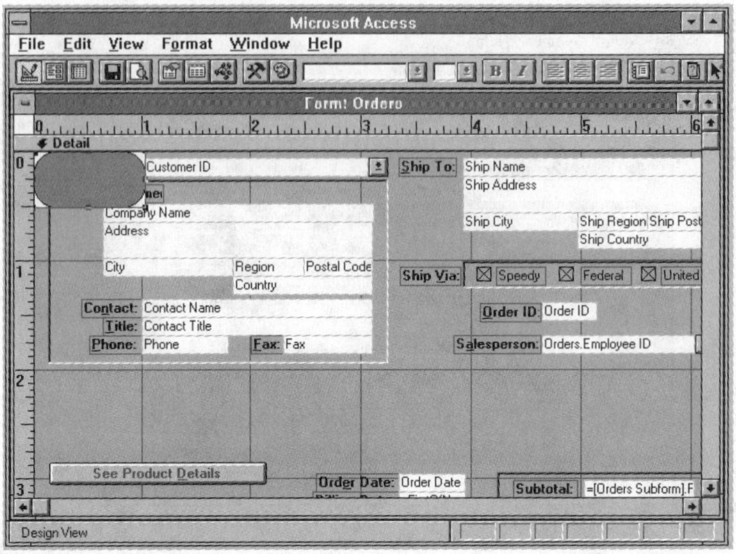

FIGURE 10-10. *The Htcd custom control is installed in a Microsoft Access sample form*

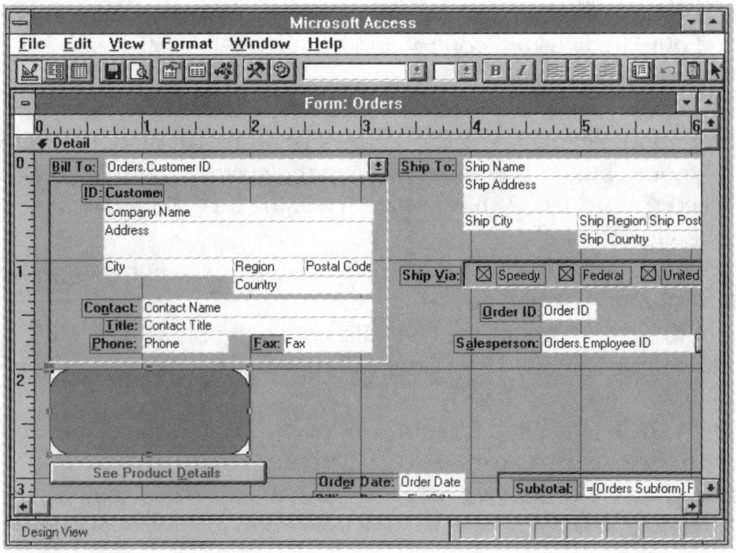

FIGURE 10-11. *The Htcd custom control is moved and sized to suit our needs*

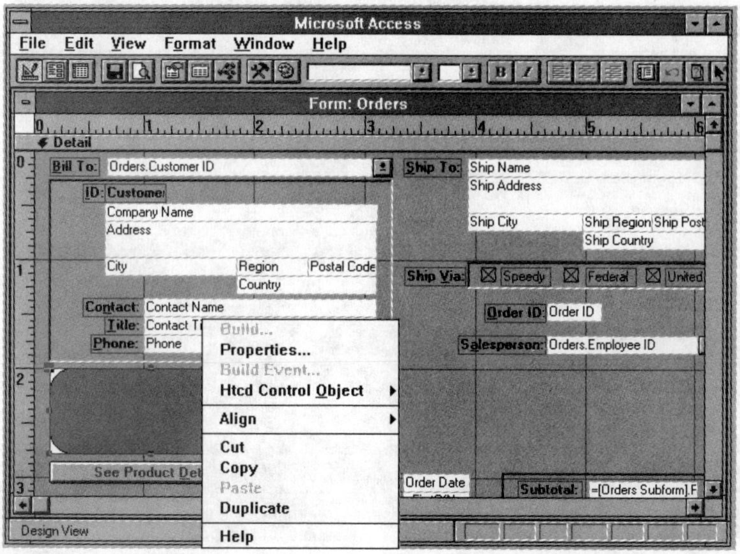

FIGURE 10-12. *To view the custom controls properties, select the Properties... dialog box item*

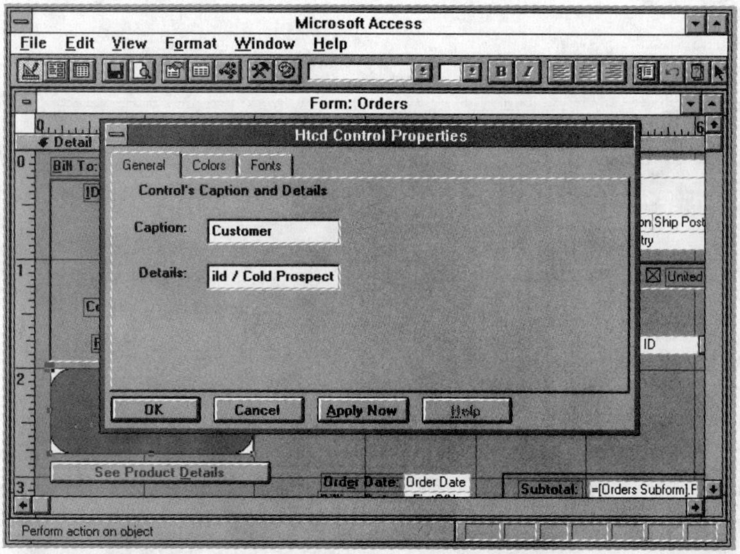

FIGURE 10-13. *The Htcd Control Properties dialog box will enable the form designer to change the caption and details strings*

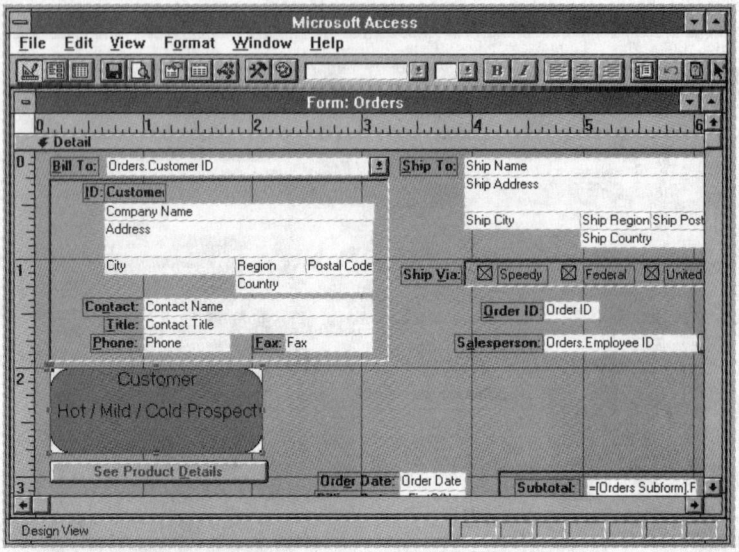

FIGURE 10-14. *The Htcd custom control is now complete, with a new Caption and Details string*

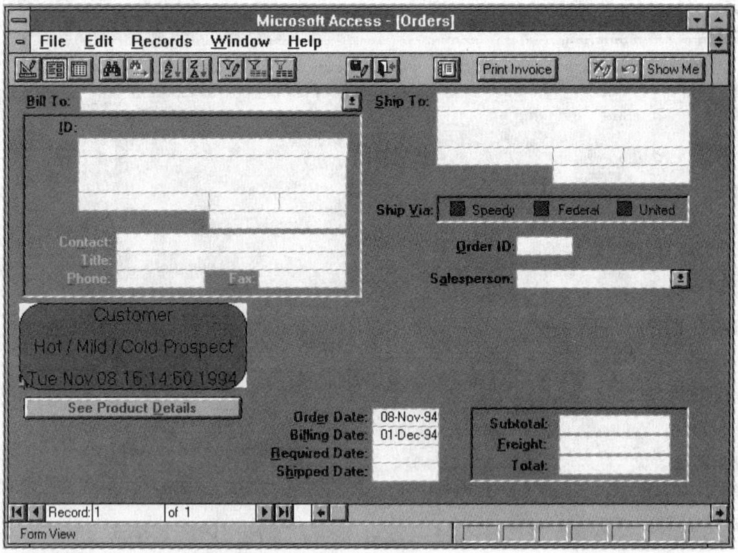

FIGURE 10-15. *Placing the custom control in a Microsoft Access form*

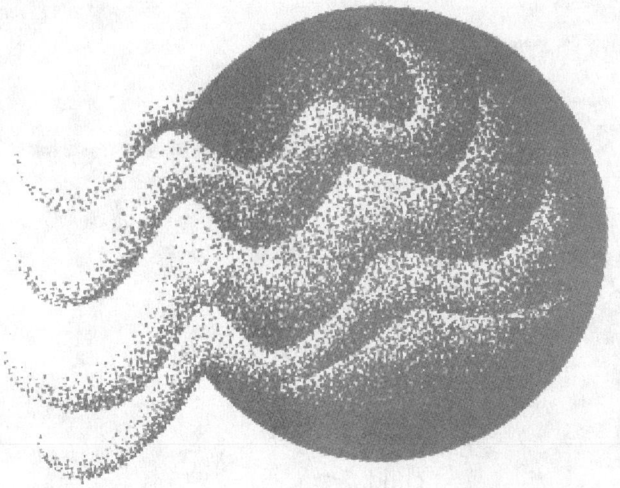

Index

C

D

E

F

G

H

I

P

R

S

T

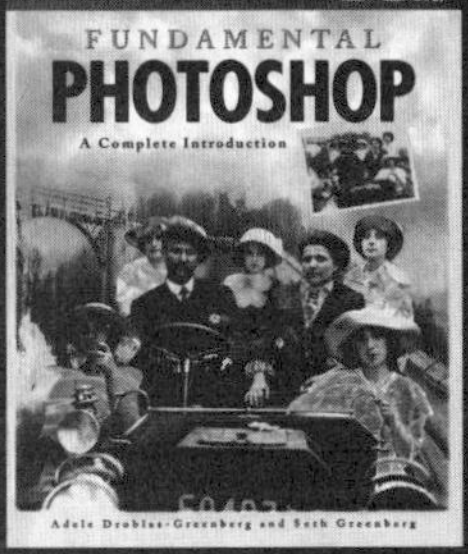

Fundamental Photoshop: A Complete Introduction
by Adele Droblas-Greenberg & Seth Greenberg
$27.95 ISBN: 0-07-881994-6

dBASE for Windows Made Easy
by Jim Sheldon
$26.95 ISBN: 0-07-881792-7

The Best Guide To Business Shareware
by Judy Heim, John Haib and Mike Callahan
Includes Two 3.5-Inch Disks
$34.95 ISBN: 0-07-882076-6

The Visual C++ Handbook
by Chris H. Pappas and William H. Murray, III
$34.95 ISBN: 0-07-882056-1

GET WHAT YOU WANT...

Expert Advice & Support 24 Hours A Day

Do you need help with your software?

Why pay up to $25.00 for a single tech support call!

Now, in conjunction with **Corporate Software Inc.**, one of the world's largest providers of tech support (they field more than 200,000 calls a month), Osborne delivers the most authoritative new series of answer books — **The Certified Tech Support** series.

- These books will bail you out of practically any pitfall.
- Find answers to the most frequently asked end-user questions, from the simple to the arcane.
- **Lotus Notes Answers: Certified Tech Support** is the next best thing to having an expert beside your computer.
- Watch for other books in the series.

Excel for Windows Answers: Certified Tech Support
by Mary Campbell
$16.95
ISBN: 0-07-882054-5

Order Today!

BC640SL